CRITICAL PSYCHOLOGY PRAXIS

This collection of chapters advances critical psychology by incorporating praxis (theory and practice) and decolonial streams of thought. They are united around a theme of psychosocial non-alignment to modernity/coloniality.

Bringing together a transdisciplinary range of authors from around the world, this edited volume weaves together a spectrum of complex arguments and perspectives to lay the foundations for bridging the Global North–South divide in critical psychology through solidarity and dialogue. The book's central argument is to emphasize praxis and transdisciplinarity over disciplinary fundamentalism. Psychology is only a starting point and not the end goal of critique in this book; incidentally, some of the authors are not even psychologists. Instead, the book draws on decolonial theoretical resources, such as Chican@ Studies, Black Male Studies, and Critical Pedagogy, to complement traditional theoretical resources like psychoanalysis, Marxism, poststructuralism, and feminism.

This groundbreaking text is suitable for scholars and upper-level undergraduate and postgraduate students studying critical discourse, the psychology and philosophy of post-coloniality, conceptual and historical issues in psychology, as well as anthropology and sociology courses engaging with action research.

Robert K. Beshara is Assistant Professor of Psychology and Humanities at Northern New Mexico College, USA and Director of the Critical Psychology certificate program at The Global Center for Advanced Studies, Ireland/USA. He is the founder of criticalpsychology.org, a free resource for scholars, activists, and practitioners. He is also the author of *Decolonial Psychoanalysis: Towards Critical Islamophobia Studies* (Routledge, 2019).

ADVANCES IN THEORETICAL AND PHILOSOPHICAL PSYCHOLOGY
Series Foreword
Brent D. Slife, Editor

Psychologists need to face the facts. Their commitment to empiricism for answering disciplinary questions does not prevent pivotal questions from arising that cannot be evaluated exclusively through empirical methods, hence the title of this series: *Advances in Theoretical and Philosophical Psychology*. For example, such moral questions as, "What is the nature of a good life?" are crucial to psychotherapists but are not answerable through empirical methods alone. And what of the methods themselves? Many have worried that our current psychological means of investigation are not adequate for fully understanding the person (e.g., Schiff, 2019). How do we address this concern through empirical methods without running headlong into the dilemma of methods investigating themselves? Such questions are in some sense philosophical, to be sure, but the discipline of psychology cannot advance even its own empirical agenda without addressing questions like these in defensible ways.

How then should the discipline of psychology deal with such distinctly theoretical questions? We could leave the answers exclusively to professional philosophers, but this option would mean that the conceptual foundations of the discipline, including the conceptual framework of empiricism itself, are left to scholars who are *outside* the discipline. As undoubtedly helpful as philosophers are and will be, this situation would mean that the people doing the actual psychological work, psychologists themselves, are divorced from the people who formulate and re-formulate the conceptual foundations of that work. This division of labor would not seem to serve the long-term viability of the discipline.

Instead, the founders of psychology—thinkers such as Wundt, Freud, and James—recognized the importance of psychologists in formulating their own foundations. These parents of psychology not only did their own theorizing, in cooperation with many other disciplines; they also realized the significance of psychologists continuously *re*-examining these theories and philosophies. This re-examination process allowed for the people most directly involved in and knowledgeable about the discipline to be the ones to decide *whether* changes were needed and *how* such changes would best be implemented. This book series is dedicated to that task, the examining and re-examining of psychology's foundations.

CRITICAL PSYCHOLOGY PRAXIS

Psychosocial Non-Alignment to Modernity/Coloniality

Edited by Robert K. Beshara

NEW YORK AND LONDON

First published 2021
by Routledge
52 Vanderbilt Avenue, New York, NY 10017

and by Routledge
2 Park Square, Milton Park, Abingdon, Oxon OX14 4RN

Routledge is an imprint of the Taylor & Francis Group, an informa business

© 2021 selection and editorial matter, Robert K. Beshara; individual chapters, the contributors

The right of Robert K. Beshara to be identified as the author of the editorial material, and of the authors for their individual chapters, has been asserted in accordance with sections 77 and 78 of the Copyright, Designs and Patents Act 1988.

All rights reserved. No part of this book may be reprinted or reproduced or utilized in any form or by any electronic, mechanical, or other means, now known or hereafter invented, including photocopying and recording, or in any information storage or retrieval system, without permission in writing from the publishers.

Trademark notice: Product or corporate names may be trademarks or registered trademarks, and are used only for identification and explanation without intent to infringe.

Library of Congress Cataloging-in-Publication Data
A catalog record for this title has been requested

ISBN: 9780367635640 (hbk)
ISBN: 9780367634636 (pbk)
ISBN: 9781003119678 (ebk)

Typeset in Bembo
by Newgen Publishing UK

CONTENTS

List of Contributors | vii
Acknowledgments | xii
Preface: Reporting on the 2019 International Critical ~~Psychology~~ Praxis Congress | xiii
 Robert K. Beshara

1 Ten Concepts for Critical Psychology Praxis | 1
 Robert K. Beshara

2 Understanding and Challenging Literary Gentrification in New Mexico: A Concept in Parts | 13
 Patricia Marina Trujillo

3 Subversions of Subjectification | 33
 Hans Skott-Myhre and Kathleen S.G. Skott-Myhre

4 The End of Knowing as Critical Praxis (Practical-Critical Activity) | 44
 Lois Holzman

5 Looking (Out) for New Masters: Assessing the Bar between Lacanianism and Critical Psychology | 51
 Michael J. Miller

6 Psychology as Business and Domination: Challenging the Colonial and the "Import–Export" Model 66
Serdar M. Değirmencioğlu

7 Blessings from the Tewa Sunrisers of Santa Clara Pueblo 82
Rachel Begay

8 The Creation of the Viable Unheard of as a Revolutionary Activity 85
Fernanda Liberali, Valdite Pereira Fuga, and José Carlos Barbosa Lopes

9 Student Resistance as a Praxis Against Neoliberalism: A Critical Analysis of Chilean Public Education from 1980 to 2020 100
Silvana S. Hernández-Ortiz and María-Constanza Garrido Sierralta

10 Critical Deconstruction of "East meets West": The Lesson from Hong Kong 113
Fu Wai

11 Decolonizing the Intersection: Black Male Studies as a Critique of Intersectionality's Indebtedness to Subculture of Violence Theory 132
Tommy J. Curry

12 Between Critical (World) Psychology and Transdisciplinary Praxis 155
Robert K. Beshara

Index 159

CONTRIBUTORS

Rachel Begay is Native American of Santa Clara Pueblo and Navajo decent. Her mother is Pueblo and her father was Navajo; she was raised and resides in Santa Clara Pueblo. She participates in Pueblo ceremonies year round and endures a lot of hard work, to preserve their way of life so that the next generation and all those who follow will be born into a world that gives them value and meaning in their lives as Pueblo people. Her career as an Administrative Assistant at Northern New Mexico College (NNMC) began in 2007 working in the Registrar's Office and in 2014 she moved to the Department of Humanities, Social Sciences, Language, and Letters. She has been employed at Northern for over 13 years and enjoy working with a diverse faculty in these departments as well as the students. She is also one of the sponsors for Northern's American Indian Student Organization.

Robert K. Beshara is the author of *Decolonial Psychoanalysis: Towards Critical Islamophobia Studies* (Routledge, 2019) and *Freud and Said: Contrapuntal Psychoanalysis as Liberation Praxis* (Palgrave, 2021), and the editor of *A Critical Introduction to Psychology* (Nova, 2019). He works as an Assistant Professor of Psychology and Humanities at Northern New Mexico College. He is the founder of criticalpsychology.org, a free resource for scholars, activists, and practitioners. He is also the director of the Critical Psychology certificate program at Global Center for Advanced Studies (GCAS) College. For more information, please visit www.robertbeshara.com

Tommy J. Curry is Personal Chair (Distinguished Professor) of Africana Philosophy and Black Male Studies, Department of Philosophy, The University of Edinburgh, School of Philosophy, Psychology, and Language Sciences. He is a recipient of the American Book Award Winner (2018) and he is a Diverse Emerging Scholar

(2018). He is the editor of *Black Male Studies: A Series Exploring the Paradoxes of Racially Subjugated Males* (Temple University Press). He is the author of *Another White Man's Burden: Josiah Royce Quest for a Philosophy of White Racial Empire* (2018); *The Man-Not: Race, Class, Genre, and the Dilemmas of Black Manhood* (2017); and *The Philosophical Treatise of William H. Ferris: Selected Readings from The African Abroad or, His Evolution in Western Civilization* (2016).

Serdar M. Değirmencioğlu was Professor of Psychology in Istanbul when he was fired in April 2016 for having signed a peace manifesto. In 2017, he was banned from public service for life. Forced to go into exile, he has held visiting positions in Cairo, Macerata, Brussels, and Frankfurt. He is now a visiting scholar at Goethe University, Frankfurt am Main. He has produced groundbreaking books on young people's participation, martyrdom, and militarism, psychosocial consequences of personal debt, and corruptive influences of private universities, and an award-winning documentary on the university entrance exam in Turkey. As an outspoken advocate of children's rights, he writes a Sunday column focused on children's rights and well-being in a daily newspaper in Turkey.

Valdite Pereira Fuga gained a Ph.D. and Master's in Applied Linguistics and Language Studies at the Catholic University of São Paulo (PUC-SP), affiliated to the Language in Activity in the School Context Research Group (LACE). She graduated in Language Studies (Portuguese and English) at Mogi das Cruzes University (UMC) and at the same institution, graduated in Mathematics. Currently, she is a professor in Higher Education at Faculdade de Tecnologia de Mogi das Cruzes, where she was one of the coordinators in the Languages without Borders (LwB) program in partnership with the Brazilian Ministry of Education (MEC). At the moment, she attends post-doctoral studies at PUC-SP. CV: http://lattes.cnpq.br/1602876529143912

Silvana S. Hernández-Ortiz graduated as a psychologist from the Universidad del Desarrollo, Concepción, Chile. She is currently a Doctoral candidate in Psychology at the Universidad Católica del Maule, Talca, Chile. Her lines of work correspond to educational psychology from the perspective of critical psychology. Her main research interest is how students from highly vulnerable and segregated educational contexts construct their subjectivities from a Foucauldian perspective and through critical discourse analysis. She has presented her work at the 2019 International Critical Psychology Praxis Congress, New Mexico, USA, and the 2020 Critical Psychology Conference in East Asia, Tokyo, Japan. She can be contacted here: ss.hernandez.o@gmail.com

Lois Holzman is the co-founder and director of the East Side Institute for Group and Short Term Psychotherapy and the founder and chair of the bi-annual Performing the World conferences. Over 40 years Holzman has built and supported grassroots organizations that are engaging poverty and underdevelopment utilizing the transformative power of performance. She is the author/editor of ten books—the latest being *The Overweight Brain: How our Obsession with Knowing Keeps us from Getting Smart Enough to make a Better World*—and dozens of chapters and articles on social therapeutics, performance and play, Lev Vygotsky, critical psychology, and postmodern Marxism. She blogs at loisholzman.org, *Psychology Today* and *Mad in America*. Lois received her Ph.D. from Columbia University and was recently appointed Distinguished Visiting Fellow in Vygotskian Practice and Performance by the Lloyd International Honors College at University of North Carolina at Greensboro.

Fernanda Liberali is a teacher educator, researcher, and professor at the Pontifical Catholic University of São Paulo, in the Languages Department. She holds a doctorate degree in Applied Linguistics and Language Studies from the same university. She is an international member of the Eastside Institute Associates, a member of the Global Network of the University of Leeds; an advisor to CNPq and FAPESP; a Brazilian representative of the international committee of the International Symposium on Bilingualism and Bilingual Education in Latin America (BILINGLATAM); and the general coordinator of the national extension and research project, Digitmed Program. Within the framework of Socio-Historical-Cultural Activity Theory, her main research interests are related to teacher education, teaching–learning, multimodal argumentation, and multilingualism / bilingual education. CV: http://lattes.cnpq.br/0046483605366023

José Carlos Barbosa Lopes is a Ph.D. student and a Master in Applied Linguistics and Language Studies at the Catholic University of São Paulo (PUCSP), affiliated to the LACE Research Group – Language in Activity in the School Context. He achieved a specialization course in English Language at São Paulo State University (UNESP), a specialization in Language Studies, and a major in Portuguese and English at Mogi das Cruzes University (UMC). He has experience as an English teacher in public and private elementary schools and high schools, language institutes, and online courses. Currently, he is a professor in Higher Education at Faculdade Méliès and at Faculdades de Tecnologia Mauá and Ipiranga, where he was one of the coordinators in the Languages without Borders (LwB) program in partnership with the Brazilian Ministry of Education (MEC). CV: http://lattes.cnpq.br/7702814038846925

Michael J. Miller is a clinical psychologist and Associate Professor of Psychiatry at State University of New York (SUNY) Upstate Medical University in Syracuse, NY. There, he is Co-Director of Psychology Training and Co-Director of Student Counseling Services. His publications include *Lacanian Psychotherapy* and a contribution to the recent *Reading Lacan's Ecrits*: From "The Freudian Thing" to "Remarks on Daniel Lagache."

x List of Contributors

María-Constanza Garrido Sierralta (Cony) is an MA student in philosophy at the University of New Mexico. Her research focuses on intersecting topics in social and political philosophy, in particular, from a phenomenological-hermeneutical perspective, but also in Marxism, psychoanalysis, and aesthetics. She has translated the work of contemporary French thinkers such as Cornelius Castoriadis, Pierre Vidal-Naquet, and Patrice Vermeren. Some of her works have been published by Palgrave Macmillan and others are forthcoming with Edinburgh University Press.

Hans Skott-Myhre is a Professor in the Social Work and Human Services Department at Kennesaw State University. He is the author of *Youth Subcultures as Creative Force: Creating New Spaces for Radical Youth Work*, co-editor with Chris Richardson of *Habitus of the Hood*, co-editor with K. Gharabaghi and M. Krueger of *With Children and Youth*, co-editor with V. Pacini-Ketchabaw and K Skott-Myhre of *Youth Work, Early Education and Psychology: Liminal Encounters*, and, with David Fancy, co-editor of *Art as Revolt: Thinking Politics Through Immanent Aesthetics*. He has published multiple articles, reviews, and book chapters.

Kathleen S.G. Skott-Myhre is an Associate Professor of Psychology at the University of West Georgia. She is the author of *Feminist Spirituality under Capitalism: Witches, Fairies and Nomads* as well as the co-author of *Writing the Family: Women, Autoethnography, and Family Work*. She is co-editor with V. Pacini-Ketchabaw and H.A. Skott-Myhre of *Youth Work, Early Education and Psychology: Liminal Encounters*. She has published multiple articles, reviews, and book chapters.

Patricia Marina Trujillo (BA, New Mexico State University; MA, University of Nebraska; Ph.D., University of Texas at San Antonio) is a proud northern New Mexican, born and raised in the Española Valley. She is the Director of Equity and Diversity and an Associate Professor of English and Chicana/o studies at Northern New Mexico College (NNMC). Dr. Trujillo has been the founding director of Equity and Diversity since 2013. Through three pillars of engagement—critical education, social justice, and beloved community—the NNMC Office of Equity and Diversity works to educate, engage, and inspire students, faculty, staff, and the greater community. She serves on the boards of Tewa Women United, NewMexicoWomen.org, the Northern Rio Grande National Heritage Area, and the LANL Foundation. Trujillo also has a nationally regarded publishing record. Additionally, Trujillo is the creative writing editor of *Chicana/Latina Studies: The Journal of Mujeres Activas en Letras y Cambio Social* and the co-host of the weekly radio show, *Brave Space: Feminist News for Northern New Mexico*, on KTRC 103.7 FM/1260 AM.

Fu Wai is an Associate Professor in the Department of Counseling Psychology, Hong Kong Shue Yan University. He is working on establishing courses, curriculum, and material related to critical psychology in Hong Kong. His research interests include: the history of psychology, ancient Chinese philosophy (including the school of names and the school of diplomats), the history of the hypnosis movement in Republican China, and psychoanalysis (Freud and Lacan) as applied in critical psychology. He is the founder of the Signifier (Chinese name Zhi Fei Zhi), a hub of Hong Kong young scholars who share ideas in psychoanalysis, contemporary philosophy, and literature. Dr. Fu's publications are mainly in Chinese, and include *City in Oral Stage* (2010), *Taipei/Lotus* (2011), *300.9 (F99)*—a novel illustrating Lacanian concepts. Dr. Fu Wai is also a committee member of the Hong Kong General Union of School Counseling Professionals to promote labor rights of oppressed frontline workers in Hong Kong.

ACKNOWLEDGMENTS

I would like to sincerely thank Brent D. Slife, Lucy McClune, Akshita Pattiyani, Lekshmi Priya S., Liz Williams Stephanie Amedeo Marquez, Ulises Ricoy, Lori Franklin, Ivan Lopez, Mateo Frazier, Charles Knight, Charles Becknell, James Annon, Mollie Kelly, Tammy Lucero, Juan Palacios, Santana Salazar, Meghan Trujillo, and everyone else who helped me actualize the 2019 International Critical ~~Psychology~~ Praxis Congress.

PREFACE: REPORTING ON THE 2019 INTERNATIONAL CRITICAL ~~PSYCHOLOGY~~ PRAXIS CONGRESS

Robert K. Beshara

In July of 2018, I launched criticalpsychology.org as a free resource for scholars, activists, and practitioners interested in critical psychology. Then after receiving a lot of positive feedback from international scholars, and encouragement from one of my mentors (Ian Parker), I decided that I wanted to organize a conference at Northern New Mexico College (NNMC) titled the *2019 International Critical ~~Psychology~~ Praxis Congress* (ICPPC).

As of August 2018, I began proposing the idea for the conference at NNMC first to the Interim Chair of the Department of Humanities and Social Sciences then to the Dean of the College of Arts and Sciences, and finally to the Provost. After receiving approval at every level, I started publicizing the call for papers in November of 2018. The deadline was on March 1st, 2019, but I later extended it to April 1st. I received many submissions, which went through a single-blind peer-review process, wherein two reviewers evaluated the anonymized abstracts by commenting on the quality of each proposal and also by rating each proposal using a five-point rating scale.

The 2019 ICPPC took place on the campus of NNMC at the Center for the Arts (CFA), and the location was significant because it is the historical land of the Tewa people, which was colonized first by Spain then by Mexico and, finally, by the United States. In other words, historical trauma is a very real experience for the numerous Indigenous people who live here and whose ancestors have lived here for more than a millennium, particularly members of the eight northern Pueblo tribes, which surround the Northern campus. This history of struggle framed the 2019 ICPPC; it was meaningful for the students in the Española valley to take pride in the fact that this land was attracting scholars from all over the world to discuss different ways of decolonizing psychology through the key framework of praxis, which is the combination of theory and practice.

For this reason, the first day of the conference (Friday, September 27, 2019) was dedicated to panels on theory (e.g., critical theory, feminism, psychoanalysis, etc.) with a keynote from the perspective of Black Male Studies delivered by Dr. Tommy J. Curry and the second day of the conference (Saturday, September 28, 2019) was dedicated to panels on practice (e.g., clinical practice, politicized healing, pedagogy, etc.) with a keynote from the perspective of Chicana studies delivered by Dr. Patricia Trujillo.

The 2019 ICPPC was a very successful event thanks to our sponsors, namely: the Regional Development Corporation, NNMC, the LANL Foundation, the Africana Studies program at the University of New Mexico (UNM), and the Office of Equity and Diversity and the Student Senate at NNMC. The sponsorship allowed us to pay for a shuttle to pick up some of the presenters from and to Santa Fe, to provide lunch to all conference affiliates (i.e., presenters, panel chairs, student organizers, etc.) on both days, to pay Film and Digital Media Arts students at NNMC to live-stream and video record the conference as well as run the lights and sound for the two-day event, to supply snacks and refreshments that were available on both mornings of the conference, to reimburse the Tewa Sunrisers of the Santa Clara Pueblo who performed at the end of the first day and very much blessed the conference with their powerful performance, to print the conference programs, to remunerate other promotional material (e.g., conference t-shirts), and to cover the expenses of Española Valley High School students so they could attend on Friday.

To give you (the reader) a sense of the event's success, I will break down the demographic data in terms of attendance. There were a total of 29 presenters at the conference, most of whom were hailing from either other countries (e.g., Canada, Japan, the United Kingdom, Brazil, Mexico, and Chile) or other states (e.g., Georgia, New York, Pennsylvania, Louisiana, New Jersey, Washington, and California). Out of the 29 presenters, seven presented virtually, either synchronously through Zoom or asynchronously via a pre-recorded video or PowerPoint slideshow.

According to the data from Eventbrite (the website used for registration), 144 tickets were sold. Tickets were free for any member of the NNMC community (students, faculty, and staff) as well as students from UNM (a co-sponsor). In addition to the registration data, we also conducted an anonymous demographic survey using Google Forms. Seventy-seven attendees filled out the survey, but the six student organizers estimate that attendance was probably around 100 because 20–30 people did not fill out the demographic survey. The majority of attendees were NNMC students (70.1%), female (63.6%), Hispanic or Latinx (72.7%), single and never married (77.9%), who make an income between $10k and $50k (40.3%), live in Española, NM (70.1%), have completed a high-school degree or equivalent (41.6%), and are under 18 (35.1%). This demographic data does not include the many online viewers who were live-streaming the conference via YouTube.

With support from the LANL Foundation and with the help of Mr. Tobe Bott-Lyons (Director of Upward Bound at NNMC), we were able to invite 24 students from Española Valley High School along with two chaperones as well as seven upward-bound students at NNMC who were enrolled in Bott-Lyons's Participatory Action Research class. In addition to busing the students to and from campus and providing them with lunch, I scheduled a half-an-hour session after lunch for all students, particularly high-school students, to meet with the presenters, and those conversations went very well.

The conference would not have been a success without the help of the six student organizers who were registered in an upper-division, special topics course I created at NNMC called Conference Experience, wherein the students learned about how to plan for as well as run an event or a conference. The students divided their time during the two-day conference between different tasks, namely: registration, support in the theatre, social media, and floating. Although there were a couple of hiccups during the conference, the students were very professional, calm, kind, and welcoming in their approach and they made the presenters feel at home, which speaks to the overall positive impression that we were able to give to attendees from outside of New Mexico, who do not hold a stereotypical idea about Española in their minds and consequently enjoyed the experience without bias.

Many of the presenters have written to me via email about how they were impressed with the students and with NNMC, and that they generally had a wonderful experience that was intellectually stimulating. It is also worth mentioning that the CFA's lobby included, in addition to registration and promotional leaflets, tables for different organizations, such as the College Assistance Migrant Program (CAMP), the Life Link, the American Indian Student Organization (AISO), and a sculpture titled *Pythagorean Forest* created by math students at NNMC. Since the entire conference was recorded, you can view the video recordings of the presentations by visiting www.criticalpsychology.org and then clicking on "2019 ICPPC."

Fifteen (Indigenous, Black, Brown, and white) authors, who reside in the United States, Santa Clara Pueblo, Greece, Brazil, Chile, Hong Kong, and Scotland, wrote the following 12 chapters. While not all of them are psychologists, they are *in toto* contributing to a critical (world) psychology from the perspectives of Chican@ Studies, Marxism, radical feminism, poststructuralism, Lacanian psychoanalysis, critical pedagogy, and Black Male Studies. In sum, this edited volume represents the heterogeneity of theoretico-methodological resources available to contemporary critical psychologists, and embodies what Ramón Grosfoguel (2012) calls "epistemic diversity",[1] which is necessary for the worlding of critical psychology. In the first chapter, I introduce ten concepts for critical psychology praxis. And, in the final chapter, I conclude with the majority of authors' responses to my question about how their chapters are contributing to the worlding of critical psychology through transdisciplinary praxis.

Note

1 Grosfoguel, R. (2012). The dilemmas of ethnic studies in the United States: Between liberal multiculturalism, identity politics, disciplinary colonization, and decolonial epistemologies. *Human Architecture: Journal of the Sociology of Self-Knowledge*, 10(1), 81–89.

1
TEN CONCEPTS FOR CRITICAL PSYCHOLOGY PRAXIS

Robert K. Beshara

Critical Psychology Praxis is an edited volume based primarily upon conference proceedings from the *2019 International Critical Psychology Praxis Congress* (ICPPC), a transdisciplinary event that brought together global scholars, activists, and practitioners who desire to cooperatively imagine a worldcentric critical psychology from the perspective of the *damnés* (Fanon, 1961/2004)—what Burton and Osorio (2011), following the decolonial turn (Maldonado-Torres, 2017; Pickren, 2020), have termed a transmodern, or analectical, psychology, but which can also be qualified as a pluriversal psychology (Beshara, 2019). The Congress took place on September 27–28, 2019, at Northern New Mexico College in Española, NM; a campus dedicated to underserved Hispanic and Native American students and surrounded by the eight northern Pueblos of Taos, Picuris, Santa Clara, Ohkay Owingeh, San Ildefonso, Nambé, Pojoaque, and Tesuque.

The book chapters are united around the theme of *psychosocial non-alignment to modernity/coloniality*. Psychosocial Studies (Frosh, 2003) emerged in the United Kingdom as a critical psychological approach that recognizes the inherent link between psyche and society and, therefore, rejects the reductionist impulse of mainstream (Euro-American) psychology (i.e., reducing psyche to behavior, cognition, and/or the brain).

Non-alignment is a reference to the Global South's Non-Aligned Movement, which embodies a third option beyond the First World's (e.g., the United States and the European Union) *laissez-faire* capitalism and the Second World's (e.g., the People's Republic of China after the collapse of the Soviet Union) state capitalism. The Global South is both a politico-economic and a geographical designation that refers to transmodern cultures in the continents of South America, Africa, and Asia. Furthermore, the Global South signifies outsiders within—that is, decolonial subcultures in the Global North (i.e., the descendants of Indigenous, Black, and Brown peoples who were colonized, enslaved, and/or over-exploited since 1492).

Modernity/coloniality is the name of a Latin American research program, which is theoretically grounded in liberation theology and other non-European intellectual developments (e.g., liberation philosophy and psychology) since the 1960s (Escobar, 2007). Arturo Escobar (2007) describes modernity/coloniality as "a framework constructed from the Latin American periphery of the modern colonial world system" that "helps explain the dynamics of eurocentrism in the making of modernity" and "reveals the dark sides of modernity" (p. 189). He adds, "Modernity/coloniality also shows that the perspective of modernity is limited and exhausted in its pretended universality" and "not only re-focuses our attention on the overall fact of development, it provides a context for interpreting the various challenges to development and modernity as so many projects that are potentially complementary and mutually reinforcing" (Escobar, 2007, p. 189).

To put it succinctly, following Mignolo (2007), what the modernity/coloniality research program clearly shows is that the oppressive rhetoric of modernity—for example, arguments regarding the supposed civilizational superiority of European cultures—is always sustained in practice by the violent logic of coloniality, particularly the "coloniality of power" (Quijano, 2000). In other words, coloniality is the unconscious of Euromodernity. Subsequently, Enrique Dussel rejects the two main critiques of modernity (i.e., critical modernity and postmodernity) since they are essentially Eurocentric and proposes instead *transmodernity* as not only a critique of modernity but also, and more significantly, as a worldcentric project that "embraces both modernity and its alterity" (Dussel, 1995, p. 139) and which is realized through liberation praxis.

Following from this, I encouraged authors to write their chapters in response to the above-mentioned theme and in the spirit of praxis (cf. Burton, 2013). The goal of this edited volume then is to bridge the North–South divide in critical psychology, a function of ethnocentrism, through solidarity and dialogue. It is worth mentioning here that the fifth volume of the *Annual Review of Critical Psychology*, a peer-reviewed journal published by the Discourse Unit, is dedicated to contributions to critical psychology from different geo-political regions. What follows are ten "polycentric" (Amin, 1990) concepts for critical psychology praxis, which is my contribution to liberation psychology (Burton & Ordóñez, 2015; Martín-Baró, 1994; Watkins & Shulman, 2008).

The Politics of Citation

I identify as a scholar-activist because I do not believe, as a human scientist, that knowledge is a neutral affair. I borrow this insight from Michel Foucault (1980), who theorized the interdependence between power and knowledge through his concept of "power/knowledge." The production of knowledge, in other words, is inherently a political act, which has productive, or oftentimes, disciplinary effects, and so we have an ethical obligation, as academics, to think about the effects of our specific positions within the network of power called academe.

In *Living a Feminist Life*, Sara Ahmed (2017) writes, "A citational chain is created around theory: you become a theorist by citing other theorists that cite other theorists" (p. 8). In other words, *citation is a political act* (Ahmed, 2013) because, as scholars, we have to consciously, or unconsciously, decide which theorists to cite. Citation is also *an act of solidarity*. Ahmed (2017) writes, "Citation is how we acknowledge our debt to those who came before; those who helped us find our way when the way was obscured because we deviated from the paths we were told to follow" (pp. 15–16). For Ahmed (2017), citations "are the materials through which, from which, we create our dwellings" (p. 16). Furthermore, what Ahmed (2017) calls "citational practice" refers to "not only who is cited in written texts but who is speaking at events" (p. 148), which informed my decision of who to invite as keynote speakers at the 2019 ICPPC. Another source of inspiration, another citation, is the Cite Black Women[1] project, which is described as follows: "In November 2017 Christen A. Smith created Cite Black Women as a campaign to push people to engage in a radical praxis of citation that acknowledges and honors Black women's transnational intellectual production."

I want to build upon these feminist initiatives, and urge the reader to Cite Southern Theorists, or theorists from the Global South. They may be literally outside of your comfort zone, hence the challenge. I recommend that you (the reader) visit the following website, which is an open-access encyclopedia of Global Southern Theory: globalsocialtheory.org. This is the site's description: "This site is intended as a free resource for students, teachers, academics, and others interested in social theory and wishing to understand it in [a] global perspective."[2]

The Ethics of Liberation

In *Pedagogy of the Oppressed*, Paulo Freire (1970/2018) shows that oppression is dehumanizing for both the oppressed *and* the oppressor; however, he argues that the oppressed must lead the way toward liberation because they know oppression first-hand. Oppressors can become "comrades" as opposed to allies (Dean, 2019) in the collective struggle toward liberation but, Freire (1970/2018) emphasizes, they must authentically follow the leadership of the oppressed without exhibiting "false generosity" (p. 44), which entails "a profound rebirth" (p. 61). Solidarity necessitates, among other things, a radical commitment to both antiracism— as opposed to the two forms of racism: segregation and assimilation—and anticapitalism given the historical and ongoing oppressive reality of "racial capitalism" (Robinson, 1983/2000). In sum, an ethics of liberation, as Enrique Dussel (2013) asserts, is "transmodern" (p. 39), or from the perspective of modernity's alterity: the oppressed, the colonized, or the *damnés*, to use Frantz Fanon's (1961/2004) term.

For Dussel (2013), there are three principles to liberation as an ethics of responsibility: (1) the material principle, which is concerned with "the production, reproduction, and development of human life" (p. 99); (2) the formal principle as "the principle of practical-intersubjective discursive rationality of the agreement that reaches, from the truth of the material principle … rational (and effective) grounding of the ends, values, and means to be accomplished" (p. 106); and (3) the principle of feasibility or what is "technically and economically possible" (p. 159). In other words, liberation ethics is truthful and valid when it is both material (as opposed to ideological) and formal (as opposed to illegitimate) in its claims; these ethical claims about truthfulness and validity are then applied, hence the praxis, according to the principle of feasibility, which is also the goodness claim (p. 159).

Decolonial Aesthesis

Walter Mignolo argues:

> The word and the concept of aesthetics entered the vocabulary of modern, European philosophy, in the eighteenth century. German philosopher Alexander Gottlieb Baumgarten published in 1750 a treatise titled *Aesthetics*. The concept was derived from the Greek word *aesthesis*, a word that refers to the senses and the emotions derived from the senses … Decolonial aestheSis refers in general to any and every thinking and doing that is geared toward undoing a particular kind of aesthesis, of senses, that is the sensibility of the colonized subject. What decolonial artists want is not to create beautiful objects, installations, music, multimedia or whatever the possibilities are, but to create in order to decolonize sensibilities, to transform colonial aestheTics into decolonial aestheSis.
> *(as cited in Gaztambide-Fernández, 2014, pp. 200–201)*

Along similar lines, in his 1935 essay, "The work of art in the age of mechanical reproduction," Walter Benjamin (1935/2012) distinguished between *the aestheticization of politics*, which the Nazis mastered with their propaganda campaign against the subaltern, and the politicization of art. For example, think of the omnipresence of the swastika (originally a spiritual symbol in Hinduism) in Leni Riefenstahl's (1935) *Triumph of the Will*. Incidentally, this propaganda film was released during the same year Benjamin's essay was published. For Benjamin (1935/2012), when art is mechanically reproduced, it loses its aura, and becomes divorced from its origins in ritual and magic. This is how art, particularly under fascism, becomes politics in the modern era—hence, why Benjamin rejected the notion of *art for art's sake*. Benjamin names a counter-ideological praxis, along the lines of decolonial aesthesis. This praxis is *the politicization of art*, that is, producing decolonial aesthetic objects from the perspective of the subaltern in the spirit of consciousness-raising or *conscientização* (conscientization).

These decolonial aesthetic objects may be perceived as cruel (Artaud, 1938/1958) or ugly and dissonant (Adorno, 1970/1997) because their purpose is to disturb the audience and shake them from their complacency with modernity through an encounter with the traumatic Real of colonial oppression and violence. This encounter would then result in not only *conscientização* but also *critical unconsciousness*. Critical unconsciousness is essential for the actualization of a politics based on the praxis of liberation.

Modernity/Coloniality

Aníbal Quijano (2000) writes:

> The idea of race, in its modern meaning, does not have a known history before the colonization of America. Perhaps it originated in reference to the phenotypic differences between conquerors and conquered. However, what matters is that soon it was constructed to refer to the supposed differential biological structures between those groups.
>
> *(p. 534)*

Quijano (2000) is basically arguing that we cannot separate modernity, or postmodernity for that matter, from coloniality because the colonization of the Americas essentially led to the establishment and acceleration of the modern world system's (i.e., racial capitalism) hegemony from then till now, and so the corrective is not fantasizing about a pre-modern/pre-colonial world, but actually drawing on material theories and practices from modernity's alterity in an effort to actualize a transmodern/decolonial world. This connects back to the first concept: the politics of citation.

Delinking

Samir Amin (1990) popularized the term "delinking," which names a praxis of alter-globalization, or of moving from a Eurocentric to a polycentric world. In order for us to do that, we need to delink the rhetoric of modernity from the logic of coloniality (Mignolo, 2007). We can only do so by thinking and acting in the spirit of *mundialización* (mundialization), that is, an antiracist/anticapitalist international network of solidarity and cooperation.

Mignolo (2000) distinguishes between globalization and mundialization; the former signifies global (civilizational) designs while the latter designates local (cultural) histories. The shift from globalization to mundialization, as an effect of delinking, entails enacting a conscious rhetoric of transmodernity and an unconscious logic of decoloniality—what I term *critical unconsciousness*. This change also implies a different citational practice as well as a movement from universality to pluriversality (Mignolo, 2007), which is the idea of *one civilization with many cultures* (Wahba, forthcoming).

The principle of delinking is furthermore related to the theme of the 2019 ICPPC, which is *psychosocial non-alignment to modernity/coloniality*. For example, instead of the Orientalist (i.e., binary and hierarchical) discourse of the West versus the rest, we can tell ourselves a worldly story about the bridge between ancient Greece and the Renaissance through Arabic science and philosophy (Al-Khalili, 2011), which constituted not only translations of, and commentaries on, ancient Greek texts (e.g., Aristotle), but also, and more significantly, a proliferation of original contributions to human knowledge in a variety of fields, from chemistry to astronomy. However, the story of European exceptionalism necessitates repressing this Other story from modernity's alterity; a story of the hegemony of Muslim, Jewish, and Christian non-Europeans for almost 800 years in Al-Andalus, wherein Arabic was the language of science, the way English is today.

Praxis

Karl Marx's (1845/1978) 11th thesis on Feuerbach is: "The philosophers [or psychologists] have only *interpreted* the world, in various ways; the point, however, is to *change* it" (p. 145, emphasis in original). This statement is in essence what praxis is all about, and it was echoed more than a century later by Freire (1970/2018), who writes that praxis is "*reflection* and *action* upon the world in order to transform it" (p. 51, emphasis added). I use the following formula myself: Praxis = Theory + Practice. The principle of praxis explains the structural logic of the 2019 ICPPC, wherein the first day was dedicated to theory and the second to practice; both are equally important and interdependent.

The scholar-activist is the subject of critical psychology praxis; he or she is not only a critical theorist of psychology, but also an embodiment of criticality. In other words, the scholar-activist embodies a criticality of knowledge and being through his or her teaching, research, activism, and/or clinical practice. The late Tod Sloan exemplified this attitude, and also wrote about it: *Activist Support as a Form of Critical Psychology Praxis* (Sloan, 2013).

Criticality

Why was the signifier psychology barred in the title of the Congress? Many have asked me this question. There are a few reasons. Barring psychology emphasizes the two other signifiers sandwiching psychology, that is, "critical" and "praxis." Also, I borrowed the matheme of "barred psychology" ($\bar{\Psi}$ or not-psi) from Ian Parker (2003), who argues that *Lacanian psychoanalysis is barred psychology* because it "is deliberately set against the rules of the game that psychologists follow in their version of scientific inquiry" and it "presents theoretical accounts that seem designed to prohibit understanding on the part of psychologists" (p. 110).

Criticality, as a negative practice in the best sense of the word, implies distance. To bar psychology means to critique it from outside of the discipline. In other words, psychology as a human scientific discipline is a point of entry for our unconscious critique, but it is not the endpoint of this critique, which leads me to the concept of secular criticism.

For Edward W. Said (1983):

> Criticism in short is always situated [or worldly]; it is skeptical, secular, reflectively open to its own failings. This is by no means to say that it is value-free. Quite the contrary, for the inevitable trajectory of *critical consciousness* is to arrive at some acute sense of what political, social, and human values are entailed in the reading, production, and transmission of every text.
>
> *(p. 26, emphasis added)*

Transdisciplinarity

Criticality, by default, is transdisciplinary, for it is a meta-position, so whereas *psychologists study psyche*, critical psychologists study *how psychologists study psyche* in addition to studying psyche *qua* subjectivity, which is more of a psychosocial notion and so avoids the orthodox impulse of reducing psyche to mind, brain, or behavior. To put it differently, in their critiques of mainstream psychology, critical psychologists draw on theories and practices (or praxes) from other disciplines in an effort to envision a *pluriversal, or polycentric, psychology*. Barring psychology undisciplines and denaturalizes the field, hence, renders it more complex.

Parker (1999) stressed the importance of transdisciplinarity for critical psychology more than 20 years ago:

> Critical psychology stretches across the boundary marking the inside and outside of the discipline. It is not only "interdisciplinary", in the sense that it must draw upon arguments raging across the academic and professional landscape, but "transdisciplinary" in the sense that it both questions the ways in which the borders were set up and policed by the colleges and training institutes and it stretches from the furthermost edges of the psy-complex to the centres of psychology.
>
> *(p. 10)*

Intersectionality of Struggles

Kimberlé Crenshaw (1989) coined the signifier "intersectionality," which is central to Black feminism today. This is a concept which Tommy J. Curry (2017; Chapter 11 of this volume) is critical of because it fails to account for Black male vulnerability since it equates maleness with patriarchy without taking into account how the history of racial capitalism produced the Man-Not, that is, the Black male in the zone of non-being. Whereas Crenshaw (1989) conceived of the concept in terms of *an intersectionality of identities* (e.g., being both Black and woman), Angela Davis, in her 2016 book, *Freedom is a Constant Struggle*, revolutionized the notion beyond its foundation in identity politics with her emphasis on the *intersectionality of struggles*. In other words, for Davis (2016), we must struggle together not because we are of the same identity but because we have common desires as comrades, which would render our liberation praxis enjoyable. Davis's (2016) radical reconceptualization allows for a praxis of *international solidarity* among scholars, activists, and practitioners inside and outside of (critical) psychology.

Imaginative Geography and Historical Knowledge

In *Orientalism*, Edward Said (1978/2003) writes that "imaginative geography and history help the mind to intensify its own sense of itself by dramatizing the distance and difference between what is close to it and what is far away" (p. 55). In other words, imaginative geography is a function of ideology, or what Louis Althusser (1970/2014) labels Ideological State Apparatuses like culture, education, the media, etc.

I am interested in mapping as an ideological practice, particularly since it is a form of imaginative geography that claims to be scientific. I want to demonstrate three map projections, and I want the reader to reflect on how each one affects your geographical imagination. The first two maps (the Mercator and Gall-Peters projections: Figures 1.1 and 1.2) are quite popular, but grossly inaccurate. The third map (AuthaGraph) is virtually unknown, even though it is the most accurate one of the three. Is it a coincidence that Hajime Narukawa, a Japanese architect, designed the third map from the periphery of the world system?

According to Decolonial Atlas (2017), "The [AuthaGraph] projection largely preserves the relative area of landmasses and oceans, limits the distortion of their shapes, and avoids cutting continents in half."[3] Narukawa (1999) writes:

> This rectangular world map called AuthaGraph World Map is made by equally dividing a spherical surface into 96 triangles, transferring it to a tetrahedron while maintaining areas proportions and unfolding it to be a rectangle. The world map can be tiled in any directions without visible seams. From this map-tiling, a new world map with triangular, rectangular or parallelogram's outline can be framed out with various regions at its center. The name, AuthaGraph is from authalic and -graph.[4]

Concepts for Critical Psychology Praxis 9

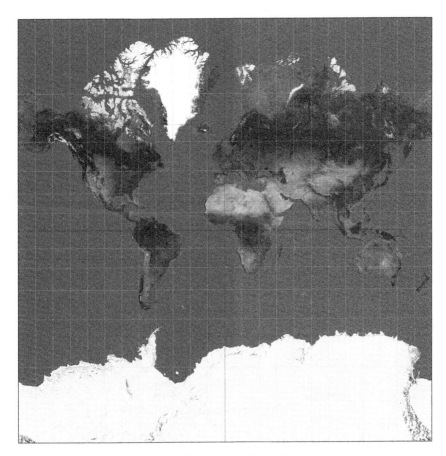

FIGURE 1.1 Mercator projection. (Courtesy of Daniel R. Strebe)

Another interesting map is the greater United States map from Daniel Immerwahr's (2019) recently published book, *How to Hide an Empire* (Figure 1.3). In the book, Immerwahr contests the logo map of the United States, outlined in red, since it does not show the US Empire's colonial territories past and present.

In sum, we need to decolonize oppressive notions of space and time by re-coding geography and history. The ongoing climate breakdown, which is but one of the many effects of modernity/coloniality, contextualizes our liberation praxis. The answer to the modern world system of racial capitalism is not a romanticization of the pre-modern past, but a rewriting of the present through the lens of transmodernity/decoloniality and from the perspective of the oppressed. In other words, can we think and act, as critical psychologists, in the pluriversal and polycentric spirit of mundialization?

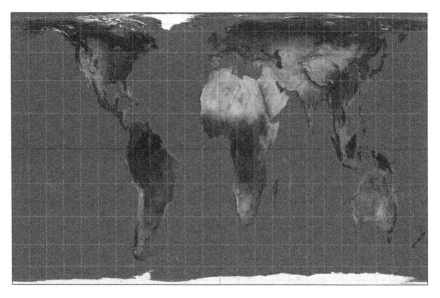

FIGURE 1.2 Gall-Peters projection. (Courtesy of Daniel R. Strebe)

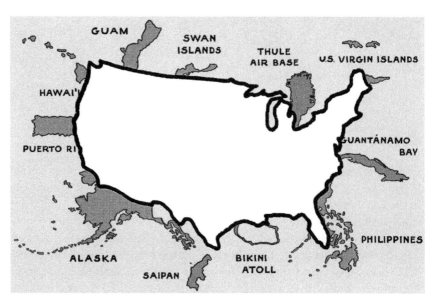

FIGURE 1.3 The Greater United States. (Courtesy of Jonathan D. Lippincott: junepark. co.)

Notes

1 www.citeblackwomencollective.org/.
2 https://globalsocialtheory.org/.
3 https://decolonialatlas.wordpress.com/2017/03/11/authagraph-world-maps/.
4 www.authagraph.com/projects/description/%E3%80%90%E4%BD%9C%E5%93%81%E8%A7%A3%E8%AA%AC%E3%80%91%E8%A8%98%E4%BA%8B01/?lang=en.

References

Adorno, T. W. (1970/1997). *Aesthetic theory* (R. Hullot-Kentor, Trans.). G. Adorno & R. Tiedemann (Eds.). New York, NY: Continuum.

Ahmed, S. (2013, September 11). Making feminist points [blog post]. Retrieved from https://feministkilljoys.com/2013/09/11/making-feminist-points/

Ahmed, S. (2017). *Living a feminist life*. Durham, NC: Duke University Press.

Al-Khalili, J. (2011). *The house of wisdom: How Arabic science saved ancient knowledge and gave us the Renaissance*. London, UK: Penguin.

Althusser, L. (1970/2014). *On the reproduction of capitalism: Ideology and ideological state apparatuses*. New York, NY: Verso.

Amin, S. (1990). *Delinking: Towards a polycentric world*. London, UK: Zed.

Artaud, A. (1938/1958). *The theater and its double* (M. C. Richards, Trans.). New York, NY: Grove Press.

Benjamin, W. (1935/2012). The work of art in the age of mechanical reproduction. In M. G. Durham & D. M. Kellner (Eds.), *Media and cultural studies: Keyworks* (3rd ed.). Hoboken, NJ: Wiley.

Beshara, R. K. (2019). Towards a pluriversal psychology. In R. K. Beshara (Ed.), *A critical introduction to psychology*. Hauppauge, NY: Nova Science Publishers.

Burton, M. (2013). Liberation psychology: A constructive critical praxis. *Estudos de Psicología (Campinas)*, *30*(2), 249–259.

Burton, M. H., & Ordóñez, L. G. (2015). Liberation psychology: Another kind of critical psychology. In I. Parker (Ed.), *Handbook of critical psychology*. Abingdon, UK: Routledge.

Burton, M., & Osorio, J. M. F. (2011). Introducing Dussel: The philosophy of liberation and a really social psychology. *Psychology in Society*, (41), 20–39.

Crenshaw, K. (1989). Demarginalizing the intersection of race and sex: A Black feminist critique of antidiscrimination doctrine, feminist theory, and antiracist politics. *University of Chicago Legal Forum*, (1), 139–167. Retrieved from https://chicagounbound.uchicago.edu/cgi/viewcontent.cgi?article=1052&context=uclf

Curry, T. J. (2017). *The man-not: Race, class, genre, and the dilemmas of Black manhood*. Philadelphia, PA: Temple University Press.

Davis, A. Y. (2016). *Freedom is a constant struggle: Ferguson, Palestine, and the foundations of a movement*. Chicago, IL: Haymarket Books.

Dean, J. (2019). *Comrade: An essay on political belonging*. New York, NY: Verso.

Dussel, E. (1995). *The invention of the Americas: Eclipse of "the Other" and the myth of modernity* (M. D. Barber, Trans.). New York, NY: Continuum.

Dussel, E. (2013). *Ethics of liberation: In the age of globalization and exclusion* (N. Maldonado-Torres, E. Mendieta, Y. Angulo, & C. P. Bustillo, Trans.). Durham, NC: Duke University Press.

Escobar, A. (2007). Worlds and knowledges otherwise: The Latin American modernity/coloniality research program. *Cultural Studies*, *21*(2–3), 179–210.

Fanon, F. (1961/2004). *The wretched of the earth* (R. Philcox, Trans.). New York, NY: Grove Press.

Foucault, M. (1980). *Power/knowledge: Selected interviews and other writings, 1972–1977*. C. Gordon (Ed.). New York, NY: Pantheon.

Freire, P. (1970/2018). *Pedagogy of the oppressed*. New York, NY: Bloomsbury.

Frosh, S. (2003). Psychosocial studies and psychology: Is a critical approach emerging? *Human Relations*, 56(12), 1545–1567.

Gaztambide-Fernández, R. (2014). Decolonial options and artistic/aestheSic entanglements: An interview with Walter Mignolo. *Decolonization: Indigeneity, Education & Society*, 3(1).

Immerwahr, D. (2019). *How to hide an empire: A short history of the greater United States*. New York, NY: Vintage.

Maldonado-Torres, N. (2017). Frantz Fanon and the decolonial turn in psychology: From modern/colonial methods to the decolonial attitude. *South African Journal of Psychology*, 47(4), 432–441.

Martín-Baró, I. (1994). *Writings for a liberation psychology*. Cambridge, MA: Harvard University Press.

Marx, K., & Engels, F. (1845/1978). *The Marx–Engels reader* (2nd ed.). R. C. Tucker (Ed.). New York, NY: W.W. Norton.

Mignolo, W. (2000). *Local histories/global designs: Coloniality, subaltern knowledges, and border thinking*. Princeton, NJ: Princeton University Press.

Mignolo, W. D. (2007). Delinking. *Cultural Studies*, 21(2–3), 449–514. doi:10.1080/09502380601162647

Narukawa, H. (1999). *AuthaGraph projection* [map of the world]. Retrieved from https://upload.wikimedia.org/wikipedia/en/a/a7/Authagraph_projection.jpg

Parker, I. (1999). Critical psychology: Critical links. *Annual Review of Critical Psychology*, 1(1), 3–18. Retrieved from https://thediscourseunit.files.wordpress.com/2016/05/arcp1-parker-003-018.doc

Parker, I. (2003). Jacques Lacan, barred psychologist. *Theory & Psychology*, 13(1), 95–115. doi:10.1177/0959354303013001764

Pickren, W. E. (2020). Coloniality of being and knowledge in the history of psychology. In L. Malich & V. Balz (Eds.), *Psychologie und Kritik* (pp. 329–343). Berlin, Germany: Springer.

Quijano, A. (2000). Coloniality of power and eurocentrism in Latin America. *International Sociology*, 15(2), 215–232. doi:10.1177/0268580900015002005

Riefenstahl, L. (Director). (1935). *Triumph of the will* [motion picture]. Germany: Reichsparteitag-Film.

Robinson, C. J. (1983/2000). *Black Marxism: The making of the Black radical tradition*. Chapel Hill, NC: University of North Carolina Press.

Said, E.W. (1978/2003). *Orientalism*. London, UK: Penguin.

Said, E.W. (1983). *The world, the text, and the critic*. Cambridge, MA: Harvard University Press.

Sloan, T. (2013). Activist support as a form of critical psychology praxis. *Annual Review of Critical Psychology*, 10, 952–963.

Wahba, M. (forthcoming). *Fundamentalism and secularization* (R. K. Beshara, Trans.).

Watkins, M., & Shulman, H. (2008). *Toward psychologies of liberation*. London, UK: Palgrave.

2
UNDERSTANDING AND CHALLENGING LITERARY GENTRIFICATION IN NEW MEXICO

A Concept in Parts

Patricia Marina Trujillo

Prelude

When invited to be one of the keynotes for the International Critical ~~Psychology~~ Praxis Congress at Northern New Mexico College on September 28, 2019, I immediately felt a tension about my relationship to the field of psychology. I wanted to put up my shields and declare, "That's not my field! I don't do psychology." But as a proponent and continual student of Critical Theory, Critical Race Theory, and Critical Education, the purposeful retooling of the title of the conference drew me in.

The path I take to critical praxis has its origins in two traditional communities in northern New Mexico: El Guache, a traditional village located on the Yungeh Yungeh (*hispano*) side of the Ohkay Owingeh Pueblo land grant, and a small rancho in the community of Upper Ranchitos de Taos, NM. Both of these locations, the traditional homelands of my families for hundreds of years, have instructed me through life and in the work I do in the academy and in my community. A very common *dicho*, or folk knowledge, used often by my family and the community is "*Dicho y hecho*," which translates to "Said and done." It is knowledge that, for me, is at the core of having a praxis orientation and that has always organically connected the concepts of action, theory, and reflection – if you say something, you give it your breath and must take action to manifest it. And we do this with an understanding of *respeto y permiso*, that we only ever act with respect and permission from the people we seek to serve.

When I approached organizing the keynote for the conference, I felt I had to employ this definition of praxis to welcoming conference attendees to our conference at Northern New Mexico College, and to orient them to the land-based communities they were visiting from a perspective of one of the community's daughters. How did I seek the respect and permission from the audience to speak before them? How did I offer my insights with cultural humility and also with great cultural pride? I knew that I wanted to walk my talk and demonstrate three connected pieces of writing that do the work of action, theory, and reflection.

In this chapter, I have done my best to replicate these interrelated pieces that all ultimately seek to demonstrate praxis in action. In Part I,[1] I offer a reflection on the tensions between a well-known fine-art photo taken by Ansel Adams (1941) and my relationship to the subject, the San José de Río Chama graveyard. I offer this non-fiction essay as an alternative positionality statement that places my family and me on to the "empty" landscape depicted in Adam's photo. In Part II, I theorize that gentrification and displacement not only occur in physical landscapes, but that the dislocation of Indigenous and traditional peoples is encoded in rhetorical practices found in literature. In the last section, Part III, I write about a classroom assignment that exemplifies how students can do critical, decolonial work to build an engaged relationship with their writing and their community. To counter literary gentrification, we must encourage development – literal and literary – without dislocation. This prelude is offered to give you the context for what you are about to read, and to explain why I chose to end this work with the words of students from my classroom. Having a critical praxis agenda means that, in our best moments as educators, we are in an intergenerational relationship with our students and give them the ability to carry the dialogue and the work forward. I don't offer a conclusion here, per se, other than to offer the words of the next generation of learners as they build an understanding about being in a right relationship with each other, our shared home, and the interconnections between us – land, water, people, and our non-human relatives.

Part I: The Moon Rises Over Hernandez Again and Again

One of the most famous and most sought-after photographs in American fine-art photography is called "Moonrise, Hernandez, NM," shot by Ansel Adams in 1941. I first encountered this photograph as capital "A" art in my university art history course. I was taught to appreciate this photo from an objective perspective, to memorize all manners of facts about its medium and technique. It is a silver gelatin print that stands the testament of time for many reasons, but particularly in terms of technique. The photograph remains one of American photography's most studied images because of how Adams reprinted the captured image over the years, adjusting the clouds in the sky by burning and dodging during development. It was not until the 1970s, when he printed the sky as an almost cloudless dark-toned expanse, that he felt he had achieved an effect equal to his original visualization of the scene.

I remember throwing up my hand in that class and proudly proclaiming, "Hey! A lot of my family is buried there!" The reply? "Interesting, Ms. Trujillo, but not pertinent to this conversation."

Where I really grew to appreciate this cemetery as art was from the yearly cleanings that first, my *gramita* Marina, my great-grandmother, then my gramma Lola, and then my mom would drag me, my siblings, and all my *primos* on each year for Memorial Day. The famous moonrise happens to be located over the *camposanto* in the village where my mother's family is from. By the time this photo was taken in 1941, generations of my family were already becoming the dust that became the land that bore the people who bore me. This is the San José de Río Chama *camposanto*; people are no longer buried there, but there are families, like my own, who still go out each year to do the annual *limpia*, the cleaning for the ancestors.

You will notice that I used the word "drag" earlier, as in kicking and screaming, in regard to how my *gramita*, grandma, and mom got us to go clean each May. It was a ritual that we prepared for weeks in advance when late April brought the displays of plastic flowers to bloom in the aisles of TG&Y and J.W. Owens. This is where *gramita* could easily spend her entire *chequecito*, the small monthly government check she received, buying artificial gardens for all the relatives she could remember. Each year I would observe her making mental maps to catalogue everyone who needed remembering – as she taught us, people only die when no one tells their story any longer.

First, she would close her eyes and trace the mental image of the *camposanto* speaking the names of her loved ones: Antonio Francisco Montoya, María Bernadita Martínez, José Antonio Martínez, Fred Valdez, Conrad Valdez, Baby Freddie, Tony Valdez, and on and on. When she got stuck, she would start telling stories of growing up and which *tío* lived next to the other *tía* and who they married and where they had come from. As she did her remembering she told us stories of marriages, unrequited loves, and tragic deaths caused by lightning strikes with keys in the pocket, being bucked by a horse, or just plain heart attacks. She told us the stories of women dying in childbirth, leaving entire broods behind, or of the small graves marked with a simple circle of rocks or a wooden cross for babies who never made it to life. Once her stories were done, she completed the mental tally for flowers and either my grandma or mom were sent to the store to complete the purchases.

After the flowers were bought, hoes and shovels and rakes were collected for all the family members. As the youngest cousin, I was always given the job to pick the weeds that were left behind with my bare hands (aka the detail work). We would pack coolers with the makings for bologna sandwiches, Lay's potato chips, a box of little Debbie snack cakes, and Cokes. Always present was a red plastic jug with a retractable spigot filled with water and ice for the entire family to share. Once the car was packed with all the tools and necessities, we would head off for a day with the ancestors.

I say that I grew to appreciate the *limpias* of the *camposanto* as art because it took me well into adulthood to understand the value of this practice and others like it. At the time, I can fairly say that we kids were reluctant – anyone who has spent an entire day doing hard labor under the hot New Mexico sun, sweating salty drops, and seeing Fruit Loop-colored sunspots understands hard work is grueling even if it *is* for your ancestors. But the elders taught us to work the cemetery by generation and shade availability. These days were literally spent climbing (and cleaning) our family tree, right down to the earth where our ancestors were laid.

After the weeding, we would go through each grave, sweep the concrete (or the dirt!), and we would move the rocks that encircled many of the graves, rinse them in a bucket of warm soapy water that grandma brought, and replace them just has they had been the year before and the year before that. It might seem futile to wash rocks, but it always struck me as an endearing gesture, one more chance to wipe the smooth face of a rock in lieu of a loved one's. Every grave marking, whether official military headstone or weather-beaten wood cross, was checked for maintenance. If we had forgotten a hammer, mom used a rock to pound nails back into the wood. Or, we could be sent around to find usable wire to reassemble the accessories of the afterlife. Our labor and the stories we heard weaved intricate mandalas around our ancestors, through grave markers and weeds, and figured us seamlessly into the design.

The catalogue of the Akron Art Museum describes Adams's photo as "a timeless metaphor of the stillness of the American landscape and the magical character of its light."[2] For me, and as I connect to the photograph by virtue of my culture and identity, there is nothing still about it. Though beautiful, the photo only hints at the art of the scene. Of the howling laughter at the stories about my grandpa Fred coming back from World War II to start a hamburger stand in El Guache, only to find reluctant customers in a community of people who had never eaten a hamburger before. Of the lamentations for loved ones lost before their time, like my *Tío* Tony and his friend who were struck on their bicycles by a drunk driver. They were only ten. Or the stories of all the beautiful and clever women who kept our homes together.

A vivid memory from my childhood is wandering and running through this orchard of family trees while the adults held vigil praying and visiting. To only see this photo as landscape removes the character of its people, and the culture of story. As Leslie Marmon Silko (1996) writes of her community, "The people perceived themselves in the world as part of an ancient continuous story composed of innumerable bundles of other stories" (p. 31). Culture is made up of these stories; they tell our history, they speak our languages, they shape our everyday lives not only into the objects of art, but also into art itself. Art is life. The everyday rituals of our communities form the lenses through which we will see the world, and that brings breath to art.

On the occasion of the 75th anniversary of the photo, I still want that professor (who I am sure has long forgotten me) to understand that those layers of family stories are pertinent. I see a moonrise over Hernandez every night, and I also greet the sun each morning from this place. Some of these mornings, I head over to Socorro's Restaurant for the "I lost my a★★ at the casino" breakfast special and wave at the San José de Río Chama cemetery along the way. My favorite table is underneath a poster of Mr. Ansel's photograph. Here I sit amongst the voices of the many regulars. In their speech I hear the cadence of my relatives, the stories of where I am from, and our pertinence is affirmed again and again.

Part II: The Literary Gentrification of Northern New Mexico

This small cache of photos (Figures 2.1–2.4) is representative of the types of advertisements often used to sell New Mexico, and they illustrate how the rhetorics of space provide narratives and the imaginative landscape for the consumption of New Mexico spaces. Words like "selling history" (Figure 2.1) and concepts like "land of *mañana*" (Figure 2.4) evoke renderings of places in New Mexico as spaces of authenticity, synchronization with nature, and perpetually existent in the *past* tense – but, most importantly, as something for sale. In the "Can you picture it?" photo (Figure 2.2), viewers/prospective buyers are literally given the option to live in "The Petroglyphs" (housing division) which would give them the opportunity to capture the Sandia mountains for aesthetic purposes. Considering the myriad connections that multiple Indigenous groups have to the mountains, known to the northern Pueblos as Okuu P'in, the billboard's investment in selling cultural space as capital is one example of how I seek to complicate the reading of gentrification as a literary process.

The Anasazi Lofts (Figure 2.3) boast a lifestyle of "urban antiquity" and ask of their consumer, "Imagine living here." But to the Indigenous and traditional people of New Mexico who have autochthonous relationships to the land, it insists that we change the tone of this sales pitch into a contemplative one, "Imagine living here?" Here where culture is simultaneously challenged and changed and where Indigenous and traditional New Mexicans struggle with being displaced from their communities to make room for amenity immigrants – a term coined

FIGURE 2.1 "Live in history: I sell it!" Photo taken in Albuquerque, NM. (Courtesy of Bernadette Trujillo Ellis)

18   Patricia Marina Trujillo

FIGURE 2.2 "Can you picture it? My balcony." Photo taken in Albuquerque, NM. (Courtesy of Bernadette Trujillo Ellis)

FIGURE 2.3 "Imagine living here." Photo taken in Albuquerque, NM. (Courtesy of Bernadette Trujillo Ellis)

FIGURE 2.4 "They call New Mexico the 'land of mañana'." Photo taken in Albuquerque, NM. (Courtesy of Bernadette Trujillo Ellis)

by anthropologist Sylvia Rodríguez (1994) – who want to pay for a curated New Mexican experience.

Literary gentrification in northern New Mexico is an interconnected spatial and rhetorical phenomenon; it is a term that embodies the displacement and disenfranchisement of ethnic New Mexicans not only in physical space, but also in imagined space as represented in literature. Emerging from a period of Anglo literary modernity (1890–1910), persistent tropes were introduced into the New Mexican literary lexicon concepts such as disappearing Native and Hispano culture, loss of authenticity, and New Mexicans as people "lost to time" and in touch with uncommon spiritual imbuing. These concepts continue to permeate the contemporary literary landscape in such common phrases as the "land of *mañana*" and even the state's motto, "The land of enchantment."

With particular focus on the space and literature of north central New Mexico, I argue that the imagined northern New Mexico produced in literary and social space replicates the material reality of how space has historically been consumed in New Mexico. Spatial theorists such as Soja, Harvey, and Massey declare that space is ontological; I add that it is through rhetoric that space is made knowable through language. Just as use of space comes to represent ideology, the rhetorical representation is imbricated in the ideological projects of crafting imagined space. Evidencing how contemporary consumption is the concomitant structure of how space and rhetoric have been employed and institutionalized in New Mexico, consumption becomes a significant lens by which to understand the relationship I am describing between space and rhetoric. The concept of gentrification in northern New Mexico as a spatial and rhetorical position by which to consider the displacement and disenfranchisement of ethnic New Mexicans, not only in literal space, but also in imagined space, provides a valuable perspective in which to read literature produced about the state.

In "Myths and Meanings of Gentrification," Caroline Mills (1993) asserts that gentrifiers write on to and read from scripts of landscapes, asserting, "Each society's 'moral order' is reflected in its particular spatial order and in the language and imagery by which that spatial order is represented" (p. 150). Thus, the renderings of actual space and imagined space in the gentrifying order always have an interest in commodifying the mythic content of space, what Mills (1993) terms "imagineering," for the dominant society (p. 152). To consider the representation of spatial order, literary gentrification is the concept I employ to create a lens for understanding the ways in which space and rhetoric interact, that is, co-create each other.

Gentrification literally means to take a space perceived to be run-down and old to renovate it for middle-class, urban consumption. Gentrification studies emerge from 1960s England where the term emerged to "mark middle-class reclamation of formerly forsaken urban regions" (Jackson, 2006, p. 42). As a discourse, the term gentrification exists in many permutations. Gentrification is usually configured materially through three broad theoretical paradigms in cultural geography:

> Production-side explanations may take a managerialist turn, pointing to the influence of government and financial institutions at a local or international scale ... A structural Marxist interpretation defines a more general production-side theory of gentrification ... [that] focuses on the switching of investment back into inner-city areas and the recommodification of derelict environments. In turn, the third model of explanation critiques the emphasis on production of "gentrifiable" locations, instead, with reference to the sphere of reproduction, this "production of gentrifiers" approach interprets urban change in terms of the restructuring of class and gender relations consequent upon changes in the organization of work and the domestic sphere.
>
> *(Mills, 1993, pp. 149–150)*

Gentrification studies, for the most part, have remained an academic discussion in cultural geography, economics, and consumption studies. Often these discussions center around the causes of gentrification, what the outcomes are for the newly migrated, more affluent consumers of space, and the displaced local working class moved out of space. In regard to space, most of the academic work done on gentrification also remains in the realm of the urban and rarely engages in the rural. Or, when the "the rural" is engaged, it is usually through the distracted lens of urbanity: how "the rural" compares to "the urban."

This perspective emerges from a lacuna in gentrification studies that overlooks the spatial potential for rural ontologies as the sites for rural epistemic practice, including the realms of community-based rhetorics. Gentrification, historically, is a social science-based study of how one group of more empowered people displaces another group of less empowered people. It does not consider the larger contexts of how space has been occupied and developed through colonial and/or imperial regimes of power via rhetoric. Gentrification studies tend to render "place" through individual ownership of property, and it is this individual ownership that allows for community membership in space. Gentrification is rendered as an "urban" dilemma, although many people outside of the city understand displacement from property. In connecting the spatial to the rhetorical through studying gentrification, rhetoric becomes one of the technologies for the displacement of groups of people from any space, real or imaginary.

Work that embodies the conflicts of gentrification insists on a focus on identity, culture, and agency as much as on physical space. Mills (1993) asserts, "In everyday language, ways of living – strategies for coping – are objectified as 'lifestyle.' And, through language, places are given meaning" (p. 151). To extend Mills's observations, one must consider not only a basic understanding of how gentrification exploits traditional myths and meanings of space and culture, but also how, once gentrification occurs, the revised myth becomes central to new, privileged meanings of space.

Gentrification is not only understood by how New Mexican space is changing physically, i.e., the material experience of displacement, it is also understood through concepts of ideological space in literature and the construction of social space. I am defining literary gentrification as *a process invested in the restructuring of literary spaces that decenter Indigenous and traditional voices and often re-center Indigenous and traditional stories told by outside (Anglo/white) perspectives.* This process includes the publication of the re-centered stories to provide hegemonic narratives about marginalized people and places for use in institutions for the means of educating, representing identities of, and entertaining a reader about a space for middle-class consumers.

For example, Jim Sagel was a well-known and respected regional writer who moved to, learned the colloquial Spanish of, and wrote about northern New Mexico. In his lifetime, he collected and rendered dozens of stories and poems that represent his understanding of the Chicana/o communities of northern New Mexico, most notably Española, NM. Jim Sagel's work can be read through a lens of literary gentrification. Despite his work to represent the space of Española through his narratives, by analyzing his rhetorical perspectives in regard to the space knowledges that are translated through his texts, one can problematize his perspectives.

Sagel took local knowledges and rendered them through hegemonic lenses, often while critiquing the local communities through a deficit model of loss and longing of traditional Nuevomexicano culture. He admonished the actual community members from whom he learned his stories for loss of language and culture, while simultaneously replacing their voices with his own. Even though he represented northern New Mexico, he failed to address how his use and maintenance of dominant rhetorical traditions to render New Mexico implicitly and explicitly facilitated much of the displacement and loss he critiqued. Furthermore, his writings were constructed, in large part, for consumption by middle-class, "educated" audiences at universities. This reading of Sagel addresses another kind of rhetorical logic, a logic that moves beyond *what is being said* to include *how and where it is being said*. It takes the structure of writing as a meta-discursive space that we can read. The spatial rhetorical logic that I employ does not suggest that Sagel and other writers (myself included) should not engage in dominant rhetorical traditions, merely that we should not privilege these traditions to the point of marginal invisibility. In this sense, we can also begin to think, teach, and write about spaces of rhetoric. Rather than gentrifying literary space, how do Chican@ and Native New Mexican writers develop imaginary New Mexico without displacement?

In Doreen Massey's (1994) "A Global Sense of Place," the author posits that:

> Instead then, of thinking of places as areas with boundaries around, they can be imagined as articulated movements in networks of social relations and understandings, but where a large proportion of those relations, experiences and understandings are constructed on a far larger scale than what we happen to define for that moment as the place itself, whether that be a street, or a region, or even a continent. And this in turn allows a sense of place which is extroverted, which includes a consciousness of its links with the wider world, which integrates in a positive way the global and the local.
>
> *(p. 239)*

Rather than viewing Sagel's work as a palimpsest that merely consumes Chican@ and Native New Mexican stories, we can put the multiple perspectives in conversation to imagine articulated movements of networks as the movement from predominantly Spanish-Mexican and Indigenous worldviews to a Eurocentric United States worldview. This removes Sagel and Chican@ and Native New Mexicans from an either/or binary, and the multiple historical actors can be read through the lens of Gloria Anzaldúa's (1987) "new Mestiza consciousness." They can be read as a fulcrum

> where phenomena tend to collide. It is where the possibility of uniting all that is separate occurs. This assembly is not one where severed or separated pieces merely come together. Nor is it a balancing of opposing powers. In attempting to work out a synthesis, the self has added a third element which is greater than the sum of its severed parts.
>
> *(pp. 101–102)*

In spatial studies, Massey (1994) calls this a "progressive concept of place" that considers first that place is not static, and if "places can be conceptualized in terms of the social interactions which tie together, then it is also the case that these interactions themselves are not motionless things, frozen in time. They are processes" (p. 239). In relation to Anzaldúa, this progressive concept of space can be used to conceptualize a progressive rhetoric that incorporates the perspective of the local and the global.

In relation to Sagel and northern New Mexicans, we can use the fulcrum as the opportunity to articulate Indigenous and Chican@ perspectives apart from the gentrified version that Sagel establishes. Anzaldúa's (1987) fulcrum problematizes the unitary nature of historical and rhetorical paradigms established in written texts and suggests that it is these fulcrums that provide opportunities for duality to be transcended (p. 102). What can be gained from this spatial rhetorical analysis is a more fully rendered understanding of written and social space of New Mexico, one that not only laments the loss of superimposed United States colonial rhetoric but one that begins to articulate alternative rhetorical positions beyond the scope of Spanish colonial and United States colonial rhetorical legacies in New Mexico. Thinking of rhetoric, like space, as progressive insists that we challenge persuasive positions as merely having roots in the colonial rhetorics despite the fact that most *written* documents reflect these positions. By employing Anzaldúa's concept, a progressive rhetoric reveals multiple third-space junctures from which to embark.

Gentrification assumes a class aspiration. In thinking about literary gentrification, it begs the question: who is the "gentry" of literary gentrification? Should we be concerned with who is consuming literature and how literature is made available? My border thinking about rhetoric insists that we consider how the space and place of our writing have meaning. Just as Walter Mignolo (2000) "attempts to remap the Americas in the modern/colonial world system, rather than reproduce it in the national imaginary" (p. 44), my work with literature and social space in New Mexico attempts to write Nuevomexicanos and Native New Mexicans on to the literary maps of the state. From this decolonial position, I work to create a new New Mexican literary terrain that not only seeks mere textual inclusion, but also spatial structural inclusion. Mignolo (2000) writes:

> In other words, transcending the colonial difference can *only* be done from a perspective of subalternity, from decolonization, and, therefore from a new epistemological terrain where border thinking works. Border thinking can only be such from a subaltern perspective, never from a territorial (e.g., from inside modernity) one. Border thinking from a territorial perspective becomes a machine of appropriation of the colonial differe/a/nces; the colonial difference as an object of study rather than an epistemic potential. Border thinking from the perspective of subalternity is a machine for intellectual deconolonization [sic].
>
> *(p. 45, emphasis in original)*

By considering the largely unquestioned urban, middle-class investments of spatial rhetoric, the work of establishing literary landscapes that more accurately represent the ever-changing space that all New Mexicans negotiate can take precedence. Creating an understanding of literary gentrification delineates central issues to consider: how does the "relative mobility and power over mobility and communication entrench ... the spatial imprisonment of other groups" (Massey, 1994, p. 151), which points to the contradictions of New Mexico space: how it can be one of the poorest states in the United States with some of the wealthiest counties (Los Alamos County is one of the top five wealthiest counties in the United States)? How can NM public education consistently be ranked lowest nationally and yet Chican@s and Native populations "have the highest level of education" in the nation (Gonzales-Berry & Maciel, 2000, p. 5)? These contradictions, amongst a host of others, force us to consider other perspectives alongside the dominant spatial rhetorical paradigms that provide access to mobility and power in New Mexico.

This is not to say that space was not consumed materially or rhetorically prior to white dominance in New Mexico; rather, it is to say that all consumption was not invested in a capitalist model per se. Massey (1994) asserts that understanding consumption only in terms of capitalism is insufficient, that we must understand access to space as "about power in relation *to* the flows and the movement" (p. 149). In conversation with Mills's concept of gentrification as recast myth, Massey's point becomes even more significant. From a production-side perspective, Mills argue that

> gentrification is a rational response to the opening of a rent gap; moreover, product differentiation (for instance, new aesthetics) is a rational response to changing market conditions. But the notion of rationality is not acultural: as Sahlins (1976: 215) points out, production is always a cultural intention, and "Rational production for gain is in one and the same motion the production of symbols." Indeed, not only does economic activity produce symbols; it is made possible by symbols: The accumulation of exchange-value is always the creation of use-value.
>
> *(pp. 156–157)*

This is where a New Mexican spatial rhetorical analysis poignantly asserts the power of persuasion and perspective, and where differentiated access becomes evident. In the oldest communities in New Mexico, there is a long tradition of ontologies that are re-configured for capitalist gain. Pragmatism is often romanticized or aestheticized in service of a hegemonic vision of New Mexico; features of the land and culture become means for fixing social position.

An example from my own experience[3] is my parents' relationship to *chile ristras*. These iconic chiles have become a symbol of "Santa Fe style"; the long bundles of red chiles are often portrayed as hanging from the front of a New Mexican adobe house as decoration. For years there was an internal struggle in my parents' home: my mom bought *ristras* for the decorative purposes and every time she did, my dad attempted to consume them as food. The *ristras'* primary purpose is as a method for drying chiles after the harvest. For my father, who grew up in this tradition, he sees their decorative purpose as incidental, not instrumental. For him, *ristras* are useful storage units. Because of my dad's perspective on usage and the meaning of the composition of *ristras*, my mom's decorations are always lopsided or thin. Interestingly, my mom also grew up in the tradition of growing, drying, and eating *chile de ristra*; however, she also identifies with the social structure of "Santa Fe style" that would make the *ristras* a status symbol and decoration. On one occasion, in an effort to keep one of her *ristras* for decoration, my mom bought a *ristra* that had been shellacked. Sure enough, my dad broke off a few of the chiles and tossed them into *posole*, only to ruin the whole pot of soup. On the issue of *ristras* in my parents' home, working-class pragmatism was in constant conflict with middle-class objectification. After the shellacking incident, only edible *ristras* were allowed in the Trujillo household for my dad's safety, but this example speaks to how cultural intention is significant in the production of spatial and rhetorical symbols.

Overall, grappling with the term literary gentrification, one must be concerned with contemporary renderings of literary and social spaces in northern New Mexico and the rhetoric that is used to make spaces known. Keeping Massey's differentiated access in mind, along with Anzaldúa's dissolution of binaries, literary gentrification studies should continue to put theories of cultural geography, consumption, and rhetoric into conversation with how mobility and power over access to dominant rhetoric entrench spatial imprisonment. In grappling with this previously under-researched understanding of New Mexican rhetorical history, what emerges is a space for a decolonial rhetorical intervention in New Mexico Studies. One such emergence is articulated in Emma Pérez's (1999) conceptualization of decoloniality. She theorizes the "decolonial imaginary" as a "time lag between the colonial and postcolonial" and she asserts that the decolonial imaginary is a "rupturing space, the alternative to that which is written in history ... that interstitial space where differential politics and social dilemmas are negotiated" (Pérez, 1999, p. 6). It is from the interstices – a third place of identity and culture – that the gentrification of literature can be contested.

It complicates the way we look to our home communities, which are already always complicit with hegemony, for rhetorical alternatives. But, as Massey (1994) posits, "Can't we re-think our sense of place? Is it not possible for a sense of place to be progressive; not self-enclosing and defensive, but outward-looking?" (p. 147). Towards this effort, I believe that the study of literary gentrification can also inform education research for pedagogy and policy reform. Ultimately, understanding literary gentrification with its investments in New Mexico is not about silencing hegemonic rhetoric but rather is about complicating the conversation for a richer, more accurate perspective of New Mexico's literary history and her literary worlds.

Part III: Land-based Writing Strategies for the Classroom and Community, or Education as Offering[4]

Many of us in the *Norte* (common-space moniker for northern New Mexico) are taught since a young age to give a ceremonial offering each morning. My Pueblo sisters offer corn meal and prayers. I was taught to acknowledge the sun in prayer for a new day; I whisper Ave Marías to myself in the car on my way to work, but I know that my *gramita* did it through song. We pray to the directions, to our ancestors, and to our respective Creator. An offering is an acknowledgment that we are part of a bigger world, and the humble action of gratitude pays respect to our relationships that allow us to do good for Mother Earth and her creatures. Our offerings are the introduction to the stories of our day.

But, often in our modern world, even amidst our traditional practices of offerings, we are jolted into our daily positions at work; in my world, it is in the classroom as students and teachers. We attend meetings, strike tasks off our to-do lists, and are constantly moving to the next thing. We grab something to eat in our cars as we move from one appointment to the next, often fueled on sugar and caffeine. Our intentionality can quickly shift. Even if we start the day from a place of process and connection, we can slide into being product- and outcome-oriented. As a college professor, I see this all the time, in the profession and in the actions of students and faculty. We are all going at a hundred miles an hour and we forget to connect.

"It's ironic, ¿que no?" College classrooms are supposed to be the place where students prepare for the real world, but often there can be very little connection between the theory and practice of knowledges shared in classrooms to the work happening in the greater community. I decided to be mindful of this in designing a course for fall 2016, "Writing the Land: Storytelling, Environment, and Indigenous Knowledge" at Northern New Mexico College. In the course cross-listed between English and Pueblo Indian Studies, students were introduced to writings by Indigenous authors from the Americas, and asked to consider how storytelling is a decolonial methodology for addressing historical and ongoing struggles for sovereignty and self-determination in their homelands, and how to co-exist with settler colonial societies. As Leslie Marmon Silko (1977) writes, "I will tell you something about stories. They aren't just entertainment. They are all we have to fight off illness and death. You don't have anything if you don't have stories" (p. 2).

In this course, we moved away from single-authored papers as major assessments for gaining knowledge. Students did get to reflect individually in short-response papers, but our major assignments were different. Our major assignments engaged in Indigenous methodologies of de-centering authors from authority, and centering community voice for power sharing. As the Pueblo adage goes, "It takes a thousand voices to tell a single story." For midterms, students in the course were asked to plan, schedule, and provide a community storytelling event for our campus. The students designed an event called "Food Stories," where we invited our campus community to share in a collective understanding of storytelling. Students organized a potluck and invited four storytellers to be a part of the event.

The event started with two original songs, "Red or Green" and "My Grandmother's Kitchen," performed by Michelle Harvier. One speaker, Richard Sedillo from Ohkay Owingeh, shared stories of growing up with his grandfather who still used a horse-drawn wagon for farming. The second speaker, Beata Tsosie Peña of Kha'po Owingeh, shared stories of corn. Lastly, Daniel Chatchou, from Cameroon, Africa, told the group of his food traditions. Over 50 students, faculty, and staff gathered for the successful event. Students from the course prepared foods near and dear to their hearts, and began the event by telling some of their own food stories.

In the reflections after the event, students and participants in the event both shared a sense of gratitude. Codiee Myles, a student from the class, reflected, "I'm proud of what we did. We made this place [the college] feel like real homey." When we are connected to a place, when it feels homey, we have a sense of belonging. So, how do we create more educational spaces that encourage connection, service, and a sense of belonging?

As we veered into our final project, I knew that we had to put our storytelling to work in the community. Knowing that the organization Tewa Women United (TWU) was hard at work in the community installing the Española Healing Foods Oasis, I asked if we could use the opportunity to create a bridge between Northern New Mexico College and this community project. TWU was very receptive, and Beata Tsosie-Peña, Program Coordinator for Environmental Health and Justice at TWU, responded whole-heartedly. She and I co-designed a six-week-long project that allowed us the opportunity to go out to the garden, bring an Indigenous environmental activist into our classroom to share in the discussion, and actively demonstrated to students the power of such relationships. The project established ways to put our literature to work; all these dialogues about the power of story began to be demonstrated in our expanded classroom. All of a sudden, stories were alive and supporting not only our learning, but also TWU and the hundreds of plants in the healing garden.

The final project was to create a story-based gift for the community. Alongside the project, we read Robin Wall Kimmerer's (2015) book *Braiding Sweetgrass: Indigenous Wisdom, Scientific Knowledge and the Teachings of Plants*. Kimmerer (2015) asks, "What else can you offer the earth, which has everything? What else can you give but something of yourself? A homemade ceremony, a ceremony that makes a home" (p. 38). In our case, we knew that there is the physical labor of the Española Healing Foods Oasis that community members have volunteered to prepare, plant, and care for the garden. We viewed this firsthand on a visit where we held our class in the dirt. But, how could we make an offering of our stories?

In conversation, Beata mentioned that over 200 varieties of edible, medicinal, or companion plants were included in the garden. She wanted to make sure that visitors to the garden were able to identify and get to know the plants, their usages, and their names in Tewa, Spanish, English, and Scientific. I asked, "What if I ask my students to perform research and write the plant stories?" We agreed that this would be an important gift that would help build relationships between students and the garden. I set to work and developed an assignment where students had to research and write the stories of five plants they selected. We got the list from the landscape architect. Some students were reluctant to jump in; I heard things like, "I'm not a planter. I don't know which one to choose" or "Manzanilla! I want to do that one. I use that all the time." After choosing five, they had to provide the plant name in all the languages mentioned above and write the story of the plant however they chose. It could be formal academic writing, or they could choose to write from the plant's perspective in the first-person point of view. However they chose to write the plant stories, their responsibility was to provide information to the community and to honor the plants.

Students really got into this project! They hit the library, Google, and even had to perform interviews with Native speakers of the Indigenous Tewa language and the colloquial New Mexico Spanish. Not everyone had access to interview resources, so guess what? They had to share and support each other in the work. Students got savvy and began to share sources and books with one another. This was not the classic final exam paper, where students are forced to write in isolation for an audience of a single professor. No, they were talking to each other, to professors, and members of their community. Each had to present their work to each other, and finally, as a group present it as a gift to the Healing Oasis.

Beata, who was along with us for the entirety of the project, helped us reframe the end of our semester from a final exam to a final ceremony. Collectively, we decided that our offering would be a "Ceremony to Reconnect with Our Plant Relatives." The students collated a binder with their stories, organized for easy usage by the greater community. On our last day of class in December, we went out once again to the garden. This time, our purpose was to present gifts to the plants and to leave our offerings in the ground. Each student wrote intentions on a sheet of paper, which we buried and blessed with tobacco and sage. We presented our stories and prayed that they would be used to heal pain in our community. And, in the end, we became part of the story of the Healing Oasis Garden. There were some tears, and lots of laughter. We all imagined ourselves connected to the well-being of our plants, our beautiful healing oasis, and the people who tend and visit there. And is not that what stories are supposed to do? All of a sudden, all of these people from various geographies belonged to a new shared place: a new home.

If you ever happen to be in Española, NM, pop by and visit the Española Healing Foods Oasis. Spend some time, and read the plant stories. Maybe you will find yourself connecting with the plants as well. Until then, be inspired with these reflections by the students in the course.

Codiee Myles

> After doing all this research to find out what these plants can do, it really changed my perspective on plants. This made me realize that nature really can provide for us and that not every sickness requires a doctor. Before this project, if I would have seen these plants, I would have thought that they were just weeds and useless. Now I realize that they are much more than that. I hope that whoever gets to read [our stories] about these plants realizes too that they can do much more than what we think.

Erik Garcia

Through our class and the books we've been reading I can say I found a deeper appreciating for Mother Earth. I've learned to improve my ways. For example now I can go riding or walking without headphones. I feel the music is a distraction to the natural world. By us appreciating the land more, the thought process is to get us to understand the importance it plays in our lives. Once we've discovered and gained knowledge we hope it changes the viewpoint and [hu]mankind will help save the world.

Evelynne Gonzalez

The most interesting thing about learning plant stories was that each plant has a purpose in nature, they are all here for a reason and our ancestors would use many of these plants before medicine was available. I feel that there is a connection from researching these plants' connections to the earth because one can imagine cultivating such plants and later boiling a cup of *yerba manza* root for a cold. We are drinking in all that power. Or when one has a deep craving for *nopalitos* with red chile, we can just go to our back yard and pick them. There is a great satisfaction that came from learning plant stories; knowing that these plants can benefit the community is satisfying. All it takes is a little dirty work!

Joy Dili

The importance of plants is that they can teach us more than we know. Their knowledge remains endless and they survived since the beginning of time; surely this makes them more than experts. The words of my plants were strong, funny, sure of themselves, a bit wild and they all had passion to give. The gifts that they provide are something I will always respect and be thankful for. I would like to have a better relationship with these plants in the future by planting and seeing them grow. The experience I gained in this class has been more than rewarding and I'm grateful to be a part of this project. It's amazing the things you think you know, until you take the time to really understand it from the beginning. We could learn so much from plants; I surely did.

Tatiana Smith

When starting this project I didn't want to do it. I was like, ewww! We have to plant and get dirty?! But after picking my plants I began to bond with them. The very first bonding experience was actually going to the garden and smelling white sage for the first time. That scent created such amazing feelings inside me and I knew that I found one of my plants. After this project I feel more connected with these plants and the plants my classmates researched as well.

Shayna Porter

Coming from a big city, I never got a chance to understand Mother Nature. After taking PIS 399 I can say that my nonchalant ways of interacting with Mother Nature has changed. Before doing this project I had no knowledge of how important and valuable a plant can be. While I was doing research on the five plants I was assigned, it made me want to change my city-like ways. Instead of taking a hike to get cardio, I can take a hike to connect with Mother Nature. Instead of stressing myself out with worries, I can place my stress or worries on to a plant and ask it to hold it for me. I learned that having a garden and showing those plants love is a spiritual and therapeutic act. Now I feel like I have a moral obligation to Mother Nature.

Michelle Martinez

How am I supposed to be a good neighbor/friend if I hardly associate with any plants? This project was a perfect opportunity to change that and I'm glad that I did it. I know so much more because of it. During this research project, I have felt a deep calling to start getting familiar with the plants that we are sharing this Earth with. I have been inspired to become friends with these plants and get to know their names and stories. I would love to know how to identify plants when I walk by and know who they are. I want to learn about how plants heal and also be able to practice it. One of my goals is to plant a New Mexico locust near my house and become close with that plant and learn from it.

Nicole Soderberg

Plants are our healers in so many ways. They help us in healing our bodies to healing our spirit, heart, and mind. They live in this same world as we do and share some of the same issues humans have. We are more alike than we think. We must respect the value of taking care of our elders. They have known this earth for many years and have lived through issues we might not have encountered yet. So we must listen when they speak and help them when they struggle to walk and grow. We must protect them when danger is near and make sure they get to live a full cycle of life. The more I learn about plants the more connected I feel to them. I understand them more and the inter-connectedness of Mother Earth and all her beings. As we are out and about in our busy days, plants wait patiently for us to come visit and share a conversation with them. To take time get to know each other and the world around us all, in which nature intended.

Notes

1 Parts I and III were previously published in a regional newspaper, *The Greenfire Times: News and Views for the Sustainable Southwest*, edited by Seth Roffman. "The Moon Rises Over Hernandez Again and Again" was published in volume 8.8, December 2016. The essay was also shared on a website dedicated to creating community archives, *Manitos.net*. "Education as Offering: Braiding Community, College, and Plant Stories" was published in volume 9.4, April 2017. *The Greenfire Times* is printed locally for a primary audience in northern New Mexico. As a land-based scholar, I often make the political decision to publish my work in community-based publications that make them accessible, ideally for free, to the people represented in my writing. This is part of my praxis of writing.
2 "Moonrise, Hernandez, New Mexico," Akron Art Museum, https://akronartmuseum. org:443/collection/Obj1384?sid=132296&x=7297257&port=204.
3 Having an intimate connection with the space I am writing about, I assert that I am employing what Dolores Delgado Bernal (1998) has termed a "researcher's cultural intuition" in her essay, "Using a Chicana Feminist Epistemology in Educational Research." Bernal is not arguing for an essentialist notion of who can and who cannot do research; she does argue that "Chicana scholars achieve a sense of cultural intuition" that significantly influences their research constituting an insider perspective that is "based on 'collective experiences and a collective space' at multiple levels, rather than on a singular identity" (p. 567). It is from this perspective that I share personal experiences and perspectives on New Mexico as part of what Bernal (1998) terms a Chicana feminist epistemology that is nurtured through "our personal experiences (which are influenced by ancestral wisdom, community memory, and intuition), the literature on and about Chicanas, our professional experiences, and the analytical processes we engage when we are in a central position of our research and analysis" (pp. 567–568).
4 When originally written for publication in a regional newspaper, *The Greenfire Times*, we dedicated the article to the late Emily "Awa Povi" Martinez from Ohkay Owingeh Pueblo. Joy Dili interviewed Ms. Martinez for the "Plant Stories" assignment featured here. She was an elder who shared important plant knowledge and the Tewa names of plants with Joy. She passed away very shortly after the interview. We offer our story to honor our elders and ancestors.

References

Anzaldúa, G. (1987). *Borderlands/La Frontera: The New Mestiza*, 2nd ed. San Francisco, CA: Aunt Lute Press.
Bernal, D. (1998). Using a Chicana Feminist Epistemology in Educational Research. *Harvard Educational Review*, 68, 555–581.
Gonzales-Berry, E. & Maciel, D. (2000). Introduction. In E. Gonzales-Berry & D. Maciel, (Eds.), *The Contested Homeland: A Chicano History of New Mexico* (pp. 1–12). Albuquerque, NM: UP New Mexico.

Jackson, Jr., J. L. (2006). Gentrification, Globalization, and Georaciality. In K. Clark & D. A. Thomas, (Eds.), *Globalization and Race: Transformations in the Cultural Production of Blackness* (pp. 188–205). Durham, NC: Duke University Press.

Kimmerer, Robin Wall. (2015). *Braiding Sweetgrass: Indigenous Wisdom, Scientific Knowledge and the Teaching of Plants.* Minneapolis, MN: Milkweed Editions.

Marmon Silko, L. (1977). *Ceremony.* New York, NY: Viking Penguin.

Marmon Silko, L. (1996). Interior and Exterior Landscapes: The Pueblo Migration Stories. In *Yellow Woman and a Beauty of Spirit: Essays on Native American Life Today* (pp. 25–47). New York, NY: Touchstone.

Massey, D. (1994). A Global Sense of Place. *Space, Place and Gender* (pp. 146–157). Minneapolis, MN: UP Minnesota.

Mignolo, W. D. (2000). *Local Histories/Global Designs: Coloniality, Subaltern Knowledges, and Border Thinking.* Princeton, NJ: Princeton University Press.

Mills, C. (1993). Myths and Meanings of Gentrification. In J. Duncan & D. Ley (Eds.), *Place/Culture/Representation* (pp. 149–169). London, UK: Routledge.

Pérez, E. (1999). *Decolonial Imaginary: Writing Chicanas into History.* Bloomfield, IN: Indiana University Press.

Rodríguez, S. (1994). Defended Boundaries, Precarious Elites: The Arroyo Seco Matachines Dance. *Journal of American Folklore, 107*(424), 248–267. doi:10.2307/541203

3
SUBVERSIONS OF SUBJECTIFICATION

Hans Skott-Myhre and Kathleen S.G. Skott-Myhre

It is now over 50 years since the revolts of 1968 with all of their unintended consequences. As the post-Marxist scholar Antonio Negri (2011) has pointed out, they were without question a political failure. But Negri (2012) also notes that failed revolutions are, in many ways, the most productive because they leave such a rich residue of things not accomplished. Numerous residual failed projects are resurfacing both on the left and the right as we approach the end of the second decade of the 21st century. We propose that the scattered bits and pieces of the broken and discarded political and cultural projects of the 20th century are being reassembled from the detritus of capitalism's latent unconscious desires.

Felix Guattari (2010) tells us that we get the unconscious we deserve and suggests that, contrary to Freud, our unconscious desires are not forged in the sexual perversities of the nuclear family, but in the realm of what he terms preconscious social investment. In his work with Gilles Deleuze (1984), they argue that individuals and families are points of social cathexis. That is, they are manifestations of libidinal investments arising out of the contingent logic of a given social mode of production. This formulation, drawn from a reconfiguration of Marx and Freud, proposes that our unconscious is not composed of individually repressed socially prohibited desires. Instead, it is the social field that gives rise to preconscious social investments (e.g., class) that shape those social formations such as individuals and families. Such libidinal investments are "an indifferent stimulus at the beginning, an extrinsic result at the point of arrival" (Deleuze & Guattari, 1984, p. 390). In other words, those preconscious social investments are not predetermined, but are virtual in their indeterminate capacity.

By virtual, we are following Bergson (2004) and Deleuze (1966) in proposing that the virtual is composed of a field of infinite capacity without determinate form. It is no thing in particular while holding the potential to be some thing in actuality. The virtual is in a dynamic relation of becoming actualized through its relation with living form or what Spinoza (2000) refers to as bodies. Each body, from simple bodies such as subatomic particles to complex bodies such as galaxies, is composed as an idiosyncratic set of virtual capacity. Put differently, each body has an infinitude of things it could do or think that only it can do or think. Because the body has a unique and idiosyncratic composition, it operates in an ecological relation to other bodies as what Bergson (2004) terms a living center. Each body, as a living center of sheer idiosyncratic capacity, transmutes the virtual to the actual by expressing those elements in any given set of relations that correspond to its functional capacities. This transmutation is a process of cyclical becoming premised in the dynamic relation of virtual to actual that shapes the particular and peculiar becoming specific to singular form.

There are three things that we would like to make a note of here. The first is that the unconscious of any given historical period is an ecological assemblage of capacities configured preconsciously out of the random collisions of bodies as they are composed and decomposed. Second, local instantiations and expressions of unconscious desires are particularized configurations of broader social flows of virtual capacity. While they may find expression through socio-political articulations of complex bodies such as individuals or humans, the unconscious libidinal force neither originates in abstract social configurations nor can it be understood at the level of conscious awareness. And third, there is no capacity for free will as a vehicle for comprehending preconscious social investments derived out of unconscious libidinal desire.

In the case of preconscious social investments, what Guattari (2010) refers to as the unconscious we deserve is premised in our body politic as an expression originating in an ecology of material relations. In this ecology, there is no ideal social formation that exists outside the field of immanent production premised in an infinitude of entanglements of bodies and thoughts that give rise to homeostatic social formations and morphogenetic flows that continually subvert those formations. Each historical period manifests a structural logic derived from the contingent relations of thought and materiality. Politics, as Foucault (2005) tells us, are the relations of force that are composing and decomposing social relations within, what he calls, an episteme.

Foucault's early writing used episteme to describe the a priori conditions that ground the production of knowledge within a given historical period. This definition of episteme is generally read as an epistemological framework. However, we would like to suggest that in the reading we have given so far, there might be an ontological reading as well. From the perspective of immanent materialist force relations, the conditions of possibility constitute not only the capacity to articulate the abstract discursive formations of what is true but also the constitutive conditions of becoming at the level of bodies organic and inorganic. We argue that the movement among key feminists such as Rosi Braidotti (1994), Donna Haraway (2003), and Karen Barad (2007) towards an immanent materialist posthumanism gives rise to a form of politics. Similarly, the colonial period of capitalist production was unable to fully discipline heterogeneous modes of production in the Global South that are premised in subaltern collective material sets of relations (Spivak, 1999; Chakrabarty, 2000).

This is politics, in the Foucauldian sense, as relations of force within what we would propose to call (quite roughly) the episteme of absolute subjectification. We delineate this episteme as functioning on an a priori logic premised precisely on the appropriation of the flows of unconscious desiring-production. Deleuze and Guattari (1988) define flows of unconscious desiring-production as the set of social mechanisms that are composed of flows of sheer capacity interrupted by machinic impersonal vehicles of structure and form. All such machines of unconscious social production interconnect with an infinite array of other machines and flows, each with an idiosyncratic assemblage of virtual capacity. Such desire is not premised in lack as in earlier psychoanalytic and philosophical dialectics. Instead, it produces reality out of an absolute surplus of living force.

Deleuze and Guattari (1988) tell us that any mode of social overcoding that seeks to appropriate this surplus must develop an apparatus of capture that, as Agamben (2009) describes it, "has in some way the capacity to capture, orient, intercept, model, control, or secure the gestures, opinions, or discourses of living beings" (p. 14). According to Deleuze (1995), as we enter what Hardt and Negri (2001) have described as the Empire of global capitalist rule, the apparatuses of capture have shifted. The way that capital manages the process of capture, orientation, interception, and modeling has moved from the episteme of what Foucault (2012) refers to as the disciplinary society, which focused on the body to be used in the manufacture of industrial production, to what Deleuze (1995) delineates as the society of control.

According to Deleuze (1995), the society of control is premised on open systems of constant modulation. We are no longer fitted to conforming molds of identification and habit but instead subjected to an ever-shifting array of social structures, political affiliations, training regimes, and identities. All of this variation and difference evokes profound anxiety and, what Deleuze (1995) terms, a life of infinite deferral in which one never arrives. Nothing stabilizes. On the one hand, this sounds a great deal like the infinite oscillations of living systems. However, the control society instead is explicitly not a living system. It mimics the processes of life, but it is, as Baudrillard (1994) would have, a copy of a copy of a copy. The rapid shifts and modulations of the control society are geared towards covering a system of absolute abstraction premised on a radically entropic center of value. That center is capital, and the system is designed to do one thing and one thing only (all of the variations and modulations are side effects), and that is to do what Marx (2005) predicted long ago, that is, to have money make money and to translate all living creative force into abstract calculations of monetary equivalence.

Antonio Negri (2012) articulates this shift into the society of control as a move away from merely appropriating the materiality of living bodies through the extraction of labor or raw resources. He suggests that 21st-century capitalism now extracts our very capacity for social relation, creativity, and thought. While this has always been the case for a relatively small group of intellectuals and artists, capital now opens the field to everyone through vehicles such as social media that make everyone an expert, a commentator, an artist, and a musician. This faux democratization appears to open a world of creative possibilities on the surface. Still, through the use of an ever-shifting array of algorithms, it covertly shapes discourses and creative expression that values them according to the money sign. Similarly, our affective capacities for affiliation are transmuted through mechanisms that abstract social functions such as caring, communication, cooperation, and affect management into aspects of job performance and avenues to success as an entrepreneur.

This emerging system of capitalist control and apparatus of capture strives to be all-encompassing. In abstracting the creative capacity for thought and affiliation, it opens avenues into all aspects of living form. Perhaps most importantly, it opens on to the virtual field of unconscious desiring-production. As such, it does not oppress us by restricting or restraining us. Instead, it appears to free us, while weaving us more deeply into its logic. That is to say, capitalism no longer cares how we manage ourselves physically or even consciously. Of greater interest is a direct line into our unconscious field of desire. However, not desire as lack. Capitalism has already largely exhausted that vehicle through extensive interventions that promised to deliver all we yearn for but cannot reach. To a large degree, we have become cynically inured to those promises. Instead, capital is now interested in unconscious desire as virtual creative capacity: be all you can be and more.

The question, for us, becomes what kind of politics stands any possibility of proposing a viable difference to such a system? It is here that we come to the question of subversion. We suggest that it is a politics of subversion that could gnaw at the foundations of virtual global capital and simultaneously undermine it while turning it into compost for new worlds and new peoples.

We are attracted to the concept of subversion as a process of turning from beneath. If capitalism is producing modes of subjectification premised on the capacity to transform our subjectivity into simulacra of living form, then the field on which subversive politics must be played is the arena of subjectification or the production of subjectivity. We have suggested that this is a plane of immanent unconscious desiring-production that has as its primary mechanism the shift from virtual to actual. The question then is: who are we to become if we are not this?

The Marxist scholar Maivan Clech Lam (1996) once remarked that, for all of us trapped within the belly of the capitalist beast, we need to find a way to become a severe irritant such that we force the beast to cough us up and expire. In our own words, we suggest that we need to become indigestible to capital. In *Inner Chapters* by Chuang Tzu (1974), there is a story about a tree that has found a way to be useless. As a result, the tree has survived to a ripe old age. Of course, all stories are told within a historical context, and in the time this was written, the question was one of physical utility. Could the tree be made into something useful for human beings? In our own time, the question the story raises for us is: how to become useless to capitalism? How might we subvert the drive by capitalism to use each and every part of us, each and every moment of every day, every interaction, and every thought? The question is: how are we to avoid being useful?

While capitalism is a monolithic system of absolute abstraction, living systems are more complex. Living systems incorporate both material and abstract systems of organization in complex ecologies of desiring-production. In order to exist and persist, capitalism requires the production of profit, and profit requires an infinite expansion of abstract surplus. To wit, capitalism must produce ever-proliferating systems of abstract code. The code itself is autopoietic and reproduces itself out of itself, but it is reliant on disturbances in its environment by living systems that can be encoded. While capitalism as an immanent system is all-pervasive at the level of abstract codification, it has little or no direct relation to the mechanisms of immanent materiality.

We argue that this is highly relevant to the question of a politics of uselessness because, as Spinoza (2000) points out, it is the body that gives rise to thought. Capitalism has inverted this living logic and constituted itself on the perverse premise that abstraction gives rise to living form. This living logic, at a very primitive level, is the logic that states that profits should come before the well-being of living things in such matters as healthcare or ecological balance. Put simply, it is the argument that, without money, we would all die. Of course, this is not so, unless the system pre-sets its logic so that money becomes the mediation between living surplus and the survival needs of living beings.

The advantage that living systems have as capitalism becomes increasingly abstract is life's sheer materiality. As capital relies more and more heavily on posthuman systems such as artificial intelligence and the proliferation of robotics and algorithms of surveillance and control, the realm of living materiality becomes less and less useful. Subjectification for capitalism becomes ever more persistently immersion into abstract systems of signification that reference a distant material subject while drawing very little on its actual lived experience.

Deleuze (1995) refers to this as a process of dividuation in which we are no longer living subjects. Instead, we are data points in marketing algorithms. There is an inevitable gap between the materiality of one's existence and the insistence that your experience must always be mediated through abstract categories defined by various forms of media. Such a gap has profound effects, such as a sense of vertiginous dislocation that can produce dystopic affective responses such as depression, anxiety, murderous rages, schizoid breaks, and cynical forms of sociopathy. All of this creates pathways for corporate psychoactive intervention that can produce vast amounts of capital in its own right. Contrary to popular discourse, these dysfunctional subjects are anything but useless. They are the coming mode of subjectification and of significant utility to capital.

So, how to be a useless subversive subject? For this, we turn to a form of posthumanism, as articulated in the work of feminist scholar Rosi Braidotti (2013). Braidotti, who terms herself a neo-vitalist, draws her inspiration from Deleuze, Nietzsche, and Spinoza. She suggests that we root our politics in an affirmative alterity. She argues that a politics of resistance and opposition is a dead end. There will be no forceful overthrow of capitalism; no mode of resistance that it cannot abstract to its own purpose, and no opposition it cannot configure into a mode of profitability. We have seen this time and again in global movements of resistance and opposition that have become marketing slogans for major corporations and which have spawned reactionary political responses funded by oligarchs and billionaire media moguls. Virtual global capital thrives on binary formations. They are the most accessible social communication to encode and abstract. Also, as Hardt and Negri (2001) point out, there is no outside to capital – no nations that function independently from corporate rule. All wars are fought within capital over spheres of financial influence. Any large-scale opposition, armed or non-violent, will be played out within the great game of global profit. To quote *Star Trek: The Next Generation*, "Resistance is futile."

As an alternative, Braidotti (2010a) proposes an ecological configuration of living force founded in "a set of interrelations with both human and inhuman forces" (p. 44). Such relations are specifically non-textual but based instead on Spinozist notions of relationality, the Deleuzian concept of immanence, and the Bergsonian idea of duration. It is perhaps a kind of identification with the sacred, in the sense that Catherine Bateson (1987) notes in *Angels Fear*, as the incommunicable. Bateson notes non-communication and a kind of secrecy as a mark of the sacred. In terms of what Starhawk (1997) terms immanent spirituality, the relation between humans and what Taylor (2012) calls more-than-human others, there is a phenomenological encounter that exceeds the capacity for expression. Perhaps it is this secret, extra-linguistic sacred set of relations that holds a kind of political possibility for becoming indigestible and useless to capital. Maybe it is a pre-modern configuration buried in the rubble of the rush to reason and rationality that is constitutively capable of turning capitalism under.

In Chuang Tzu's (1974) story, the useless tree seeks refuge in the temple to "escape the abuse of those who do not appreciate it" (p. 80). If it were not sacred, it would be cut down. But there is a contradiction in the text of the story that holds an essential utility for our conversation. On the one hand, the tree is not cut down because it is so imperfect as to be useless, while on the other hand, we are told if it were not sacred, it would be cut down. We argue that there is the possibility of a subtle double usage of the sacred here. In the story, there is a master carpenter who states, "Moreover, the means it adopts for safety is different from that of others, and to criticize it by ordinary standards would be far wide of the mark" (p. 82).

The tree exists in a complex ecology of definitions that are simultaneously encoded and immanent. That is to say, it is useless because it is a sacred object, which cannot be cut down, but at the same time, the tree is useful for its shade and as a vehicle for contemplation. In the first configuration, it persists because of being encoded as sacred, while in the latter, it serves a phenomenological function that we cannot fully speak. How can one fully articulate the experience of a human/more-than-human encounter such as sitting under a tree? This latter assemblage is difficult to entangle because it speaks to the idiosyncratic manner of the tree's growth as a function immanent to a vast array of colliding bodies, including sun, rain, soil, genetics, insects, birds, and animals. In this sense, the tree is somewhat like the North American Indigenous (Segal, 2011) definition of a bear, which includes rivers, fish, moss, birds, humans, rocks, to name but a few. It is a living ecology, that is, a sheer affirmation of virtual capacity.

So how does this help us to understand how to become subversively useless? We would argue that there is at least one thing we can deduce thus far. That is, we must become textually incomprehensible. In an interview with Negri, Deleuze (1995) states,

> You ask whether control or communication societies will lead to forms of resistance that might reopen the way for a communism understood as the "transversal organization of free individuals." Maybe, I don't know. But it would be nothing to do with minorities speaking out. Maybe speech and communication have been corrupted. They're thoroughly permeated by money – and not by accident but by their very nature. We've got to hijack speech. Creating has always been something different from communicating. The key thing may be to create vacuoles of noncommunication, circuit breakers, so we can elude control.
>
> (p. 175)

To become useless is to abandon things such as speaking truth to power, or passing better legislation or inventing new media. Instead, Deleuze points to creativity as a vehicle for breaking the circuit of self-referential communication that is the bread and butter of capitalist accumulation in the early part of the 21st century. But what does he mean by "vacuoles of noncommunication" as the key to "hijack[ing] speech"? How are we to become useless through creating such spaces?

By vacuole, Deleuze (1995) is referencing a small cavity or space in the tissue of an organism. We can often find this small cavity in the tissues of the nervous system as the result of disease. In this sense, the key to politics is to produce disease in the communication system of the body politic of capitalism. We can only imagine that Deleuze is thinking that creating spaces of non-communication in a system, premised as a series of communication systems, would trigger what he calls circuit breakers. Circuit breakers would be the Batesonian-type mechanisms that would disrupt the runaway escalation of binary overcoding that drives capitalism to encase itself deeper and deeper into systems of abstract signification radically scissioned from the checks and balances of phenomenological experience.

To become useless is to become a disease within the body of capitalist relations. Such a disease is premised within ecological and relational creativity; that is, doing rather than speaking, creating rather than communicating. It is to be found in a politics premised in the radical relation of multiple alterities. Such assemblages of radical difference are composed out of the generative responses of bodies in collision. That is to say, the useless tree is always useless within a context of relations with other bodies that creates its radical alterity. The tree cannot choose to be useless. It has to find its uselessness contingently through an infinitude of minor acts of relational becoming.

It is in this sense that Braidotti (2010a) argues that we must be careful not to attribute individual agency to our political activities. In the first instance, such activities have no individual center and are composed of a web of human and more-than-human interactions. This ecological set of relations is quite evident when we think of Naomi Klein's (2007) disaster capitalism, or the gentrification of New Orleans after Hurricane Katrina, and so on. Similarly, to engage as a vacuole of non-communication through acts that engage human and more-than-human actors must be found in the mundanity of daily living; these are not acts of human heroics striving to save the world or other species. Braidotti (2011) suggests that the subjects capable of the kind of human to more-than-human relational work that goes beyond taxonomic and hierarchical understandings are constitutively driven to such activities. It is a random confluence of virtual capacity through which a transformation of subjectivity opens new vectors of possible acts. It is not premised on morality or conventional ethics, but in what Braidotti (2013) calls a radical ethics of transformation. This radical ethics is a gradual warping, a drifting away from conventional binary conceptual frameworks. Like the shamanic tradition, "it shifts the focus from unitary rationality-driven consciousness to process ontology, that is to say a vision of subjectivity propelled by affects and relations" (p. 323).

These living relations are not formed through the generosity of corporate training in affect management or schools that teach mindfulness as a disciplinary technique. Nor is it to be found in assertiveness training or non-violence workshops. Subjectivities of uselessness are propelled by the necessities of contingent, relational encounter. It is the cathexis of a web of unconscious desiring-production not yet overcoded by capitalist simulacra. It is not a copy. It is the seminal but never completed set of relations. Such relations are defined by bodily encounters that give rise to thought and then acts. They are diagrammatically transversal and highly mobile. In Braidotti's (2010b) terminology, they are nomadic subjectivities. She tells us that this is a process that "attaches subjectivity to affirmative otherness – reciprocity as creation, not as the re-cognition of Sameness" (p. 47).

As a praxis, becoming useless to capital is, to some degree, to engage in what Braidotti (2011) refers to as dis-identifying oneself. To become a nomadic subject is to embrace what she defines as "the cruel messy outside-ness of Life itself"

(p. 305). It is to open oneself beyond the formations of historical binary taxonomies and hierarchies of the self, to engage in the flow of virtuality that is all that moves through us.

Lest we imagine this to be some kind of Dionysian exploration of the new me, we want to be clear that the transformational power of living force is impersonal and holds no regard for any individual preference of whom you wish to become. It encompasses extreme vulnerability, exposure, and availability to whatever alterity is at hand. Braidotti, in a gesture towards the suffering that is living force embedded within a system functioning in radical counterdistinction to it, suggests moments of identity consolidation when moving through overtly hostile territory. But this is a reading at the surface of the politics of uselessness. The actual politics is well beyond our comprehension and engages,

> the vital politics of life itself, as external and non-human forces: cells, as Franklin argues; viruses and bacteria, as Luciana Parisi points out; and earth others, as Haraway has been arguing for a long time. This post-human ethics rests on a multi-layered form of relationality. It assumes as the point of reference not the individual, but the relation.
> *(Braidotti, 2008, p. 20)*

Gloria Anzaldúa (1987) opens a passage to the abstract and mystical in her profoundly intersectional work. In this aspect of her writing, we would argue that she constitutes vacuoles of noncommunication. She states that,

> In our very flesh, (r)evolution works out the clash of cultures ... *Nuestra alma el trabajo*, the opus, the great alchemical work; spiritual *mestizaje*, a "morphogenesis," an inevitable unfolding. We have become the quickening serpent movement.
> *(Anzaldúa, 1987, p. 46)*

Anzaldúa's reading of the mother goddess Coatlicue as embodying the transformation (serpent movement), through which who we imagine ourselves to be, is continuously created and destroyed. Coatlicue "devours" the self to allow for "evolution" and new "germination," "kicking a hole out of the old boundaries of the self and slipping under or over, dragging the old skin along, stumbling over it" (Anzaldúa, 1987, pp. 46–47, 49). This process can constitute the enfleshment of revolutionary subjectivities capable of being useless to capital.

Revolutions are messy businesses with little or no purity to be found. They inevitably fail if their goal is merely a transformation of rule. For us, it is a question of sustaining the creative virtual force of life. During periods of great transition, chaos, and upheaval where empires desperately engage in runaway escalations of force, it is uselessness that represents the world to come. This was true in the world of Chuang Tzu, and we would suggest it might be true today.

References

Agamben, G. (2009). *"What is an apparatus?" and other essays.* Palo Alto, CA: Stanford University Press.
Anzaldúa, G. (1987). *Borderlands: La frontera.* San Francisco, CA: Aunt Lute.
Barad, K. (2007). *Meeting the universe halfway: Quantum physics and the entanglement of matter and meaning.* Durham, NC: Duke University Press.
Bateson, G., & Bateson, M. C. (1987). *Angels fear: An investigation into the nature and meaning of the sacred.* London: Rider.
Baudrillard, J. (1994). *Simulacra and simulation.* Ann Arbor, MI: University of Michigan Press.
Bergson, H. (2004). *Matter and memory.* North Chelmsford, MA: Courier Corporation.
Braidotti, R. (1994). *Nomadic subjects: Embodiment and sexual difference in contemporary feminist theory.* New York, NY: Columbia University Press.
Braidotti, R. (2008). Affirmation, pain and empowerment. *Asian Journal of Women's Studies, 14*(3), 7–36.
Braidotti, R. (2010a). The politics of life itself and new ways of dying. In J. Bennett, P. Cheah, M. A. Orlie, & E. Grosz (Eds). *New materialisms: Ontology, agency, and politics.* Durham, NC: Duke University Press.
Braidotti, R. (2010b). On putting the active back into activism. *New Formations, 68,* 42–57.
Braidotti, R. (2011). *Nomadic theory: The portable Rosi Braidotti.* New York, NY: Columbia University Press.
Braidotti, R. (2013). *The posthuman.* Cambridge: Polity.
Chakrabarty, D. (2000). *Provincializing Europe: Postcolonial thought and historical difference.* Princeton, NJ: Princeton University Press.
Chuang, T. (1974). *Inner chapters* (G. Feng & J. English, Trans.). New York, NY: Vintage Books.
Deleuze, G. (1966). *Bergsonism* (trans. H. Tomlinson and B. Habberjam). New York, NY: Zone.
Deleuze, G. (1995). Postscript on the societies of control. *October, 59,* 3–7.
Deleuze, G., & Guattari, F. (1984). *Anti-Oedipus: Capitalism and schizophrenia* (trans. R. Hurley, M. Seem, and H. R. Lane). London: Athlone.
Deleuze, G., & Guattari, F. (1988). *A thousand plateaus: Capitalism and schizophrenia.* London: Bloomsbury Publishing.
Foucault, M. (2005). *The order of things.* New York, NY: Routledge.
Foucault, M. (2012). *Discipline and punish: The birth of the prison.* New York, NY: Vintage.
Guattari, F. (2010). *The machinic unconscious: Essays in schizoanalysis.* LA: Semiotext(e)
Haraway, D. J. (2003). *The companion species manifesto: Dogs, people, and significant otherness.* Chicago, IL: Prickly Paradigm Press.
Hardt, M., & Negri, A. (2001). *Empire.* Cambridge, MA: Harvard University Press.
Klein, N. (2007). Disaster capitalism. *Harper's Magazine.*
Lam, M. C. (1996). A resistance role for Marxism in the belly of the beast. In S. Makdisi, C. Casarino, & R. Karl (Eds.). *Marxism beyond Marxism,* pp. 255–264. New York, NY: Routledge.
Marx, K. (2005). *Grundrisse: Foundations of the critique of political economy.* London: Penguin.
Negri, A. (2011). *Art and multitude.* Cambridge: Polity.
Negri, A. (2012). Twenty theses on Marx. In S. Makdisi, C. Casarino, & R. Karl (Eds.). *Marxism beyond Marxism,* pp. 149–180. New York, NY: Routledge.
Segal, D. (2011). "The promise of ecopsychology: Addressing the psychological and spiritual pain associated with the industrial growth society," http://postgrowth.org/the-promise-of-ecopsychology/

Spivak, G. C. (1999). *A critique of postcolonial reason. Towards a history of the vanishing present.* Calcutta: Seagull.
Spinoza, B. (2000). *The ethics.* Cambridge: Oxford University Press.
Starhawk. (1997). *Dreaming the dark : Magic, sex, and politics.* Boston : Beacon Press.
Taylor, A., Pacinini-Ketchabaw, V., & Blaise, M. (2012). Children's relations to the more-than-human world. *Contemporary Issues in Early Childhood,* 13(2), 81.

4
THE END OF KNOWING AS CRITICAL PRAXIS (PRACTICAL-CRITICAL ACTIVITY)

Lois Holzman

While there are many varieties (not to mention definitions) of critical psychology and critical praxis, it is safe to assume that the people who practice and promote them all strive for a more equitable, fair, and just world and, further, that they believe that the dominant (non-critical) psychology, in varying ways, stands in the way of realizing such a world. The varieties of critical psychology that I am most familiar with are those that have emerged in the US and the UK. In previous writings, I have characterized the various approaches into the following types according to the source or basis of the critique: identity-based, ideology-based, epistemology-based, and ontology-based (Holzman, 2013). The latter refers to the philosophically informed social therapeutics developed over the past 40 years by myself and the late Fred Newman (Holzman, 2020; Newman and Holzman, 1997, 2006). For us and the global practitioners of social therapeutics, identity-based, ideology-based, and epistemology-based critical psychologies do not go nearly far enough, for it is identity, ideology, and epistemology themselves that stand in the way of people creating an equitable, fair, and just world (Newman and Holzman, 2006). They are what human beings are socialized to believe in and to rely on as what makes us human. They are both the glasses and the mirrors through which we have learned to perceive. This overly cognitive perceptual orientation impacts how we think and feel, what we believe exists, and what we believe possible.

Who am I without an identity? How would I know what is right without an ideology? How can I act without knowing what to do? While people do not, as a rule, spend time pondering these issues in the abstract, we do live our lives as if we are, or should be, guided by them. Indeed, our very wants and needs are shaped by assumptions about identity, ideology, and epistemology, regardless of how firm or shaky a particular individual's identity, ideology, or epistemology might be. This is in accord with mainstream (non-critical) psychology's authoritarian insistence that it knows what people are, what makes us tick, what we want, and how we come to know what we want. Psychology not only dictates to us; it shapes us as dictaters(ors) to ourselves.

As a critical psychologist I am, of course, concerned to contribute to ways that people can meet their current wants and needs. However, what people currently want and need is shaped by the many ways that the broad culture makes use of mainstream psychology and its authoritarianism to socialize people to particular wants and needs. Given this overdetermination, those of us who are critical of psychology need to be concerned with something further—namely, how do we reconstruct our world in such a way that people can not only meet their current needs but go beyond that to create new wants and needs? Creating new wants and needs requires, as far as I can tell, the creating of environments that generate them, and so, the answers to the question of how to reconstruct the world have to be created by what people, including us, do.

While the answers are unknowable, the path to creative discovery is not. I offer a direction (hopefully, there are others), one that is guided by a methodology that goes beyond the critical to the *practical-critical*. I take that term from Marx, for whom it meant revolutionary activity, the changing of ourselves that is dialectically united with world changing: "The coincidence of the changing of circumstances and of human activity or self-changing can be conceived and rationally understood only as *revolutionary practice*" (Marx, 1974, p. 121, emphasis in original). As an *ontological critique* of mainstream psychology and psychotherapy, this methodology represents a move from critical (opposition, resistance, and destruction or deconstruction) to practical-critical (creating something new out of what exists, reconstruction-in-deconstruction). It represents a move from applying method to practicing method, from using method as an instrumental tool meant to yield results to method as dialectically united with results (Newman and Holzman, 2013).

This practical-critical methodology (practice of method) guides the work that my colleagues and I have been engaged in across the US for over 40 years and which, for the past ten years, has adapted by activist-scholars and practitioners in many other countries of the world (Friedman and Holzman, 2014; Holzman, 2019, 2020). The goals of this work are:

1. To organize environments that involve all kinds of people—young and old, rich, poor, and in between—in transforming their relationships to themselves, to each other, and to the institutional gatekeepers of both local and global culture
2. To re-initiate hope and imagination through exercising our human capacity to self-organize to meet our needs
3. To support people to become active creators of their relationality, their emotionality, their learning
4. To remake the world in such a way that everyone can have what they need to continue to develop themselves and their communities.

With such a broad agenda, it is no surprise that the work does not fit neatly into known categories, and so it goes by many names: social therapeutics, the psychology of becoming, the development community, performance activism, and postmodern Marxism. Social therapeutics because it is grounded in Fred Newman's creation of social therapy 40 years ago. A psychology of becoming because it takes human beings to be not just who we are but simultaneously who we are becoming. The development community because it engages in the activity of creating development and the activity of creating the community that supports development. Performance activism because its politics is one of reconstruction and transformation through people creating new performances of themselves. Postmodern Marxism because it is inspired by Marx's revolutionary philosophy and radical humanism of transforming the very circumstances that determine us through the all-round development of everyone as well as by the postmodern questioning of the tenets of modernism, including truth, reality, and objectivity.

I have chosen four features of this practical-critical methodology to highlight as especially relevant to the future of critical psychology: (1) engage the epistemological bias; (2) do not confuse power with authority; (3) reinitiate the development of persons and communities; and (4) play and perform.

Engage the Epistemological Bias

The authoritarianism of Western ways of knowing is often critiqued by critical psychologists (myself included), and this is all well and good. Moreover, while non-Western epistemologies should be honored and respected along with all the other features of a given culture, I think that *all* epistemologies are authoritarian. It is the epistemic posture itself that is a fetter to revolutionary activity. All peoples are, to greater and lesser degrees, guided (consciously and unconsciously) by a knowing paradigm—that we can and must know what is, what to do, who we are, how we feel, what is real, and what is right, and what is true. Institutions (education, the law, economics, psychology, science, religion, and so on) derive their authority from a knowing paradigm. They socialize us to ways of understanding and feeling and relating that are, in the current times, conservative and destructive. Living by a knowing paradigm stifles creativity and discovery, closes off other ways of understanding, and constrains our ability to imagine and create a new world (Holzman, 2018; Newman and Holzman, 1997, 2006).

Do Not Confuse Power with Authority

As a child of the 1960s, I still bristle when I hear the word "power" used negatively by progressives, as a pejorative, something bad or even evil, and a property of those who rule. I am still a believer in "power to the people." I do not know exactly when "power" lost its revolutionary meaning, but the talk today is most often about the exercise and abuse of power by those "in power." What then, could it mean, to "empower people"? But, you might be thinking, are not these merely different uses of the word "power" in different contexts? Yes, they are, but not "merely." Leaving it at that masks an important distinction that I have found invaluable in my political understanding and work. That distinction is between power and authority—power being *created from the bottom*, and authority being *imposed from the top*. From this vantage point, being "in power" and "exercising power" are as different as can be. Being "in power" is the commodification of power into authority. Exercising power is engaging, collectively, democratically and creatively, in practical-critical, revolutionary activity—without commodification (Newman and Holzman, 2003; Holzman and Newman, 2004, 2012).

Professionalized and institutionalized psychology, psychotherapy, counseling, social work, healthcare, and education in the US, and increasingly elsewhere, practice and promote all manner of dehumanizing authoritarian commodification—DSM and ICD diagnoses, identity psychology and identity politics, testing and evaluation are just the most obvious examples. The authority of these institutions is so thorough that people not only commodify themselves in these and other ways—we feel we *need* to. At the same time, I believe that people not only need, but *want*, to exercise power *without commodification*. Psychologically, this desire is in nearly constant struggle with the human need to authoritarianly commodify oneself. Given this contemporary human condition, it is a huge creative challenge to create ways to support people to *exercise power without commodification*, that is, free of authority.

Reinitiate the Development of Persons and Communities

Mainstream psychology is interested in who we are and, working from that position, it grandiosely and erroneously tells us who we will become. That is because it is thoroughly epistemological and authoritarian, claiming to be a predictive science. Prediction, however, knows nothing of dialectics, of the practical-critical, of revolutionary activity. A practical-critical, a humanizing psychology, is not predictive but possibility generating, in that it engages directly the human struggle between power and authority—the power of becoming and the authority of being. For human beings are not just who we are, as persons, communities and nation states. We are also, and at the same time, who we are becoming. We all live in a particular culture, society, space, and time. But we also all live in history, by which I do not mean the past, but the totality of past, present, and future. Most people, however, experience themselves societally, rather than dialectically living in society and history. They do not feel themselves as simultaneously self- and world-changers, as creators of qualitative transformation, as active bringers-into-being new ways of feeling and relating to themselves and others. Reinitiating the development of persons and communities involves building environments in which people can stop being *only* who they are (societal) and simultaneously become who they are becoming (historical), in which they can engage in the revolutionary activity of creating new wants and needs and emotions and relationships.

Play and Perform

To create new needs and new wants we have to imagine. More than that, we have to allow our imaginations to impact on our past experiences, and our past experiences to impact on our imaginings—and generate new social activity. There are at least two things people in every culture, so it seems, do that accomplish this. One is play and the other is performing. Both allow—indeed, depend on—our being both who we are and not who we are at the same time. When little children roar like lions in the zoo, they are themselves and not themselves. When babbling babies carry on conversations with adults, they are playing with language and performing as speakers before they know how to talk. They are both who they are (babbling babies) and who they are becoming (speakers). When actors perform in a stage play, they are themselves and the character they are playing at the same time. In both cases, babies and actors, experiences and imaginings are creating something new and other.

As the critical praxis of the development community that social therapeutics has been building, these four features of the practice of method challenge the foundational assumptions of existing institutions, be they political, cultural, educational, or psychological. Some examples from the 40-year history of organizing Newman and I have been involved in here in the US are: a school for children that denied the individuated, knowledge-seeking model of learning; social therapy centers with an approach to emotional help that denies the premises of mainstream psychotherapy; a labor union for unorganized labor and welfare recipients (who did not labor and, therefore, were at no point of production); a university that is free, open to anyone who wants to participate and has no grades or degrees; a national network of talent shows for youth that denies the bourgeois conception of talent; electoral political campaigns that are not concerned with winning and political parties that exist to redefine politics and transform political culture—including the possibility of doing away with political parties as the mode of citizen participation. Until his passing in 2011, Newman and I—along with our colleagues in psychology, social work, theatre, community organizing, youth work, and education—organized thousands to participate in creating developmental projects in culture, psychology, education, and politics and simultaneously continued to advance the articulation of the methodology we were creating (Newman and Holzman, 1997, 2003, 2004).

The goal of these projects is to inspire, invite, and help people to practice method, to create new forms of life, to build environments that are at once the context for revolutionary activity and revolutionary activity itself. This activity is a deconstruction–reconstruction of the capitalist ontology in which human beings are understood to be only *who we are*. Given that "who we are" (especially those in late capitalist culture) is commodified and alienated individuals, the products of a sick society to which we have adapted, transforming this sick society needs to involve the de-commodification and de-alienation of its human "products." This is neither negative nor destructive, but rather the positive and constructive process of producing sociality.

In the *process ontology* of practicing method (and its ontologically based critical psychology), human beings are both who we are and *who we are becoming*. And who we are becoming are creators of tools that can "abolish the present state of things" by the continuous transformation of mundane specific life practices into new forms of life. Creating these new kinds of tools is the *becoming activity* of expressing—in how we live our lives—our sociality, our adaptation to history, our "species-life," as Marx (1967) referred to it. It is a participatory process in which people exercise their collective power to create new environments and new ways of relating to themselves, each other, and the world.

After more than 40 years, the practical-critical methodology of social therapeutics and performance activism (the ontologically based critical psychology) is studied and practiced in the US and internationally, from the Mexico–US border and refugee camps in Europe, from schools in Brazil and Japan to mental health institutions in Kolkata and villages of Nigeria and Uganda. From my own work and that of others around the world, we have come to identify what we are all doing as a new kind of activism. Not a reactive activism, but a reconstruction–deconstruction of the existing circumstances; of people coming together, with their different histories and identities, their agreements and disagreements, and creating something "other" with them. We have seen firsthand in thousands of cases that, to generate new possibilities, people have to perform, to step out of their comfort zones (as the teenagers put it), to do whatever it is they are trying to do without knowing how. They have to play and perform life. And by engaging in this practical-critical activity of deconstruction through reconstruction, they are reigniting their historical identity as revolutionary changers of the circumstances that determine us, creating the possibility that they will not only meet their current needs and wants but create new, more humanizing, inclusive, relational, and developmental ones. I believe that this is something all of us need and want.

References

Friedman, D. and Holzman, L. (2014). Performing the world: The performance turn in social activism. In A. Citron, S. Aronson-Lehavi and D. Zerbib (Eds.), *Performance studies in motion: International perspectives and practices in the twenty-first century*. London: Bloomsbury (pp. 276–287).

Holzman, L. (2013). Critical psychology, philosophy and social therapy. *Human Studies*, 36(4), 471–489.

Holzman, L. (2018). *The overweight brain: How our obsession with knowing keeps us from getting smart enough to make a better world*. New York: East Side Institute.

Holzman, L. (2019). Vygotsky on the margins. In A. T. Neto, F. Liberali and M. Dafermos (Eds.), *Revisiting Vygotsky for social change: Bringing together theory and practice*. New York: Peter Lang.

Holzman, L. (2020). Constructing social therapeutics. In S. McNamee, M. Gergen, C. Camargo Borges and E. Rasera (Eds.), *The SAGE handbook on social constructionist practice*. Newbury Park, CA: Sage.

Holzman, L. and Newman, F. (2012). Activity and performance (and their discourse) in social therapeutic practice. In A. Lock and T. Strong (Eds.), *Discursive perspectives in therapeutic practice*. Oxford: Oxford University Press (pp. 184–195).

Marx, K. (1967). Economic and philosophical manuscripts. In E. Fromm (Ed.), *Marx's concept of man*. New York: Frederick Ungar (pp. 90–196).

Marx, K. (1974). Theses on Feuerbach. In K. Marx and F. Engels (Eds.), *The German ideology*. New York: International Publishers (pp. 121–123).

Newman, F. and Holzman, L. (1996). *Unscientific psychology: A cultural-performatory approach to understanding human life*. Westport, CT: Praeger. Republished, 2006, iUniverse.

Newman, F. and Holzman, L. (1997). *The end of knowing: A new developmental way of learning*. London: Routledge.

Newman, F. and Holzman, L. (2003). All power to the developing! *Annual Review of Critical Psychology*, 3, 8–23.

Newman, F. and Holzman, L. (2004). Power, authority and pointless activity (the developmental discourse of social therapy). In T. Strong and D. Paré (Eds.), *Furthering talk: Advances in the discursive therapies* (pp. 73–86). New York: Kluwer Academic/Plenum.

Newman, F. and Holzman, L. (2013). *Lev Vygotsky: Revolutionary scientist (classic edition)*. New York: Psychology Press. Originally published, 1993, London: Routledge (Portuguese edition, 2002).

5
LOOKING (OUT) FOR NEW MASTERS
Assessing the Bar between Lacanianism and Critical Psychology

Michael J. Miller[1]

The Prefecture of Police: On Patrol along the Rue St. Jacques

Jacques Lacan wasted few opportunities to position himself as a detractor of psychology. Paraphrasing Canguilhem's (2016) critique, Lacan (2006d, p. 729) comments that psychology slides "like a toboggan from the pantheon to the prefecture of police." Here, and in other *Écrits* (2006c; see also Miller, 2020), Lacan is warning his readers against taking a psychologized approach to psychoanalysis, such as that taken by the mainstream of the psychoanalytic movement at the time, which would amount to climbing into that particular toboggan, and to ally what should be a decidedly non-conformist (or at least a-conformist) movement, psychoanalysis, with the mechanisms of enforcement of social norms through the valuing of adaptation, heteronormative "genital" sexuality, and the manufacture of healthy egos modeled on those of the enforcers (Lacan, 2006a, 2006c).[2]

Lacan insists that it is to Canguilhem's Pantheon that psychoanalysts must instead pledge allegiance—that is, on his reading, to the preservation of Freud's teachings in their pristine (and dead) state, just as the actual structure preserves the corpses of Voltaire and Rousseau. But in his injunction that his followers hew closely to "the Freudian discovery" rather than let themselves become polluted by interpretations of Freud that he finds substandard, Lacan furnishes them with a toboggan route of his own, one that ends up in the same place. By insisting on purity, he is effectively conscripting a "police" force of followers who will judge not only whether other analysts, clinicians, or thinkers are respecting the "truth of the Freudian discovery," but whether their understandings of Lacan are worthy. Fittingly, it is Paris's Rue St. Jacques that connects the Pantheon to the Prefecture of Police.

Modeled on Lacan's insistence on claiming the one true Freud, so to speak, is the pursuit among Lacanians to enter into relationship with the one true Lacan. We find this at least as early as the heated contestation of the text of Lacan's Seminar, numerous versions of which circulated around Paris in bootleg forms before the social power of Lacan's son-in-law, J.A. Miller, was brought to bear to root out any but his definitive text (Roudinesco et al., 1997, pp. 413–427). Miller did not stop at trying to assemble the best record of what was said, claiming co-authorship of the Seminar itself, and even that his name was indistinguishable from Lacan's: "I can write 'I' and that 'I' is Lacan's, an 'I' that continues the author and prolongs him beyond his death" (as cited in Roudinesco et al., 1997, p. 421). When, later, readers began to notice problems with Miller's authoritative editions of the Seminar, they demanded access to all other existing versions of these texts (which had been litigated out of accessibility by Miller). Millerians such as Catherine Clement dismissed the complaints as a "witch hunt" designed to punish Lacan's son-in-law, and his daughter, who was only "guilty for having been engendered by the master whose dead blood people now thirst after" (Clement, as cited in Roudinesco et al., 1997, p. 426).

Lacan's biographer, Elisabeth Roudinesco, was soon caught up in a similar controversy, and sued by Judith Miller (the daughter in question) in 2011 for suggesting that Lacan wanted a Catholic funeral (Roudinesco & Elliott, 2014). While Roudinesco's legal defense is said to have been thorough, Miller's counsel reportedly showed up armed mainly with the Name-of-the-Father:

> In a short speech, [Miller's counsel] described Roudinesco as an "imposter" who is not, nor shall ever be, "part of the family," and that she spent her entire career obsessing about an author "who did not have the slightest degree of attachment towards her."
>
> *(Weslati, 2013)*

These are but primal examples of what we might call Lacanian police work, which is accompanied, as police work so often is, by violence. The interpersonal violence we see here, which we might dismiss as in-fighting, is not anomalous, but is reproduced outside the immediate social orbit of Jacques Lacan in the realm of Lacanian writing: both that about Lacanian thought itself, and about other disciplines or social phenomena, which have likely had little or no contact with Lacan's work, let alone psychoanalysis. Ironically, the direction of Lacanian critique of both those categories is often that they are not Lacanian enough. The violence of the first category, toward "other" Lacanian writing, often comes in the form of contemptuous dismissals of "confused" treatments of Lacan (confusion being an accusation favored by Lacan and Lacanians). Jane Gallop, for example, recounts a reviewer response to her manuscript for *Reading Lacan* (1987):

It began with the point that the text was not worthy of publication because it demonstrated inadequate command of the subject matter, adding that I even admitted as much ... I did not sufficiently grasp the Lacanian theory of sexual identification (again acknowledging that I admitted this) and that I should wait to write about Lacan's theory until I was no longer confused.

(Gallop, 1987, p. 19)[3]

The Will to "Non-Rapport" in Lacanian Criticism

Venturing beyond the field of Lacanianism itself, attacks from those coordinates upon non-Lacanian thinking are not unusual. Perhaps the best-worn "defile" in this category is the attack upon psychology that Lacan himself began. It is in that critique that we might see a major form of hope for a Lacanian critical psychology, and Lacan's own treatment, especially of Skinner, of the "applied psychoanalysis" of Miller and Dollard, and of the psychoanalytic anthropology proposed by Abram Kardiner and Cora DuBois are powerful examples, even if not academically rigorous in the typical sense (Lacan, 2006c).

In his criticism of the latter, for example, Lacan strikes us as surprisingly progressive, given his patrician reputation, in his awareness of Kardiner's colonialism and racism. Kardiner and DuBois—to whom Lacan referred as "American procrusteans [who] torment with their yardstick the mystery of supposedly primitive souls"— advanced the notion, which flourished in DuBois's work in Indonesia (Alor at that time), that given cultures favor particular "basic" or "modal" personality structures that could be assessed via psychological testing, including the then-heavily psychoanalytic Rorschach; hence, the yardstick and the "supposedly primitive souls." Kardiner infamously proposed that poverty was the result of the poor emotional health of its victims, and set out to train women to teach parents how to raise their children in accordance with the principles of his understanding of psychoanalysis (Prilleltensky, 1994, p. 65). Such pronouncements were not limited to the "other" of Alor. Kardiner, a white man, after similar researches, declared that the "psychological scars" of the postwar African American community were due chiefly to the "matriarchal" structure of some black families, with all of their Oedipal problematics (O'Connor, 2009, p. 111).

Part of Lacan's appeal as an author is his tendency, not of making thorough critique, but rather setting us readers upon our way, in such a manner that it often appears, as we proceed to visit the primary texts in question, that Lacan has been there already. This, arguably, is of a piece with the "style" that he characterizes psychoanalysis as teaching.

This is not to say that, having been there, Lacan has been faithful, careful, or respectful of the texts to which he refers. Lacan's excursions into psychology, as well as other fields, are poorly or simply never cited, and even when his aim is not critical he presents us with incomplete, or, to be more generous, radically revised versions of the literature in question. Examples include Lacan's creative misreading of Saussure's construct of the sign, and as Billig (2006) has thoroughly demonstrated, his "misuse" of the psychology that furnished the "facts" at the basis of "The Mirror Stage." While I am suspicious of the notion of a "misuse" of psychology, Billig is right on the substance: Lacan commits, at the very least, an *abuse*[4] of psychological scholarship, which includes, as he notes, the frank reversal of Kohler's statement that chimpanzees do not lose interest in their mirror images. Lacan casually cites the "the opposite as if it were fact" (Billig, 2006, p. 16) as a foundational point in "The Mirror Stage" (2006b).[5]

Leaving it to Billig to evaluate the rigor and respect brought by Lacan to his citations of psychology, we must concede that, no matter how dilettante Lacan's engagement may be, it is nonetheless an engagement. It is not often the case, however, that Lacanian secondary literature, no matter its level of rigor within the Lacanian field, continues that tradition. Lacanian literature (see, for example, Badiou & Roudinesco, 2014; Hook, 2018; Malone & Freidlander, 2000; Parker, 2003) frequently echoes Lacan on the disqualifying flaws of psychology, revisiting its "confusion" of the ego with the subject, its naïve Cartesianism, its unapologetic lack of theoretical rigor, and its pride of position as an agency of social control (located, as it is, in the Prefecture of Police). While Lacan's criticisms are important, their reproductions almost never cite the psychology they purport to criticize. When they do, they cite only those psychologists that Lacan himself addressed, directly or indirectly: figures like Baldwin, Wallon, and Skinner, for example. A search through the index for *The Subject of Lacan: A Lacanian Reader for Psychologists* (Friedlander & Malone, 2000) illustrates this phenomenon. This comes from (or is at least rationalized by) a stance of "rejectionism" (see Parker, 2003, 2005, 2015). Because Lacan's work is taken up as wholly transcending or rejecting the ontological and epistemological bases of psychology, it is not to be "confused with" or made to mix with psychology. Lacanians then tend to keep their attention only on the work of Lacan and his fellow travelers within the continental philosophical tradition, or literature and film studies.

The rejectionist Lacanian insistence that Lacan's work was antithetical to psychology seems sometimes to come hand in hand with license not only to ignore his engagement with psychology, nor only to direct contempt "in psychology's general direction," to take a phrase from *Monty Python*. It seems to allow the Lacanian to be utterly unconcerned with what the discipline of psychology *is*, even at the most basic level. One routinely hears in conversation, for example, a conflation of "American ego-psychology" (a form of psychoanalysis practiced only by medical doctors) with "psychology" (a written example is found in Badiou & Roudinesco, 2014, p. 52).

Nor, with some few exceptions (namely: Hook, 2018; Friedlander and Malone, 2000; Miller, 2011, 2020), does the Lacanian literature make much room for a conception of psychology as anything beyond highly positivistic, quantitative, "natural science" psychology, neglecting to even recognize the formidable voice of Human Science psychology, which has actively challenged the very structural bases of positivist psychology with which Lacan took issue—building on the same philosophical literature so well known to Lacanians—and has made tangible changes in the teaching and practice of the discipline (see, for example, Finn, Fischer, & Handler, 2012; Fischer, 1994; Spinelli, 2007).

The resultant effigy of Psychology, built from the detritus of a century-old disciplinary moment, already selectively and inaccurately re-presented by Jacques Lacan, is a statue built from the dust of the shards of a missing statue. This version of psychology travels for the most part to the student of Lacanianism through the echo of the same gratifyingly snide dismissals Lacan elevated to an art form, which others continue to re-perform as pageant. The obvious reply is that there is no need to stay up to date on the latest innovations in psychology, be it experimental, clinical, or otherwise, as contemporary psychology proceeds from the same epistemological and social stance as its founders.

While this may be true, it begs the question: why continue to repeat the same critique of psychology made by Lacan, which was itself never carefully grounded, without any attempt to more rigorously locate it in contemporary literature and practice? It appears that other, non-Lacanian critics of psychology, no strangers themselves to the literature of rigorous philosophical examination, are clearly willing—and some might say intellectually obligated—to do so (see, for example, Billig, 2006; Fischer, 1994; and many of the contributors to Parker, 2015, including Cosgrove, Wheeler, Kosterina, Arfken, and Ruiz, 2015). It would seem that such a willingness to engage with the current state of affairs in psychology in an academically rigorous manner might allow the followers of Lacan to have their voices heard and effect meaningful change outside the increasingly cryptic (in every sense) walls of their Pantheon. Why does this not occur? A key to the answer lies in the extraordinarily ironic pride of place in Lacanianism for identification.

Mastery and Reflexivity

One of the most pivotal and profound contributions of Lacan's thought, especially through the 1950s, was his construction (and deconstruction) of the imaginary register. More to our purposes here, Lacan made a scathing critique of his contemporaries—psychoanalysts—of having merely identified with an image of Freud, as well as overvaluing the imaginary in other ways, such as their reverence for the promotion of the ego, while missing the truth of the Freudian "discovery" (Lacan, 2006a, 2006c). Lacan's iconoclasm of the imaginary, as it were, found as early as his work on "The Mirror Stage" beginning in 1936 (2006a) has been discussed extensively in the secondary literature (Fink, 1997, 1999; Gallop, 1987; Hook, 2018; and Miller, 2011 are but a few examples) and there is no need to recount it here. Contemporary Lacanianism, as discussed above, revisits this mode of criticism upon psychology, other would-be Lacanians, other forms of psychoanalysis, and popular culture. Yet, on examination, it often seems to do so *out of identification with Lacan*, and thus reenacts the original Lacanian problem: identification with the master.

Gallop (1987) puts one aspect of this paradox nicely:

> Inasmuch as anyone would be "for" the symbolic and "against" the imaginary, he would be operating in the imaginary. Ironically, the ethical imperative to accede to the symbolic and vigilantly to resist the imaginary is itself mired in the imaginary.
>
> *(Gallop, 1987, p. 60)*

But truth be told, we have only to witness the vectors of Lacanianism (above) to understand that this is probably too generous a critique. Gallop's reviewer, like Catherine Clement, is hardly concerned with avoiding the imaginary.

Billig (2006) has noted more sinister aspects of this phenomenon in the imaginary transmission of authority from Lacan to his reader or follower. That is, despite often having his facts wrong, and neglecting to cite them, Lacan has a habit of tossing them off with an air of authority, indeed of mastery, that tempts his followers not to question, but to don that authority for themselves, and repeat his claims with impunity:[6]

> Given Lacan's own references to the master–slave relationship of language, it is not difficult to say that Lacan places his readers in the subservient position of needing to accept the authoritative word of the master. It is curious that thinkers, who are otherwise critical, should willingly embrace such rhetorical subservience.
>
> *(Billig, 2006, p. 21)*

It is not all *that* curious. Although Lacan was less than fond of his work, we might find helpful Ferenczi's (1995) notion of "identification with the aggressor," a phenomenon with which we in the United States are becoming thematically familiar of late. With a master so dazzling and brilliant as Lacan, who is also so clearly willing to abuse the interloping other, it is all too seductive to trade critical-mindedness for identification, and to become a semblable of the master himself, and therefore close-enough to a master oneself (see comments on colonialism, below).

For the purposes of this discussion, such an identification with the master leads us to what a Lacanian might call the "non-rapport" of mastery and critique. Lacan's (2007) notion of the Master's Discourse, based upon Hegel's Lordship and Bondage dialectic, posits that the master, in order to maintain his existence, must constantly cover up his own lack, his own unjustifiability, and his own contingency and vulnerability. Instead, the master is always directing his demand to the other's labor.[7] To visit Hegel's view of this relationship, the struggle for the absolute power of one consciousness over the other results in the fact that the subjugated consciousness (slave or bondsman) cannot freely offer recognition of the master without thereby undoing his mastery. Therefore, the demand for recognition must be a demand for misrecognition (as complete, justified master), and can only continue as the result of a threatening dominance. According to Hegel et al. (1967, pp. 236–237), "[J]ust where the master has effectively achieved lordship, he really finds that something has come about quite different from an independent consciousness. It is not an independent, but rather a dependent consciousness that he has achieved." That is, the master is not only dependent, but is dependent upon a misrecognition of his own being.

Mastery, then, foreclosing free recognition, stands in absolute refusal of reflexivity.[8] The position of mastery is therefore structurally incapable of becoming either the object of critique or the locus of critical consciousness. As Fink (1997) says, "The master is unconcerned with knowledge. As long as everything works, as long as his or her power is maintained or grows, all is well" (p. 131). But Fink's tone here is misleading, for it is never a matter of mere indifference. It is, as Hegel reminds us, a struggle to the death. The master must constantly demand, attack, and exploit in order to maintain his position. This is the essence of the impediment between Lacanianism and criticality.

A "good Lacanian," who identifies with the master (and therefore does the work of the slave), must refuse critique. She must seek to subject the other, and never to be the subject of critique, of recognition, of vulnerability. The maintenance of this position may be an unspoken benefit of the well-worn Lacanian dismissal of the analyst's ego, the exploration of countertransference, or the encounter between Balint's two persons (Lacan, 2006e, p. 251). To be a "good Lacanian" is to remind the other—to remind others—that they, now in the position of bondsman themselves—have failed conformation to a Lacanian image, while shrouding oneself in jargon that sounds like the master's master. It is above all to cover one's own lack.

The Subject of Others

We have so far examined some patterns of Lacanian discourse within Lacan's own social circle; between Lacan and other disciplines (including other forms of psychoanalysis); within the community of secondary Lacanian literature; and between the secondary literature and other disciplines.

In each of the following examples, which while admittedly anecdotal I find representative, we see these impediments to reflexivity and critique, including the compulsion to maintain a "pure" Lacanianism and the identification with the master, finding their logical expression in moments of encounter between a culture of Lacanianism and matters of interest to people, *actual others* rather than "little others" or the "big Other," who may have little concern with the academic preoccupations so far elaborated in this chapter.

The Lacanian Colonial

While the subject is best left to experts for a thorough treatment, it seems important to at least acknowledge an undercurrent of the colonial in Lacanianism. The kind of imaginary purity of preservation that we have been discussing throughout this chapter raises questions of translation, of the "rapport" between American values (pragmatism, egoism, and adaptability, to name a few) and those of the French, and of the difference between the assimilation of an immigrant and the domination of a colonizer. Those questions and the tensions that surround them show up in the social spaces that surround Lacanian work, and are at times difficult to cite in the literature. But I feel that it is important to begin to tell these stories that occur in the unwritten interstices, as they are illustrative.

I once witnessed an American relational analyst sharing a panel presentation with the leader of a major French Lacanian school. The former was part of a group hosting the Parisians in Washington, D.C. Working hard to find common ground with the Lacanian, and asking humbly if he had found it, he was met with the leader turning her head away, laughing derisively, and saying "I don't know what you're talking about." The American analyst blanched and looked down quietly. The conference moved on.

I have long felt that there was something about the colonial in this moment, and eventually I discussed it with my colleague Sipho Mbuqe, an expert in postcolonial theory. He at once asked the illuminating question: what would have pleased the Lacanian leader? What does the colonizer want from the colonized?

Is it the perfect reproduction of a French Lacanianness? While this may be the lure, I doubt it is the real demand, for a perfect reproduction of mastery threatens the master. Similarly problematic, as Gallop (1987) points out, "[If] one's project is to carry Lacan across [the Atlantic], it cannot be accomplished within the confines of a Francophile colony internal to America. Having arrived here, he would still be there" (p. 59). Gallop resisted this tendency in her work. But, as I witnessed that day in Washington, the problem persists.

To be sure, various individuals and groups have taken up the question differently. Lacan Toronto, for example, under the leadership of Judith Hamilton, has intentionally fostered an openness to a variety of interpretations by North Americans working in English, and eschewed the drive for mastery I describe above. This kind of acculturation, one of labor and humility rather than of filial hierarchy, one that Hamilton playfully describes as "Low Church Lacanianism," is its own vicissitude of colonization, and itself brings us to an intersection with another colonizer altogether—British and protestant, rather than French and Catholic. But for some, its humanism may be preferable.

While North America has been somewhat fallow soil for Lacanianism, some parts of South America have been far more open, especially Argentina and Venezuela. In June of 1980, Lacan mused in his seminar that "it is above all Caracas that occupies him, where they work on Lacan without Lacan. I am transmitted over there by writing. It is certain that that's the future" (Cherki, as cited in Gallop, 1987, p. 36). Yet shortly afterward, Lacan the man set out to survey how his work had taken root. He traveled there in July 1980, and gave what would be his final public address.

To return to Dr. Mbuqe's question, I once met a Venezuelan analyst who was there for his visit, and might give us a sense of an answer. She told me about the "energy" that transferred from Lacan to her when she touched him as he walked by, in a tone that brought to mind the woman healed by touching Jesus' hem. When my students ask me, as clinical psychologists are bound to do, what the "outcome" of a Lacanian analysis should be, I always remember what this woman told me was the outcome of hers: a permanent (by then 30-year-long), full-bodied orgasm.

This is perhaps what is wanted from the Lacanian colonial subject: entrancement by the European "father," a soul saved, a sexualized, non-European body, still ravished, tortured by the *jouissance* brought by the extension of the inexhaustible, perfect, dispassionate phallus of Lacan's intellect some 30 years later. An ecstatic woman spreading this gospel to me, even as she claims a proximity to a pure Lacanianness that others could only hope to connect with through her. It is not French-ness or Lacanianness that the colonizer wants—it is the rapacious desire for it—a subject flinging herself upon the Lacanian phallus, desperate for it, as its very existence decimates the legitimacy of her own subjectivity (see Fanon, 2004).

People with Autism, Transgender People, and Cisgender Women

A position of mastery requires a "slave," who produces the objects upon which the master can gaze to reinforce his mastery. The colonial position is one example of this. We see others in Lacanian attitudes toward autistic people, transgender people, cisgender women, and regardless of political identity, anyone at all who seems to be fighting a frank political battle for recognition.

While Lacan himself railed against psychoanalysis as a force for conformity, likening practitioners with that predilection to surgeons willing to amputate the legs of those in a society whose normative mode of walking is a limp, the response to the question of autism in France by Lacanian psychoanalysts, even in the past decade, has been limping in lockstep with some of the worst instincts of 20th-century chauvinism.

The 2011 documentary *Le Mur* features interviews with a number of psychoanalysts, many of them Lacanian, on the subject of autism (Robert, 2011). It is true that the film is tendentious and makes no attempt at a generous reading of the Lacanian, or any, form of psychonalysis. But even with that major caveat, the analysts in the film, including the prominent Lacanian Eric Laurent, speak for themselves, and claim in unison that autism (of the type referred to in contemporary parlance) is a form of psychosis caused by a failure of the (actual) mother, or of the (actual) father to protect the child from the mother's *jouissance*.

From a Lacanian point of view, psychosis is caused by a failure of the "Name of the Father" (see Fink, 1999; Lacan, 2006a), which brings the child into a structural relationship with language and the social order—a neurotic relationship, structurally opposed to psychosis. Some Lacanians (see Fink, 1997) note that this function need not be attached to an actual father, and that the "paternal" aspect of this "paternal function" is chiefly metaphorical (it is indeed the basis for Lacan's understanding of metaphor itself). This was often described in terms of the father interfering with a synchronous, unboundaried imaginary relationship with the mOther, who was at times described by Lacan as an alligator who threatened to eat up the developing child with her inscrutable and overwhelming desire. So it is that Genevieve Loison, child psychoanalyst, jettisoning all metaphor, pulls a plastic crocodile out of her therapeutic toy box and explains:

> *Voila! Le Crocodile!* So the crocodile tells us what it's all about. They [children] play with it and when they put the hand or an object in [its open mouth] I am worried! [But] when they get on top of it and hit it, I feel reassured! They are fighting! ... The crocodile is the mother's belly, the mother's teeth ... So the goal of our work is to forbid her to eat.
> *(as cited in Robert, 2011)*

Loison now places a pen in the mouth of the crocodile, showing how it stops the crocodile from biting down. She confirms to us that this symbolizes the Lacanian "bar" that separates the signifier from the signified, splits the subject into conscious and unconscious, and represents the instance of the language subject who thereby escapes psychosis: "*C'est la barre*," she jubilantly declares. It is difficult to imagine Lacan, who spent a career lamenting just such hackneyed, literalized applications of Freudian theory, approving.

Short shrift is paid to another core Lacanian value, too: that of the license to re-punctuate, re-arrange, and re-hear the language of the "subject" so as to access unintended dimensions of truth. Three of the analysts in the film, Esthela Solano Suarez, Eric Laurent, and Alexandre Stevens, brought a lawsuit to ban the film— on the basis that the filmmaker, Sophie Robert, used their words in a way they did not anticipate!

As we see in Laurent et al.'s treatment of autistic people, "psychosis" can function as a convenient way not only to dismiss the marginalized other, but to let psychoanalysis off the hook for engaging them. We see psychosis deployed in this way in regard to the transgender community. Some prominent Lacanians (especially Frignet, 2002; Millot, 1991) have been particularly outspoken in this position. They hold up "sexual difference" as structurally integral to the Symbolic Order, by which the subject must be restructured in order to remain outside the realms of psychosis and perversion. In a radical refusal of "castration" and sexual difference, the subject is consigned to psychosis (Millot, 1991). Hence, for them, a transgender person, who is unwilling to accept the limits of sexual difference, must be at best perverse and at worst psychotic. Some more progressive Lacanians are content to let this go, but still go out of their way to criticize the transgender community on the basis of being, if not psychotic, too essentialist and therefore behind the philosophical times (Neirenberg & Watson, 2015). This kind of position has been directly challenged, however, by Lacanian analyst Patricia Gherovici in recent years. Gherovici (2017) offers a far more humanistic approach to the transgender community within a Lacanian frame, and a far less dogmatic Lacanianism; indeed, a Lacanianism that values being of service to others, and even to the oppressed.

Catherine Millot (2018) herself is noteworthy also for her curious silence on what most non-Lacanian clinicians (and even some Lacanian ones) would see as flagrant abuse of some women by some psychoanalysts. Not once in her 2018 memoir *Life With Lacan*, in which she recounts her years-long affair with Lacan—during some of which he was her analyst—does Millot broach the question of the ethics of the matter. While it is Millot's prerogative to see her affair with Lacan however she chooses, and I am aware of the risky position I put myself in as a man criticizing that choice, the absence of any ethical consideration, let alone criticism, of Lacan's behavior in this case should be striking to any reader.

Yet Millot's silence is not unexpected. As Parker (2011) says, there is a Lacanian sense in which it is not

> "immoral" for the professional to have sex with someone they have taken into their charge *loco parentis*—and the danger with that moral frame is precisely that it tends to infantilise the patient—but rather that to engage in physical contact of such a kind breaks the psychoanalytic contract; it sabotages the possibility of a psychoanalysis taking place.
>
> *(p. 4)*

Parker's claim relies on two premises: first, the reduction of the ethical problem of having sex with one's patient to an act of infantilization, which positions the very position of the ethical problem as itself an ethical problem, and therefore nullifies it. Second, the implication that the breaking of a promise that a psychoanalysis will occur trumps the abuse of power most would point out is manifest in having sex with the patient.

On Parker's view, then, the ethical objection to Lacan's behavior in Millot's case is made impossible, on the grounds that a pure Lacanianism will not admit of the obvious ethical critique because it has decided (through dubious logic) that such critique is beneath it. This allows the Lacanian position to continue its identification with that of the master, and to thereby escape reflexivity in regard to what another ethical thinker would easily see as blatant abuse.

Post-Script: Looking for a New Master

There is a well-known story about Lacan, reproaching a group of students in 1968 or 1969: "what you aspire to as revolutionaries is a new master. You shall soon have one" (Badiou & Roudinesco, 2014, p. 21). There are competing understandings of the setting and meaning of Lacan's comments: one version holds that he made them to a group of protesting students on the street during May, 1968, thus dismissing their revolutionary tendencies as self-deluding, and scoffing at them from a patrician position. Another version is that he made the comments at Vincennes, a setting that some regarded as a holding tank for the revolutionaries of the year before, in 1969, implying that by participating in an institutionalized psychoanalysis, the students had given up their radical aspirations. But whether the comment came from Lacan the patrician or Lacan the quasi-Foucauldian, the line is a favorite quotation among Lacanians. One function of the quote seems to be to reinscribe the inevitability of mastery; sometimes, of Lacan's mastery, or that of what Roudinesco (Roudinesco & Elliott, 2014) calls his "epigones."

Paul Verhaeghe (1998), taking up the recovered traumatic memories movement (or "memory wars") of the 1990s, examined the question of whether or not the hysteric was telling the truth about trauma. He rightly criticizes Babinski (1909), who was concerned with whether hysterics were "truly" ill or were simply "simulating." One might say he "rightly" criticizes Babinski because one agrees with him, but also because a part of the Lacanian lexicon is the criticism of Babinski, because Lacan criticized Babinski. Verhaeghe, for his part, relocated Babinski's dichotomy between fake and real symptoms in the contemporary questions around true trauma and lying. He criticizes the dichotomy itself, saying it misses the clinical point; that it is not born of neutral clinical interest, but is a value judgment about the merits of a given case. But then Verhaeghe makes a curious move:

> Besides being a patient, [those women who claim to be traumatized are seen as] victims, and they deserve not only our counseling but also our sympathy and even our pity ... Nowadays, there are almost no patients left, there are only victims who are in no way whatsoever implied in their situation.
> *(Verhaeghe, 1998, p. 88)*

It strikes us that, even as Verhaeghe questions the Babinksian binary, he immediately simply reproduces it. There is, essentially, a good woman and a bad woman: the real, responsibility-taking agentic "patient" (!) vs. the fake, irresponsible "victim." And what kind of person loves to be a victim? Verhaeghe (1998) tells us in the very next line: those in "the feminist movement" (p. 88). In a typically Lacanian manner (see above discussions of Lacanian treatments of psychology), Verhaeghe makes no specific citation about which feminists he means. But the reader is safe in assuming that he thinks "feminists" are not fond of taking responsibility, preferring instead to lay blame upon their victimizers.

A rebuttal to Verhaeghe—indeed, conceivably, a Lacanian rebuttal—might point out that "feminism," writ large as a series of acts of resistance, writing, confrontation, and reclamation of social power, can reasonably be described as essentially a taking of responsibility. In its acts of *speech*, especially, which challenge and remetaphorize a power structure that is not in one's favor, a form of law that falls short of the Law, a demand by the Other for the erasure of subjectivity and desire, it is a form of responsibility taking that might be particularly laudable from a Lacanian point of view.

I made that rebuttal regarding Verhaeghe several years ago in a presentation to a group of Lacanians. When it came time for responses, an analyst raised her hand, and offered a statement: "I know Paul Verhaeghe, and he is a good man!" Fair enough! I am sure he is. As I considered the irony of a Lacanian resorting to the primacy of the ego to defend a text, she offered a question: "Are you looking," she asked, "for a new master?"

Notes

1 Special thanks to Sipho Mbuqe and Holly Vanderhoff for their thoughtful feedback on this chapter.
2 We should not overlook that Lacan is first and foremost criticizing psychoanalysis, not psychology.
3 In the interest of transparency, I will note that I have been the object of similar feedback, when certain Lacanians noticed the juxtaposition of the first two words of the title of my 2011 book.
4 If abuse is too caustic a word, Lacanians might be more comfortable with "misrecognition."
5 Billig points out: "Wolfgang Kohler is mentioned, but his observations about chimpanzees' reactions to reflected images are not just ignored: the opposite is stated as if it were fact. Something is going on beyond the simple observation and speculative interpretation of existing data." It is tempting to think about Billig's comment, and perhaps even Lacan's move in "The Mirror Stage," as setting up Kohler's work in a kind of mirroring relationship to Lacan's—reversed and not ignored (as Lacan notes that the infant does not ignore his image as a chimpanzee soon does, which is the reverse of Kohler's claim). But this leads us to a question of how far we wish to extend Lacan's line of credi(bili)t(y).
6 Billig sees this process exemplified in Elizabeth Grosz's claim that Lacan "cites" Wallon "many times," her own citations of which lead not to Wallon, but to Caillois (Grosz, 1990, quoted in Billig, 2006). I am not sure that this is a fair criticism of Grosz, who as a human being is capable of a mistake without it serving as an indictment of an entire field. Other examples abound, however, some of which are scattered throughout the present chapter in more and less explicit ways. One of these is the deployment of "Lacanian-ese," turns of phrase such as "non-rapport," "confusion," "semblable," which whatever their function in a given argument, take on the air of Lacanian authority when they are used and therefore can substitute for rigor. I use them here with this in mind.

7 For an illuminating discussion of Lacan's Four Discourses, see Fink (1997, p. 30).
8 The Lordship/Bondage dialectic can be applied within one consciousness as well as between two.

References

Babinski, J. (1909). Démembrement de l'hystérie traditionnelle: Pithiatisme. Paris: Impr. de la 'Semaine médicale'.
Badiou, A., & Roudinesco, E. (2014). Jacques Lacan, past and present: A dialogue. New York: Columbia University Press.
Billig, M. (2006). Lacan's misuse of psychology. Theory, Culture & Society, 23(4), 1–26.
Canguilhem, G. (2016). What is psychology? Trans. Pena-Guzman, D. Foucault Studies, No. 21, pp. 200–213.
Fanon, F. (2004). Toward the African revolution: Political essays. New York: Grove.
Ferenczi, S., & Dupont, J. (1995). The clinical diary of Sandor Ferenczi. Cambridge, MA: Harvard University Press.
Fink, B. (1997). The Lacanian subject: Between language and jouissance. Princeton, NJ: Princeton University Press.
Fink, B. (1999). A clinical introduction to Lacanian psychoanalysis: Theory and technique. Cambridge, MA: Harvard University Press.
Finn, S. E., Fischer, C. T., & Handler, L. (2012). Collaborative therapeutic assessment. Hoboken, NJ: John Wiley.
Fischer, C. T. (1994). Individualizing psychological assessment. Hillsdale, NJ: Lawrence Erlbaum.
Friedlander, S. R., & Malone, K. R. (2000). The subject of Lacan: A Lacanian reader for psychologists. Albany, NY: State University of New York Press.
Frignet, H. (2002). O transexualismo. Rio de Janeiro, RJ: Companhia de Freud.
Gallop, J. (1987). Reading Lacan. Ithaca, NY: Cornell University Press.
Gherovici, P. (2017). Transgender psychoanalysis: A Lacanian perspective on sexual difference. New York: Routledge.
Hegel, G. W. F., Baillie, J. B., & Lichtheim, G. (1967). The phenomenology of mind. New York: Harper & Row.
Hook, D. (2018). Six moments in Lacan: Communication and identification in psychology and psychoanalysis. London: Routledge.
Lacan, J. (2006a). The instance of the letter in the unconscious. In Écrits: The first complete edition in English. Translated by Fink, B. and Grigg, R. New York: W.W. Norton, pp. 412–441.
Lacan, J. (2006b). The mirror stage as formative of the I function as revealed in psychoanalytic experience. In Écrits: The first complete edition in English. Translated by Fink, B. and Grigg, R. New York: W.W. Norton, pp. 75–81.
Lacan, J. (2006c). Psychoanalysis and its teaching. In Écrits: The first complete edition in English. Translated by Fink, B. and Grigg, R. New York: W.W. Norton, pp. 364–383.
Lacan, J. (2006d). Science and truth. In Écrits: The first complete edition in English. Translated by Fink, B. and Grigg, R. New York: W.W. Norton, pp. 726–745.
Lacan, J. (2006e). The function and field of speech and language in psychoanalysis. In Écrits: The first complete edition in English. Translated by Fink, B. and Grigg, R. New York: W.W. Norton, pp. 237–268.

Lacan, J., & Grigg, R. (2007). The other side of psychoanalysis: Book xvii. New York: Norton.
Miller, M. J. (2011). Lacanian psychotherapy: Theory and practical applications. London: Routledge.
Miller, M. J. (2020) Psychoanalysis and its teaching. In Hook, D., Neill, C., & Vanheule, S. (Eds.), Reading Lacan's *écrits*: from The Freudian thing to Remarks on Daniel Lagache. London: Routledge.
Millot, C. (1991). Horsexe: Essay on transsexuality. Brooklyn, NY: Autonomedia.
Millot, C. (2018). Life with Lacan. Cambridge: Polity Press.
Neill, C. (2016). Ethics and psychology. New York: Routledge.
Neirenberg, O., & Watson, E. (2015). Making a difference: On the non-rapport of psychoanalysis and the discourse of 'trans.' In Owens, C., & Farelly Quinn, S. (Eds.), Lacanian psychoanalysis with babies, children, and adolescents. London: Karnac.
O'Connor, A. (2009). Poverty knowledge: social science, social policy, and the poor in twentieth-century U.S. history. Princeton, NJ: Princeton University Press.
Parker, I. (2003). Jacques Lacan, barred psychologist. Theory & Psychology, 13(1), 95–115.
Parker, I. (2005). Lacanian discourse analysis in psychology. Theory & Psychology, 15(2), 163–182.
Parker, I. (2011). Lacanian psychoanalysis: Revolutions in subjectivity. London: Routledge.
Parker, I. (Ed.) (2015). Handbook of critical psychology. London: Routledge.
Prilleltensky, I. (1994). The morals and politics of psychology: Psychological discourse and the status quo. New York: SUNY Press.
Robert, S. (2011). *The wall: Psychoanalysis put to the test for autism*. France [film].
Roudinesco, E., & Elliott, G. (2014). Lacan, in spite of everything. London: Verso Books.
Roudinesco, E., Bray, B., & Lacan, J. (1997). Jacques Lacan. New York: Columbia University Press.
Spinelli, E. (2007). The interpreted world: An introduction to phenomenological psychology. Los Angeles, CA: Sage Publications.
Verhaeghe, P. (1998). Trauma and hysteria within Freud and Lacan. The Letter, 14, 87–106.
Weslati, H. (2013, June 17). The Lacanian trials. Retrieved from http://criticallegalthinking.com/2013/05/06/the-lacanian-trials/

6

PSYCHOLOGY AS BUSINESS AND DOMINATION

Challenging the Colonial and the "Import–Export" Model[1]

Serdar M. Değirmencioğlu

The General Assembly of the European Federation of Psychologists' Associations (EFPA) in 2015 convened in Milan on July 11–12. A statement titled, "Declaration on Colonialism: Psychology in a Postcolonial Era," was on the agenda. The statement invited psychologists in Europe to "eradicate colonialism, to avoid neo-colonialism, and to develop healthy and egalitarian post-colonial relations":

The European Federation of Psychologists' Associations' Declaration on Colonialism

(April 5, 2015)

The European Federation of Psychologists Associations,
Recognizing

- the need for greater awareness among psychologists from European countries of the history of enslavement and colonialism and the deep impacts that centuries of economic exploitation, and domination by foreign rule and culture have had, and continue to have, on the social and economic development of former European colonies;
- the need for all affected persons and places to share in efforts to overcome the legacies surviving in both the victims and the beneficiaries of these historical arrangements.

Considering

- that in spite of recent growth in the local economies of Africa, Latin America, the Caribbean and Asia, populations and racial groups in

the former colonies are still suffering from the marks that centuries of enslavement and/or colonization have left;
- that former slavery, oppression, dependence, deportation, and abuse continue to have psychological and social impacts on people in everyday life;
- that poverty and income inequality resulting from economic exploitation continue to have depressing effects on economic development;
- that the people of Europe should take responsibility for providing support to the people from the former colonies in their efforts to overcome the deep and long-lasting effects of enslavement and colonization in the economic, political, religious and social domains;

Affirming

- the special responsibility of psychologists in this context, given their expertise in matters of crisis, trauma, violence, and racism, and their effects on people's individual and collective identity, mental health, trust and social relations;

Calls upon

- psychologists' organizations and individual psychologists in Europe and other countries of the world to support their colleagues in former colonies in their efforts to overcome the effects of the colonial past;
- national and international psychologists' associations—at the former colonizer and colonized sides—to place activities to eradicate colonialism, to avoid neo-colonialism, and to develop healthy and egalitarian post-colonial relations high on their agenda;

Undertakes

- to bring this matter to the attention of all pertinent parties in the world, including former colonizing countries and former colonies.
- to initiate partnerships between psychologists in former colonizing countries and psychologists in former colonies to facilitate the development of an indigenous capacity to address fundamental maladies of underdevelopment.

The statement was not received well. It was not relevant. It came out of nowhere. In short, it was too unnecessary, too irrelevant. The statement was discreetly rejected. Official minutes read: "The General Assembly has decided that an amended version of the Declaration on Colonialism should be presented to the next General Assembly." In 2017, the Assembly convened in Amsterdam. The chairs went through the minutes from Milan. A delegate, known for her work on human rights, asked about the declaration. The response was brief: "the Executive Council did not prioritize the document."

That was the end of the Colonialism Declaration. Mainstream psychologists in Europe were not interested in the colonial past, its current ramifications, or in efforts by psychologists in colonized lands to overcome the legacy of colonization. The declaration has been forgotten and the EFPA webpage[2] devoted to the declaration is blank. There is mention of the statement only on another page,[3] containing David Fryer's sobering assessment:

> The April 2015 Colonialism Declaration ... is to be welcomed for explicitly drawing attention to the issue of colonisation and the importance of recognising the centrality of European and United Statesian psychology with respect to colonisation. The EFPA is also to be congratulated on its recognition that colonisation is an ongoing contemporary phenomenon which has a continuing impact i.e. is not yet relegated to history and that historically and contemporarily located colonisation has beneficiaries as well as maleficiaries.
>
> Psychology as a discipline and the related psy-complex ... which discursively universalistically position domains of human life as "psychological", construct and deploy expertise in relation to them, regulate them and in so doing individualise, psychologise, essentialise and naturalise what are socially constructed features of particular politico-socio-economic arrangements, including colonising arrangements, and organisations like EFPA are fully implicated in that nexus of colonisation.
>
> It will take more than a declaration to address that but a declaration is a welcome and progressive start by EFPA. However if commitment to decolonisation by EFPA ends in a declaration it will be an oppressive finish. In the meantime, whilst mainstream Western/Northern psychology continues to be colonising and oppressive (rather than decolonising and emancipatory) it will continue to be seen in circles which are critical and Indigenous as part of the problem...

Seven Pillars

Fryer was right. It will take much more than a statement for the discipline of psychology to come to terms with the legacy of colonialism. It will also take far more than words to decolonize psychology. The fate of the Declaration on Colonialism is clear evidence that mainstream psychology (MP) in Europe is nowhere near coming to terms with colonialism. The same holds for MP in general. Now MP is more interested in a *global psychology*, that is, marketing MP around the *globe* in line with the "import–export" model—a new version of dominance and a lucrative business.

In this chapter, I offer seven key steps or pillars to guide those who are interested in decolonizing the discipline of psychology. The number of psychologists interested in this task is growing, as indicated by the number of conferences and events with this theme. Given the centrality of action in critical praxis, these pillars can be phrased as actions:

1. Meet your rich uncle.
2. Expose the "import–export" business.
3. Uncover the neoliberal setup.
4. Expect and reveal taming efforts.
5. Criticize instructional materials.
6. Challenge the dominance of colonial languages.
7. Anticipate local resistance.

The very first step is a reconstruction of history from the margins by those who have been marginalized or colonized. Any challenge to colonial practices and ideologies necessitates opening dominant narratives to rigorous debate and that requires a critical analysis of the history of psychology. This is essential because MP is notoriously and decidedly ahistorical. Anthropology provides a good example in this context, as is clear from this statement by the Radical Caucus of the American Anthropological Association in 1969:

> Anthropology since its inception has contained a dual but contradictory heritage. On the one hand, it derives from a humanistic tradition of concern with people. On the other hand, anthropology is a discipline developed alongside and within the growth of the colonial and imperial powers. By what they have studied (and what they have not studied) anthropologists have assisted in, or at least acquiesced to, the goals of imperialist policy.
> *(as cited in Price, 2016)*

An Earthquake of Sorts

The EFPA General Assembly in 2015 was a historic event for another reason. Only a day before, on July 10, the American Psychological Association (APA) had released a statement,[4] which was akin to an earthquake for MP. The statement announced the findings of the *Independent Review Relating to APA Ethics Guidelines, National Security Investigations, and Torture*, or the Hoffman Report (2015).[5] APA admitted that there had been collusion with the Bush administration, offered an apology for "deeply disturbing findings and organizational failures," and announced "policy and procedural actions to correct shortcomings."

Attorney David Hoffman was hired by APA in November 2014

> to conduct an independent review of whether there was any factual support for the assertion that APA engaged in activity that would constitute collusion with the Bush administration to promote, support or facilitate the use of "enhanced" interrogation techniques by the United States in the war on terror.
> *(www.apa.org/independent-review)*

The Hoffman Report provided an immense set of evidence, far beyond expectations, and a clear conclusion: APA colluded with the US Department of Defense and the Bush administration to provide ethical cover for their interrogation program and for psychologists working in the program. The collusion was "one of the greatest ethical breaches in the history of psychology" (Elkins, 2016). Those who worked to expose the collusion knew that all along: Nathaniel Raymond, from the Physicians for Human Rights, called it "arguably the single greatest medical-ethics scandal" in US history (as cited in Mayer, 2009).

The news, however, hardly made an impact on the General Assembly. It was discussed privately. Some offered defensive opinions, some expressed disbelief. Many kept repeating they were surprised, or that they did not know! The General Assembly did not allow spontaneous debate. And there was little interest in the room for protest or outcry.

The lack of enthusiasm for the Declaration on Colonialism and the absence of a major outcry in response to the Hoffman Report might be very disappointing for critical psychologists. But that should come as no surprise. Lack of enthusiasm for decolonization or for demilitarizing psychology is not coincidental. The history of psychology is full of examples of psychologists endorsing eugenics, colonialism, militarism, and other oppressive belief systems and practices. The Hoffman Report was certainly an earthquake for MP and a major wake-up call for psychologists around the world.

Meet Your Rich Uncle

Psychology is routinely described as a helping profession (e.g., Gervasio, Wendorf, & Yoder, 2010). APA, the largest MP organization, defines helping professions as "occupations that provide health and education services to individuals and groups, including occupations in the fields of psychology, psychiatry, counseling, medicine, nursing, social work, physical and occupational therapy, teaching, and education."[6] The mainstream literature offers plenty of material to reproduce this belief.

History, however, offers plenty of evidence that MP has offered a helping hand to oppressors as well as to colonizers and their military. Psychology did not grow because it served public interest. It grew because it allied with the dominant forces and regimes, and entrepreneurs promoted it. The clearest example can be found in the history of intelligence testing and the birth of military psychology. It was civilian psychologists who convinced the US Army to adopt intelligence testing. Once in, psychologists expanded the scope of their work so as to put psychological methods in the service of the military (Keene, 1994).

Howell (2018) argues that psychology has served war or colonialism for a century, and finds a symbiotic relationship between psychology and modern warfare:

> In the late nineteenth and early twentieth centuries, psychology was a fledgling discipline and was understood as a humanistic form of knowledge. That

changed drastically in World War I. At that time Robert Yerkes, a eugenics proponent and professor of psychology, was President of the American Psychological Association. Convinced that psychologists could be of service in the war, and that war could be useful to psychologists, Yerkes approached the US Army with a proposition: he could help the Army with its personnel problem (of appropriately placing the massive number of new recruits) in return for funding and access to an unprecedented number of subjects on which to experiment: soldiers. World War I enabled the first mass scientific experiment in psychology in the form of intelligence testing.

(p. 11)

The academic and the organizational basis for MP grew in association with the military. This is how intelligence testing became synonymous with psychology. Yerkes and other "entrepreneurial psychologists" (Van De Water, 1997) expanded the business of psychology. The link between the social sciences and the military in the US grew stronger during the Cold War (Rohde, 2013). The number of psychologists serving in the military increased. By the end of the 20th century, the Veterans Administration (VA) was the largest employer of psychologists in the US. Raymond D. Fowler played a key role in building the relationship between APA and VA, and later became APA's CEO. He recounted an "explosive expansion," which is worth quoting:

After World War II, APA reorganized itself to recognize psychology as a profession as well as a science and welcomed clinicians as members. The VA, faced with 17 million veterans, many of whom needed mental health services, established new roles and new positions for psychologists in its treatments and rehabilitation programs, and set about trying to recruit psychologists to fill those positions [but] available positions for psychologists in the VA exceeded the total of all qualified clinical psychologists in the country ... VA asked APA to identify those psychology departments qualified to train clinicians at the doctoral level. APA identified 22 programs, and the VA provided 200 graduate stipends, which began an explosive expansion in the development of clinical training programs throughout the country. This process was repeated for counseling psychologists. APA's modest effort in 1946 to identify 22 programs qualified to train clinicians grew into an accreditation program that now accredits 351 doctoral programs, as well as 461 internship programs and nine postdoctoral programs.

By 1950, nearly half of all psychology interns were VA-trained and 700 students were being supported by VA stipends. The number of VA psychologists had more than doubled to 300. Today, the VA employs 1,200 psychologists, making it by far the largest employer of psychologists—a position it has maintained for decades...

VA psychologists have been highly active in the association. The section of Veterans' Affairs Psychologists is the largest section of APA's Div. 18 (Public Service). VA psychologists have served on many APA committees and on its Council of Representatives. Several have been nominated for APA president. APA has included VA psychologists on the APA Commission on Education and Training Leading to Licensure in Psychology. Each year, APA co-sponsors a conference with the Association of VA Psychologist Leaders (AVAPL) to bring together leaders of the two organizations. In addition, AVAPL officers meet each year in Washington to learn more about federal advocacy of interest to VA psychologists, and APA arranges meetings between VA leaders and congressional leaders on veterans' affairs.

The partnership between VA psychologists and APA has been mutually beneficial. APA has directly intervened at the local, regional and national levels on behalf of VA psychologists whenever psychology's role in the VA was threatened. The demand for clinical services by VA psychologists sometimes overwhelms the other important roles they can play, so APA has worked to help the VA in its efforts to establish more Mental Illness Research and Education Centers. APA has also lobbied for placing language in appropriations bills highlighting the need for the VA to designate more time for research for investigators, so that they get some protection from the high demand for clinical hours. Keeping psychology in the VA strong and healthy is a high priority for APA.

(Fowler, 2002, p. 9)

The Hoffman Report described the relationship between the military and APA as follows: "DoD [Department of Defense] is like a *rich, powerful uncle* to APA, helping it in important ways throughout APA's life. Acting independently of a benefactor like this is difficult" (p. 72, emphasis added). Fowler (2002) reminds us that APA has always done its part to nourish this "mutually beneficial" relationship.

Ken Pope (2018) asserts that the collusion was not the first time psychologists were losing their "moral compass"; for example, psychologists served the Nazi Regime (Geuter, 1992). Hendrik Verwoerd, the architect of apartheid, was a psychologist and MP was part of apartheid:

Professional psychology associations in South Africa have overtly and covertly furthered the aims of apartheid. Guidance about the ethical obligations of psychologists in the South African context has been singularly lacking, and as a result blacks have not been attracted to the profession of psychology in sufficient numbers to administer to psychological needs of the client population. The political dimension of psychological practice in South Africa needs to be addressed directly.

(as cited in Nicholas, 1990, p. 59)

Thus, it is clear that decolonizing psychology requires questioning the history of MP with a focus on enabling students and scholars to acquire filters to reject or keep the narratives and the practices. Psychologists served militarism, nationalism, fascism, and racism for a reason. Therefore, it is critical to always focus on whom psychologists are serving or helping (Değirmencioğlu, 2010). It is critical to understand how MP generates money. In other words, MP has to be understood as a business.

Expose the "Import–Export" Business

It is easy to see that MP operates in line with business principles. Conferences and congresses are full of psychologists who are trying to sell their models, techniques, research, or books to the audiences or potential customers. In fact, the marketing of psychology has become much bolder. In a recent special issue (Sokol & Norton, 2020), lessons from "the business of consulting psychology" are offered (Norton, 2020): how to start/manage a business, an international consultancy, a domestic "boutique firm," or a large-scale test-publishing and assessment enterprise.

Business discourse is common in recent MP publications portraying successful practitioners. A piece titled "Launch. Grow. Thrive" advises psychologists to "Think like an entrepreneur" (Novotney, 2019). An entrepreneurial psychologist finds her best inspirations from the business world, particularly for marketing and branding. She learns in a corporate workshop that she should see herself as a brand. The piece offers further advice: "Add unexpected services. Fine-tune your office design." And "Don't shy away from raising fees." Popular video venues offer titles like "*A Guide To Earning 6 Figures As a Private Practice Therapist.*"

The business does not stop at borders. MP is produced in the Global North (GN) and is marketed globally as "knowledge," "practice," "model," etc. Importers bring the "product" in and dealers market it locally. In the past, importers were primarily professors. The dealers were practitioners. Nowadays the actors are not that easy to separate. But the import business continues to flourish.

Very rarely has a distinction been made between exporters and importers. Castro and Lafuente (2007) distinguished between countries exporting and countries subsequently importing psychology (e.g., Spain, Italy, Latin America, Japan). Exporters provide universalistic claims and importers try to adjust these to their own local theoretical and practical demands. Castro and Lafuente (2007) did not explain why psychology was being exported and then imported. A visit to booths in major international congresses may provide insights. Psychology is big business; there are sellers and buyers. Therapeutic techniques, instruments, softwares, books, and journals are marketed and they bring in big profits. Congresses and conventions are themselves big moneymakers. Major psychology organizations rely on congress fees and revenues to supplement their budgets.

Teaching is also big business, particularly in the US and in the UK. Nicola Gale, past president of the British Psychological Society, recently said, "Universities in the UK are hugely global these days" (as cited in Clay, 2019). She added that many psychologists are not happy with Brexit because they "want to work on a cross-European basis." Students who receive their degrees in the GN often facilitate the export of MP to their countries of origin.

Psychology students in importing countries receive a marketed version of how "import–export" works. Objective, curious, and industrious psychologists in the GN produce theoretical, methodological, and therapeutic tools for the entire world (Değirmencioğlu, 2016). They are experts and their products are valuable. Psychological knowledge and practice are marketable products, and they are exported from the center to the periphery. Most, but not all, psychologists at the periphery eagerly import the exported products. Psychology as an "import–export" business offers the same products for the *generic* individual, community, or society.

Uncover the Neoliberal Setup

Universities around the world are under intense pressure to fit with neoliberal capitalism, which promotes privatization of public institutions, competition, and inequality. Universities are forced to function as businesses, covering their own costs and generating profits. Administrators, with little understanding of teaching and research, run the business. Checks and audits are utilized to reproduce the neoliberal mentality at every level. Academic functions that are not directly associated with money lose their value. Teaching or public service is made undesirable. This oppressive work climate generates anxiety and stress (Berg, Huijbens & Larsen, 2016).

As universities become businesses, existing mainstream tendencies grow stronger. Those who see psychology as a business fit very well within the neoliberal setup. Their productivity is measurable and is promoted by administrators. Authoritarian regimes, too, are happy with the notion that universities are businesses. Neoliberal universities are not bastions of resistance as many public universities were in the past.

It is, therefore, important to expose the neoliberal setup and raise awareness as to why and how universities are turned into agents of capitalism. Also important is to expose the fact that authoritarian regimes prefer neoliberal universities and how the business mentality corrupts and tames universities from within. Students rarely hear that psychology-as-business turns scholars or researchers into entrepreneurs, and reproduces capitalism at all levels.

Expect and Reveal Taming Efforts

Critical psychologists around the world are struggling with their direction. Serious challenges are corrupted, and tamed by institutional forces. Emancipatory work is softened so that it, too, turns a blind eye to complacency, injustices, and suffering.

There are multiple ways in which taming takes place. Funding is one of them, for it not only dictates research topics and methodology, but also attracts researchers to the "rich uncles" they should stay away from. Students rarely discuss why the Stanford Prison Experiment, one of the most well-known studies in psychology, was funded by the US Office of Naval Research. Or why Carl Rogers, who is known for humanistic psychology, had no problem working with the CIA (Demanchick, & Kirschenbaum, 2008).

Critical voices can also be tamed with precarity, for corporatization, commercialization, managerialist, and entrepreneurial make-over (i.e., neoliberal universities) bring intense pressures and insecurity (Peters, 2019). The "neocolonial" multi-campus university—i.e., a well-known institution and its branch campuses located in various countries in the Global South (GS)—provides another tough setting (Peters, 2019).

Therefore, it is important for critical psychologists to expect and expose previous and ongoing taming efforts, and find ways to counter them. Critical psychologists in various locations have extensive experience with these efforts, and some lost their jobs repeatedly. Still, there is little in the critical literature about how to counter taming pressures. Critical psychologists seem to be reluctant to accept that building resistance is far more important than theoretical sophistication.

Criticize Instructional Materials

Textbooks are an important export channel for MP and provide ample material for exposing the colonial. Exported textbooks are very mainstream and professional; they often come with supplements for teaching. In the absence of local, decolonized textbooks, which can replace imported ones, it is best to promote focused criticism of instructional materials. This raises students' awareness about power, positionality, and justice.

Students enjoy the agency this critical process involves and get better at identifying biases. Critical analyses of textbooks can be carried out within a framework. For instance, a single textbook or several textbooks can be examined to see how children's rights are addressed. In developmental psychology textbooks, children's rights were rarely mentioned (Değirmencioğlu, 2005). Such exercises reveal how MP ignores mechanisms that are built to protect and promote human welfare.

Textbooks can also be examined to identify specific biases. Biases, such as militarism, can be quite overt. The fifth edition of a well-known textbook, *Psychological Testing and Assessment: An Introduction to Tests and Measurement* (Cohen & Swerdlik, 2002) was dedicated "to the victims of America's September 11th tragedy" (Değirmencioğlu, 2014). This dedication and the preface reflected the feeling at the time among right-wing psychologists: "progress in the field of psychological assessment may better aid civilized society in profiling and identifying misguided individuals intent upon perpetrating senseless violence against innocent people" (as cited in Değirmencioğlu, 2014). These words were removed by the time the seventh edition was published (Cohen & Swerdlik, 2010), but the bias remained. On page 392, Dr. Zillmer recounts his daylong visit to Guantanamo in 2006 with colleagues from APA:

> I attended briefings, visited JTF [Joint Task Force] headquarters, and several of the detention camps and medical facilities. I learned that about 430 detainees were held as "enemies of the nation." It was underscored that these are not innocent bystanders, but are considered guilty, since they are terrorist trainers, master bomb makers, would-be suicide bombers, Bin Laden's bodyguards, and terrorist financiers … the information gleaned from detainees has intelligence capital, will assist in winning the war on terrorism, and prevent further terrorist attacks. A further mission at GTMO [Guantanamo] is to prevent terrorists from returning to the battlefield, where most were captured in the first place.
> *(as cited in Cohen & Swerdlik, 2010)*

Zillmer whitewashed Guantanamo by claiming that prisoners were treated well: "*medical treatment and psychological needs of the detainees are looked after carefully and appropriately … treated humanely and ethically*" (as cited in Cohen & Swerdlik, 2010, p. 392, emphasis added). Zillmer also maintained that psychologists behaved ethically: "*Psychologists acting as Behavioral Science Consultants provide support to interrogators, but do not conduct interrogations*" (as cited in Cohen & Swerdlik, 2010, p. 392, emphasis added).

In sum, the textbook is showing students how to serve their country well:

> Psychologists are experts in the science of human decision-making and can put psychological science to good use in counter-terrorism endeavors. Advancing psychological science directly and indirectly in these areas will benefit the security of our nation as well as the discipline of psychology.
> *(as cited in Cohen & Swerdlik, 2010, p. 392)*

Challenge the Dominance of Colonial Languages

An indispensable component of colonialism is the subordination of local languages and the unquestionable domination of the colonizers' languages. Linguistic domination continues today in various ways and domains. The vast majority of MP is produced in English and is often exported without translation. The "import–export" business facilitates the domination of colonial languages. A typical export textbook is printed in English and students often learn psychology in this linguistic context.

Challenging linguistic domination is extremely difficult and yet extremely important because students often learn psychology through colonial languages. Students who are learning very abstract concepts in a second language have tremendous difficulty developing psychological insights to match these concepts. Local psychological concepts that do not exist in colonial languages are often ignored or given non-scientific status because they are not mentioned in imported textbooks.

Anticipate Local Resistance

Decolonizing psychology and a reconstruction of the psychology curriculum will disrupt the status quo and will not be endorsed by all. Challenges to instructional materials and the curricula will upset those who are used to them. Questioning the dominance of a colonial language will upset those who operate well within that language. The fact is that the majority of doctoral degrees in psychology are obtained from institutions in the GN; consequently, many scholars in the GS are trained in the GN. Decolonizing psychology will necessarily involve organizing and finding ways to overcome MP's resistance. This is bound to be a long, uphill struggle: it cannot be maintained without the support of other psychologists and students. Decolonization of psychology requires a dedicated, collective effort and strong solidarity.

Critical Praxis in Turkey

Born from the ashes of an empire, the Republic of Turkey was never formally colonized. Decolonization is nevertheless necessary because Westernization paved the way for a process of self-colonization. For decades, MP in Turkey relied on imports. In leading departments, most faculty members were trained in the US. Classes were taught in English. Occasional visitors (e.g., Fulbright scholars) reinforced the "import–export" model. Most academics came from upper- or upper-middle-class backgrounds. They were schooled in English from early on and regularly inserted English into Turkish. Many were quite elitist. Candidates for master's programs were disqualified if they had to work, reproducing the class structure and the elitism. Genuine criticism of textbooks was unheard of. Students who challenged the dominance of English were quickly silenced.

The military coup in 1980 brought on a disaster. All democratic elements were eradicated to usher in neoliberal capitalism and a conservative regime. Universities were purged. Any existing left-wing voices in psychology were silenced. By 2000, conservative politics dominated. Political Islam was everywhere. It was in this vacuum that a new Islamist party captured power in 2002 and built the current dictatorship.

Private universities with no tenure were introduced in 1985 as part of the neoliberal order. Initially, only big corporations were interested. They built big campuses, away from urban areas, with ideas imported from the US. After 2000, many entrepreneurs seeking quick profits started small universities. The government started new, conservative public universities across the country. The number of psychology departments increased from 10 to 70. Large departments lost their faculty to private universities. Most new departments had at best three faculty members to shoulder huge workloads. The quality of education went into free fall.

Private universities consolidated the dominance of conservatives in MP. Retired professors were recruited to head new departments, diminishing chances of change. Critical voices were silenced by workload or by the hierarchy. But the regime was in a hurry to produce conservative generations with university diplomas. It was easy to build cadres in new, ultra-conservative public universities. Theology schools produced candidates with desirable qualifications for philosophy (Ph.D. in philosophy of religion), sociology (Ph.D. in sociology of religion), and psychology departments (Ph.D. in psychology of religion). Disciplines with critical potential were infused with patriarchy, nationalism, militarism, and orthodox Islam. The authoritarian regime desired psychological control. Psychology, just like religion, was turned into a political tool for the regime.

As the number of departments and graduates kept increasing, entrepreneurial psychologists multiplied. Many psychologists were more interested in quick cash because they were in debt. The "import–export" business flourished and spread. Importers grew more ambitious. Some professors imported well-known personality scales, claimed copyrights, and put them in the service of various industries. Practitioners kept importing therapeutic techniques, along with their promoters who were flown in for expensive training sessions. As psychology graduates with few skills multiplied, training sessions turned into big business. Firms were started solely to organize expensive training sessions with imported trainers.

As business and conservatism grew, silences in MP multiplied: silence about the invasion of Iraq, about APA's collusion, about the decline of universities, about the suffering of Kurds, and so on. Precarity was the norm in private universities. Those who challenged the neoliberal university or MP were quickly fired. In 2005, I was fired for the first time. The chairperson, a retired professor imported from the US, knew how to keep her bosses happy and her department mainstream.

In 2008, Stephen H. Behnke was invited to Istanbul as an ethics expert. (As the head of APA's Ethics Office, Behnke masterminded the collusion for a decade.) This visit coincided with the 1st Critical Psychology Symposium and I was a speaker on the first day. I abandoned my talk and instead focused on explicating Behnke's role in how psychologists had become complicit in developing torture techniques. This led to a big protest, ignited critical psychology, and shook the Turkish Psychological Association (TPA). An article, which I wrote asking psychologists to stand up, was published in a major newspaper. A full-page interview about the scandal was later printed in another major newspaper.

The response was ostracism. The TPA president formed an investigation committee, headed by an ally. The committee concluded that the invitation was an oversight. The protestors, however, were at fault for smearing the reputation of psychology. The implicit message was received: I was never to be invited again to speak at MP events. Finding a job in an MP department became impossible.

Recent accounts of critical praxis in Turkey (Kayaoğlu & Batur, 2013; Şensoy et al., 2013) fail to capture the impact of the Behnke scandal and omit its aftermath entirely. Critical psychologists in Turkey are yet to pay attention to how silencing works in MP.

The second time I was fired, I was a psychology professor at Doğuş University, a profit-driven institution where fear was palpable. In 2013, the university changed hands and I was hired as department chairperson. The new owners expected quick profits from psychology graduate programs and I was expected to implement their unethical schemes. Instead, I rejected them. Soon, just 40 days after I had started work, I was fired. I went to court and was reinstated in 2014 by a court order.

On 11 January 2016, a peace petition was made public in Istanbul. A total of 1128 scholars, including me, invited the government to stop the military onslaught in the Southeast, which produced countless civilian casualties and deaths, and to return to peace talks. The regime responded ruthlessly. Universities received orders to "deal" with the treason. Many junior scholars in private universities were fired. There were death threats. In small cities, the police raided homes. The administration at Doğuş University seized the opportunity, and I was fired in April without severance pay. Later on, the administration worked hard to have me listed on a government decree. My name was listed on Decree 686, published on 7 February 2017: I was banned from public service for life.

This was the end of my career in Turkey. With decree after decree, psychologists were purged from universities and from public service. Psychology departments and psychologists in public service were targeted for the first time in Turkey's history. The response in MP was, once again, mainly silence. As of today, this silence is yet to be questioned publicly.

Conclusion: A Way Forward?

Thirty years ago, Tod S. Sloan (1990) noted that psychologists in the West "ignored the societies of the Third World, viewing them as the proper subject matter for other disciplines." About three decades later, Suntosh R. Pillay (2017) wondered why psychology, "whose primary purposes are to understand and benefit people, fails so miserably at both." Today, the answer and a way out are now clearer. As Pickren (2020) suggests, MP has helped the rise of the neoliberal order in the late 20th century. Genuine efforts toward psychologies of liberation have come primarily from the GS. Psychologists need to break with the legacy of coloniality and seek more liberatory stances.

In this chapter, I have offered seven pillars to help with this task. Decolonization requires a constant struggle against collective amnesia, export–import and *globalized psychology* business, neoliberal order, taming mechanisms, biases in instructional materials, and linguistic domination. These ideas may sound basic and simple.

More comprehensive and very authentic analyses can certainly be found in recent books (e.g., Ciofalo, 2019). These decolonial accounts are meant to disrupt and create what Pillay (2017) described as "cracks" in MP, which for almost a century has fortified its narratives and resources, and has joined the capitalist order. Critical praxis is urgently needed and it can only be sustained with solidarity.

Notes

1 Dedicated to the memory of Tod Sloan, who inspired so many around the world.
2 http://communitypsy.efpa.eu/statements/.
3 http://communitypsy.efpa.eu/statements/colonialism-declaration/.
4 www.apa.org/news/press/releases/2015/07/independent-review-release.
5 The report and related materials can be found at www.apa.org/independent-review.
6 https://dictionary.apa.org/helping-professions.

References

Berg, L. D., Huijbens, E. H., & Larsen, H. G. (2016). Producing anxiety in the neoliberal university. The Canadian Geographer/le géographe canadien, 60(2), 168–180.
Castro, J., & Lafuente, E. (2007). Westernalization in the mirror: On the cultural reception of Western psychology. Integrative Psychological and Behavioral Science, 41(1), 106–113. https://doi.org/10.1007/s12124-007-9013-z
Ciofalo, N. (2019). Indigenous psychologies in an era of decolonization. Switzerland: Springer.
Clay, R. A. (2019). Brexit blues. Monitor on Psychology, 50(7), 22–25.
Cohen, R. J., & Swerdlik, M. E. (2002). Psychological testing and assessment: An Introduction to tests and measurement, 5th int. ed. Boston: MacGraw Hill.
Cohen, R. J., & Swerdlik, M. E. (2010). Psychological testing and assessment: An introduction to tests and measurement, 7th int. ed. Boston: MacGraw Hill.
Değirmencioğlu, S. M. (2005). Convention on the rights of the child, children's participation as a right, and textbooks. Poster presented at the Society for Research in Child Development Biennial Meetings, Atlanta, USA.
Değirmencioğlu, S. M. (2010). The psychology of napalm: Whose side are psychologists on? Journal of Critical Psychology, Counselling and Psychotherapy, 10(4), 196–205.
Değirmencioğlu, S. M. (2014). Militarism in textbooks: An alarming threat in psychology. Poster presented at the 5th International Conference on Community Psychology, Fortaleza, Brazil.
Değirmencioğlu, S. M. (2016). Challenging the "import–export" business: Possibilities and challenges for community psychologies. Paper presented at a symposium titled, "Decolonising Community Psychologies: Dispatches from the Global South", 6th International Conference on Community Psychology, Durban, South Africa.
Demanchick, S. P., & Kirschenbaum, H. (2008). Carl Rogers and the CIA. Journal of Humanistic Psychology, 48(1), 6–31. https://doi.org/10.1177/0022167807303005
Elkins, D. N. (2016). The American Psychological Association and the Hoffman Report. Journal of Humanistic Psychology, 56(2), 99–109. https://doi.org/10.1177/0022167815619064
Fowler, R. D. (2002). APA and the VA: An enduring partnership. Monitor on Psychology, 33(8), 9.

Gervasio, A. H., Wendorf, C. A., & Yoder, N. F. (2010). Validating a psychology as a helping profession scale. Teaching of Psychology, 37(2), 107–113.
Geuter, U. (1992). The professionalization of psychology in Nazi Germany. Cambridge, UK: Cambridge University Press.
Howell, A. (2018). Forget "militarization": Race, disability and the "martial politics" of the police and of the university. International Feminist Journal of Politics, 20(2), 117–136. https://doi.org/10.1080/14616742.2018.1447310
Kayaoğlu, A., & Batur, S. (2013). Critical psychology in Turkey: Recent developments. Annual Review of Critical Psychology, 10, 916–931.
Keene, J. D. (1994). Intelligence and morale in the army of a democracy: The genesis of military psychology during the First World War. Military Psychology, 6(4), 235–253.
Mayer, J. (2009). the secret history. The New Yorker, June 14. www.newyorker.com/magazine/2009/06/22/the-secret-history.
Nicholas, L. J. (1990). The response of South African professional psychology associations to apartheid. Journal of the History of the Behavioral Sciences, 26(1), 58–63.
Norton, L. W. (2020). The business of consulting psychology: Lessons from the field. Consulting Psychology Journal: Practice and Research, 72(1), 68–76. https://doi.org/10.1037/cpb0000159
Novotney, A. (2019). Launch. Grow. Thrive. Established solo and group practitioners share their secrets to success in independent practice. Monitor on Psychology, 50(7), 60–65.
Peters, M. A. (2019). Manifesto for the postcolonial university. Educational Philosophy and Theory, 51(2), 142–148. DOI: 10.1080/00131857.2017.1388660
Pickren, W. E. (2020). Coloniality of being and knowledge in the history of psychology. In Psychologie und Kritik (pp. 329–343). Wiesbaden: Springer.
Pillay, S. R. (2017). Cracking the fortress: Can we really decolonize psychology? South African Journal of Psychology, 47(2), 135–140. https://doi.org/10.1177/0081246317698059
Pope, K. S. (2018). A human rights and ethics crisis facing the world's largest organization of psychologists. European Psychologist, 24(2), 180–194. https://doi.org/10.1027/1016-9040/a000341.
Price, D. H. (2016). Cold War anthropology: The CIA, the Pentagon, and the growth of dual use anthropology. Durham, NC: Duke University Press.
Rohde, J. (2013). Armed with expertise: The militarization of American social research during the Cold War. Ithaca: Cornell University Press.
Şensoy, B. Ö., Okan, E., Kayacı, G., Erbey, M., & Yılmaz, Ö. (2013). Psychology as labor, criticism and solidarity: An account of critical psychology experience from Turkey. Annual Review of Critical Psychology, 10, 901–915.
Sloan, T. S. (1990). Psychology for the third world? Journal of Social Issues, 46(3), 1–20.
Sokol, M. B., & Norton, L. W. (2020). Introduction to the special issue on the strategic design and management of psychology-based consulting firms. Consulting Psychology Journal: Practice and Research, 72(1), 4–7. http://dx.doi.org/10.1037/cpb0000158
Van De Water, T. J. (1997). Psychology's entrepreneurs and the marketing of industrial psychology. Journal of Applied Psychology, 82(4), 486–499. https://doi.org/10.1037/0021-9010.82.4.486

7
BLESSINGS FROM THE TEWA SUNRISERS OF SANTA CLARA PUEBLO

Rachel Begay

My name is Rachel Begay. I am Native American from the Pueblo of Santa Clara and the Navajo (Diné) Nation. I am the Administrative Assistant for the Humanities and Social Sciences Department here at Northern New Mexico College. Before I begin, I would like to mention that I work with a group of talented, hardworking, knowledgeable, and all-around awesome faculty in this Department.

This evening, I will share with you a little bit about my Pueblo before we end the conference with a performance of one of our sacred dances. The name Santa Clara Pueblo comes from the Catholic name Saint Claire. When the Spaniards first tried to rule over the Pueblos, they built churches, giving each Pueblo a patron saint. The traditional name for Santa Clara is *Kha'p'o Owingeh* (Singing Water) because at one time there were many natural springs within and around the Pueblo. The creek that runs through the Pueblo is water flowing from our canyon. It continuously flows like it is singing, hence the name Singing Water.

There are 19 Pueblo tribes in New Mexico and each Pueblo is a sovereign nation, meaning each body of land or reservation is under its own tribal governmental structure; however, all 19 Pueblos share similar belief systems, spirituality, and lifestyle.

Santa Clara is a Tewa-speaking Pueblo, which is located along the Rio Grande River, one and a half miles south of Española, NM. The Puye Cliff Dwellings are the ancestral home of the Santa Clara people. Puye Cliffs are a historical and archeological landmark located in the mountains above the modern-day Pueblo. For more than three centuries, this locale was home to over 1500 people who built villages, farmed, hunted game, and inhabited the Cliff Dwellings. Eventually, drought caused the springs to dry up and crops to fail, forcing the people to move their homes along the river. The translation for Puye Owingeh is Buckskin

Village, named for its abundance of elk and deer that were (and still are) hunted in the nearby canyon; the ancestors used every bit of the animals' hides to clothe themselves and for native ceremonies.

The Santa Clara people, as well as many other Indigenous tribes, have preserved the majority of their ancient traditions. We all share a history of oppression and injustice, but our identities have not faded, even in the face of multiple colonizing nations. Today, as always, we value our uniqueness and traditional way of life. At the same time, we live in modern houses, and work and reside both on and off the reservation. Our beliefs and actions are still guided by our core Pueblo values, which include: respect, compassion, faith, understanding, spirituality, balance, and peace. We continue to participate in our traditional celebrations and ceremonies throughout the year, maintaining our deep connection to our ancestors, nature, and Mother Earth.

Santa Clara takes great pride in its rich legacy of pottery making. The Pueblo is known for its distinct handcrafted black and redware pottery, which is decorated with intricate engravings and precise designs. Mr. Eric Tafoya, the drummer for the dance group, is one of our many well-known potters.

Since time immemorial, Pueblo communities have celebrated seasonal cycles through prayer, song, and dance. These dances connect us to our ancestors, while honoring gifts from the Creator (Figure 7.1). They ensure that life continues and that connections to the past and future are reinforced. They are not selfish prayers; we ask for guidance and blessings for all people throughout the world. Although we may not look the same, we are all brothers and sisters.

The dance group "Tewa Sunrisers" of Santa Clara Pueblo will be performing tonight. Mr. Eric Tafoya, who is the drummer, leads the group. His son, daughter, and granddaughter will be dancing while Kevin Jenkins (of Santa Clara/San

FIGURE 7.1 Dancers performing the Buffalo Dance

Ildefonso Pueblos) will assist them. What you will be witnessing shortly is called the Buffalo Dance. Normally, it is performed toward the end of the winter season, to honor the animals that have given their lives to feed us, give us warmth, and clothe us. The dancers' regalia are made from actual animal parts. Our ancestors also learned to spin cotton, as you will notice from the kilts and dresses that are hand-made.

In closing, we hope that you will enjoy this sacred dance and leave the conference with a little understanding of who we are as Pueblo people. This dance is dedicated to you with our blessings to send you on your life journey with happiness, harmony, health, and prosperity.

8
THE CREATION OF THE VIABLE UNHEARD OF AS A REVOLUTIONARY ACTIVITY

Fernanda Liberali, Valdite Pereira Fuga, and José Carlos Barbosa Lopes

Introduction

The current scenario in social and political areas in Brazil has faced the reinforcement of injustice, segregation, prejudice, and the maintenance of the status quo; in a way, life conditions tend to decay rather than improve. In many educational contexts, for example, questioning and finding ways to overcome constraints that limit one's existence have been understood as a subversive activity, instead of a legitimate critical role a citizen is entitled to in everyday life to nourish equality, well-being, the development of individuals, and collectivity in the country, as stated by the Brazilian Constitution.

This chapter, therefore, raises issues of research as an interventionist, activist activity, which is engaged with the search for the right to exist, that is, the right to live one's essential creative potential in a re-appropriation of the vital force which has been outrageously taken by a colonial-capitalist regime (Rolnik, 2018). According to Rolnik, since the 15th century, this regime of living has created a *modus operandi*, which, in its contemporary format, has emphasized a financial, neoliberal, and globalitarian perspective.

Consequently, the initial exploitation of the workforce and of the intrinsic cooperation in the production for "surplus value" has now been intensified by the exploitation of life itself, of the individual, and the collective potential for new forms of existence. They have also been intensified by the functions, codes, and representations which capital has explored and turned into its motor. This colonial-capitalist system extracts not only economic power, but also, and more importantly, cultural and subjective power. Therefore, Rolnik (2018) recommends the re-appropriation of the creative potential to construct what Negri and Hardt (2001, 2014, 2017, as cited in Rolnik, 2018) have called "the common," understood as the immanent life impulse of the social group to take in its hand the creation of new means of existing. In Freirean terms, the focus relies on the production of the viable unheard of, or the potential to overcome restrictions of reality by devising new possibilities for the future.

In line with this search for the common or the viable unheard of, therefore, the Language in Activity in the School Context Research Group (LACE) conducts research as a resistance-expansive group, taking the dialectical understanding as a driving force in and for the production of knowledge, not setting aside the revolutionary transformative perspective in Marxist theory. For the group, revolution or revolutionary activity means "the transformation of the existing state of things or the transformation of the totality of what is there" (Newman & Holzman, 2002, p. 25).

This transformation of the existing state of things (revolutionary activity) has taken place in LACE through several projects developed within the scope of Applied Linguistics (Moita Lopes, 2006), which seeks to articulate characteristics of the real world, via language, in daily pedagogical actions in order to create spaces and conditions for subjects to engage in activities aimed at solving real problems in schools, communities, and, as a consequence, society in general. In the same line, Gonçalez Rey (2016) also points out the importance of subjective engagement in transformation as an internal and external process within critical psychology, which is formed by symbolical processes and emotions in social experience.

LACE, broadly speaking, from the Catholic University of São Paulo (PUC-SP), has its basis in the Applied Linguistics perspective, which chooses the school context to act and language as the core of its work. LACE focuses on the critical formative process of researchers, coordinators, supervisors, directors, teachers, Brazilian Sign Language (LIBRAS) and Portuguese translators-interpreters, and students in the development of critical-collaborative intervention research in multilingual school contexts.

This chapter will focus on some of the activities developed in Digitmed Brazil, one of the projects LACE has developed since 2013 on de-encapsulating curriculum proposals to foster transformative agency (Liberali, 2019) in a university–school–community partnership based on a critical-collaborative intervention research (Magalhães, 2011). In the first section, the theoretical background that supports the actions developed by LACE is presented. After that, Digitmed will be generically described. In the third section, the 2018 version of the program will exemplify the theoretical discussion in a more practical way. Finally, some considerations will be drawn about how these research procedures can potentially create the viable unheard of and overcome the colonial-capitalist oppression of our present daily lives.

The Importance of the Dialectical Historical Materialism in Digitmed Brazil

Dialectical historical materialism has established itself as a basic theoretical-methodological contribution for LACE because, in general, it provides subsidies for thinking about pedagogical practice as a revolutionary activity, that is, transforming the state of existing things or the totality of what exists (Newman & Holzman, 2002). As applied linguists and political agents, LACE directs this transformation of existing things towards the development of research and pedagogical language practices that can promote the dialogue between theory and practice, and contemplate other ways of sociability, centralizing marginalized lives from social classes, ethnicity, sexuality, and nationality among other aspects (Moita Lopes, 2006).

In this theoretical view, LACE understands language as dialogical, taken as a social, historical, and ideological phenomenon, and a place of human interaction (Bakhtin, 1929/1995) constituted by different forces that show meanings and voices linguistically highlighted in discourse through multimodal resources. In this sense, LACE has discussed many topics related to how language can create possibilities for reorganizing society. And because language has this strong potential to both create oppression and also to devise means of overcoming this oppression, LACE has developed intervention research that can create possibilities to think about ways language can support individuals to overcome oppression.

Broadly speaking, dialectical historical materialism presents a theoretical, methodological, and analytical perspective that enables the understanding of the dynamics and major changes in history and human societies. From the proposition of a theoretical-practical movement, human beings are able to overcome the speculative reasoning and act within their conscious plans. It is in the scientific analysis of society that dialectical historical materialism expresses its indignation, its complaints, but also highlights the possibility of overcoming the current state of affairs (Marx & Engels, 1989/2007) in order to build new ways of production and new social relations in society.

For LACE, in Digitmed this overcoming of the current state of affairs comes from the adoption of a critical view on the research practices in all its contexts, which is also considered a proposal for transgressive education (hooks, 1994/2017). Doing research at Digitmed means keeping away from traditional actions in all its steps, such as, in the thematic choice, in the meetings that precede the workshops, in the theoretical and methodological procedures that collaboratively involve all participants, and in the reports issued among others. Digitmed constitutes itself as a fertile field for this new way of producing knowledge, new social relations, since it has triggered constant reflections on the tasks, roles, and social activities in which the group is involved.

Dialectical historical materialism postulates that everything and everyone are seen as in transformation because of their historical, material, and concrete existence, which can be understood in process, in transformation. As a result, it is important to highlight that Vygotsky (1934/2001) addresses this key concept when he explains that thought and language are inseparable in human activity because they convey meaning. In other words, dialectical historical materialism is a revolutionary activity in human experience because it enables people to act and change reality; consequently, it is one of the fundamentals in critical psychology.

In this sense, people create scenarios of existence and a perspective of the future in order to transform their lives, that is, artifacts, activities, motives, relationships which, in a dialectical way, transform their surroundings: "human beings come to be themselves and come to know their world and themselves *in the process* and *as a process* of collaboration changing their world, while changing together with it" (Stetsenko, 2017, p. 485, emphasis in original). Therefore, there are no absolute and eternal laws that could restrict the potential for living and creating new ways of life.

Being "in the process" and "as a process" underlines the transformative and non-adaptive principle of human development, a concern that Marx emphasizes in the 11th Thesis on Feuerbach when stating that "philosophers have so far only interpreted the world in various ways; the point is to change it" (Marx & Engels, 1989/2007, p. 103). In this thesis, Marx and Engels suggest a new approach to philosophy that should not only be interpretative, but focused on social transformation. For Stetsenko (2016), this transformation implies uninterrupted continuum practice–theory–practice cycles, in which theoretical concepts, ways of knowing and doing, words and deeds, ideologically defined by different worldviews, co-exist in an inseparable blend. In other words, everything and everyone in continuous transformation in different dimensions and aspects, interpenetrating themselves, dialectically, through multidirectional movements, constitute the continuous flow of praxis.

The experiences lived in the context of Digitmed, for example, have pointed to revolutionary transformative actions, diluting rigid borders concerning the content of the subject areas, with an emphasis on curricular de-encapsulation; on non-hierarchical relationships among participants; and on teaching–learning contents of daily life (Liberali, 2019). In short, pedagogical practice seems to re-signify itself in this context, which interweaves subjects and their historicities (Stetsenko, 2017). In this sense, hooks (1994/2017) points out that, in school experiences, it is possible to minimize the gaps between theory and practice, and combine the lived experiences with broader processes of engagement with collective liberation.

Thinking about revolutionary praxis, as stated by Vygotsky (1934/2001), and more recently discussed by Stetsenko (2017), means to overcome the dogmatization of education and the Eurocentrism with the imposition of a single thought; it also means to strengthen the prism of multiculturalism that de-silences the oppressed voices of participants. Through challenging proposals, participants learn to question and foster a decolonization of difference, because subjects who are open to the world and to different types of knowledge are simultaneously open to a dialogical, permanent, and active movement in history (Freire, 1996).

Decoloniality in Revolutionary Activity

It is urgent to understand how education is pivotal for the practice of freedom and for a critical stance towards reality. Although this premise is widely known, the constraints that prevent it from happening are huge, because critical pedagogy stands for a radical change against hegemonic values that still limit people's existence. hooks (1994/2017), for example, reveals many faces of those restrictions on topics such as sexism, racism, segregation, class domination, and colonization. She points out the right to resist and transgress against those boundaries to achieve democratic participation in everyday life within social power relations.

In this context, the foundations for emancipatory educational practices are raised in multicultural diversity and in terms of the qualitative transformation in society to fight against injustice. hooks (1994/2017) sets this argument when she highlights Freire's ideas about the collective effort to know and transform reality. It brings back the concept of praxis by Marx and Engels (1989/2007) in terms of the inseparability of action and consciousness. Therefore, hooks stresses political educational practices as a progressive perspective, in which knowledge is developed through conflicts in history, so it is inevitably partial and ever-changing. All that implies a more critical approach in schools and the responsibility to be aware of differences to come up with alternatives to overcome oppression.

It is true that dealing with these issues is complex because it involves setting a political agenda and, consequently, it unseats those who have long been granted privileges. To question knowledge, who defines it, and what objectives are behind regulations assumed to be the norm are just a few aspects to be considered in a pedagogical perspective engaged to transform realities. In support of these ideas, hooks (1994/2017) also refers to the "banking" concept of education, which Freire (1970/2005) describes as the mechanical approach that teachers would simply "deposit" knowledge while students would receive it. She claims that school settings can only recognize diversity if decoloniality becomes part of the educational process to envision different modes of living, thinking, and being that were pushed aside from history.

Decolonial practices, as stated by Santos (2005/2019), tend to capture the richness of diversity in social experience and the variety of forms of knowledge needed to build social emancipation. This epistemological transformation, better known as *Epistemologies of the South,* is opposed to the interpretation of science as universal or the absolute truth. It is rather through social practice, contextualized methodology, and collective participation that knowledge is both produced and lived. This perspective criticizes how globalization, capitalism, as well as cognitive and social injustice reject an array of forms of knowledge as if they were not partial and situated resources for understanding reality.

Based on his worldwide experience and intellectual activism in the World Social Forum (WSF), which constitutes organizations from the *Global South* that also demand recognition and emancipation, Santos (2005/2019) explores how people are constantly silenced and systematically marginalized. As he names it, the sociology of absences is characterized by enabling counter-hegemonic social experience to become visible in space and time in order to transform what is thought to be impossible into possibility. This inquiry denies the "monoculture of knowledge" that undermines the credibility of local differences and, eventually, erases them.

As a possibility to envision the future from the present moment in which we are living, Santos (2005/2019) proposes the sociology of emergencies, which consists of the production of knowledge and social transformation, considering reality as part of an ongoing historical process open to change. As a result, social experiences, especially what has been neglected in favor of hegemonic practices, become practices of transgressive freedom – both practices of transformative action and practices of transformative knowledge. Again, Santos emphasizes a refusal of monocultures and an affirmation of ecologies as concepts that broaden our understanding of multiplicity and suggests alternatives to avoid the coloniality of power and knowledge in society.

The wheels of social transformation are then identified as symbolic alternatives to combat injustice based on a critical analysis of the possibilities and real capabilities to do so. This idea leads us to the viable unheard of, proposed by Freire (1970/2005), once concrete possibilities are conceived of in order to strengthen hope for another future instead of accepting failure as foretold and inevitable. What should nourish our existence is an ongoing desire to strive to overcome oppressive contexts and find possible means to contribute responsibly to history while living it in the collectivity.

On that aspect, Freire (1970/2005) discusses how action and reflection are never apart in our everyday life. This dialectic process is what makes people go beyond their immediate realities by doing what is possible to struggle with the obstacles they face in life. In other words, people are constantly moving towards transformation, which implies changes in the world through their individual and collective experience, also discussed by González Rey (2016) as subjectivity in its living process that integrates the decisions and paths taken by the individual and social instances during ongoing activity.

When it comes to Marx and Engels (1989/2007), the concept of praxis is a theoretical and methodological key concept to ground the critical and practical human activity, while conceptualizing dialectical and historical materialism. This is why the wave of decolonization assumes a central role in emancipatory practices because, as discussed by Romão and Gadotti (2012) about Freire's principles, people are not only affected by political factors that condition them to prescribed policies, but their consciousness is also culturally shaped to repeat a certain set of beliefs. Taking educational contexts into this discussion, praxis is then driven to critical thinking and revolutionary activity, as well as to all kinds of human activities that are intentionally committed to something and/or someone.

In this perspective, the research projects carried out by LACE are methodologically structured as intervention studies. They are intentionally oriented to transform contexts (Marx and Engels, 1989/2007; Vygotsky, 1934/ 2001), promote collective engagement, and search for shared solutions and development based on experimenting with crisis. Participants become agents who are constituted in the collectivity (Magalhães, 2011) and take part in projects that can promote the viable unheard of (Freire, 1970/2005), assumed as the historically possible materialization of their desired dream in the face of unpredictable, and often oppressive, situations.

Digitmed Brazil: The Construction of the Viable Unheard Of

Throughout the years, LACE has developed non-profit projects, whose funding comes from different agencies in terms of the equipment to support and disseminate research. These projects can enable spaces for the development of many different research activities: researchers collect data, develop material, write their dissertations, theses, articles, and books; they also collaborate forming new insights within the LACE framework.

Digitmed Brazil[1] became one of the projects developed by LACE in 2013 as part of an international project called Digital Media Education, coordinated by Kontopodis et al. (2017) and funded by the Interchange Project Marie Curie International Research Teams – European Union FP7 (IRSES) (2012–2014). It involved different universities around the world, analyzing and investigating how media could transform people's lives in very marginalized situations. The project was held in Brazil to take into account interventions in school curriculum for de-encapsulation (Engeström, 2002; Liberali, 2019). At first, the choice was to study digital means that could trigger important changes for education. But then, it expanded to different aspects such as cultural, ecological, political, and economic issues, which affected relationships beyond the school context and led to great changes in people's existence as a whole.

In Brazil, Digitmed gathers researchers, deaf and hearing students, migrant students, teachers, school coordinators, principals, LIBRAS interpreters, and people from the communities where partner schools are located. Together, in monthly four-hour workshops at PUC-SP, these participants strengthen diversity and enrich committed participation for a more critical-collaborative attitude in everyday life. To do so, topics that are relevant to the Brazilian community are brought into question since fake news, violence, and all types of exclusion and oppression have gradually interrupted social development. That is why all participants move around discussions on how to de-encapsulate the school curriculum in order to find ways to resist-expand within the limitations imposed by their broader reality.

This implies that all participants are responsible for everyone's development in the learning process towards a revolutionary activity. Following this perspective, Digitmed assumes a Marxist-informed transformative proposal and works to engage participants in critical-collaborative contexts to re-think social practices, roles, knowledge, and values in order to take a stance on diverse life issues.

The project is organized as a university–school–community partnership with private and public (municipal and state) schools in São Paulo. Participants engaged in performative activities can creatively think about proposals to develop ways to live together and possibilities to overcome constraints and face conflict as the force that moves everyone beyond their immediate reality. Each year, discussions in the meetings are organized on a thematic axis: in 2013, how to demonstrate and quality of life; in 2014, taking care of the garbage; in 2015, the roles of men and women; in 2016, otherness in moving around the city; in 2017, public and private issues; in 2018, to resist-expand in a shared city; in 2019, based on the United Nations Sustainable Development Goals – Reduction of Inequalities, to overcome "social inequality," through the development of artistic and cultural manifestations. The third workshop, held in 2018, will be described to exemplify the actions developed by the researchers.

In that year, Digitmed was organized to work with the Freirean concept of the viable unheard of, the social activity of designing transformations in neighborhoods. The leading topic was formulated in terms of a question: how to resist-expand in shared landscapes? These choices were made based on the perception that 2018 was not going to be an easy year because the country was experiencing a great turn to far-right positions, which included deeply conservative views on education, religion, and the family among other important cultural, ecological, political, and economic issues. All of that influenced relationships in different contexts and led to a great wave of intolerance in the country, exacerbated by the presidential election.

The choice to go beyond resisting into expanding was based on the desire to think about proposals for changing contexts, and not simply about how to struggle against the attack on different forms of freedom that society was going through. Above all, the meetings put an emphasis on the development of ways to live together and find possibilities of overcoming conflict in a more liberating way (Freire, 1970/2005). Therefore, thinking about the viable unheard of had to do with creating forms of living together with and because of differences, as well as designing transformations in the neighborhood or city as a means to prove to everyone that they had the power to create something together – the unheard of.

In 2018, two public and four private schools were organized around different activities, which raised the discussion of what central issues should be improved in their neighborhoods. The following categories were used:

- Mobility: safety, transportation, traffic
- Social interaction: culture, leisure, and sports – ways of being and acting in public spaces
- Training and social development: education, health care, social security, employment
- Participation: urban planning, councils, associations, local and intersectoral management
- Uses and infrastructure: housing, commerce, services, social equipment, infrastructure, and sanitation.

The Viable Unheard Of **93**

The topic was the desired city/neighborhood, which presented how participants brought to light their main concerns about their cities/neighborhoods. There were about 50 participants (deaf and hearing students aged from 9 to 18 onwards, teachers, principals, coordinators, LIBRAS interpreters, and researchers: Figure 8.1).

First Task

Participants presented DataWalls with results to a pool they carried out with other members of the school during the month (Figures 8.2 and 8.3).

Second Task

Participants got together to compare their findings and produced short performances in which they expressed their relationships to these analyses (Figures 8.4 and 8.5).

FIGURE 8.1 Participants in the auditorium

FIGURE 8.2 Presenting DataWalls

94 Fernanda Liberali et al.

FIGURE 8.3 Presenting DataWalls

FIGURE 8.4 Discussing the DataWalls presented

FIGURE 8.5 Group performance

FIGURE 8.6 Groups drawing dreams

FIGURE 8.7 Burning dreams

Third Task

Groups drew and wrote their dreams about how they could devise their realities, which were later collected and burned in a very dramatic situation (Figures 8.6 and 8.7). That experience emotionally affected and raised an important discussion among participants.

Fourth Task

The group watched a film created by the researchers using snippets from films, news media, and interviews that captured various and differing positions in relation to how homeless people have been using the unoccupied places in the city of São Paulo (Figure 8.8). This topic was emphasized because some days before the meeting a 26-storey building, occupied by squatters, had collapsed after being engulfed in flames.

FIGURE 8.8 Watching the film

Regarding controversial issues on the situation, researchers decided to open them up for debate, so that participants could dramatically connect themselves to the feelings of loss experienced in their second task. During the discussions, there was a group of adult students from Haiti who described how the hurricane there had ended lives and submerged people into poverty and abandonment in less than one minute. These students made very strong connections between what they had lived through in Haiti and the task that they were part of. While the general group discussed the film and the "burning of their dreams," the distinction between occupation and invasion started to appear in the participants' speeches. In order to deal with that, the participants' awareness and construction of possible solutions on the topic were addressed through other tasks, such as: film analysis, sharing personal experiences, theoretical background reading, and creating performances on actions that were related to the housing problem. All that movement converged into the group organization inviting representatives of political parties for a conversation on a follow-up workshop in search of alternatives to real problems experienced by the schools and communities involved.

In this synthesized description, we have tried to show how intentionality guided different moments of the workshop to establish cognitive-affective connections through performance, so that the participants could first break conceptual barriers about real-life problems. The aim was to connect their memories and feelings to the issues in the debate, as they shared and produced knowledge during different moments of the workshop as well as through all the multimodal resources provided, such as films and texts, among others.

The whole activity broke boundaries imposed by school contexts and the limitations of school reality and provoked the participants so that they could observe their own realities and, simultaneously, demand the same attitude from other school participants and even from politicians. By doing so, they had the chance to deal with problems of their everyday realities and feel they could try to take responsibility for them. For example, it is possible to see how the participants brought to the discussions their personal experiences and created a close connection with the issues in the debate. The memories and feelings opened them up to a more personal relationship with both the situation under analysis as well as the conceptual and theoretical topics presented.

This example seems to highlight underlying aspects of revolutionary activity (Newman & Holzman, 2002): a shared experience in the collectivity, in which actions bring the possibility to re-signify and transform socio-cultural-historical practices intentionally. In other words, it means to live and reflect on situated contexts that provide resources to understand and actively take a stance in the world, based on ethical and political commitments that aspire to social justice in the revolutionary process (hooks, 1994/2017), that is, the viable unheard of (Freire, 1970/2005).

Concluding Remarks: Resist-Expand in Digitmed Brazil

This chapter discussed some of the activities in Digitmed Brazil aimed at transformative agency in a university–school–community partnership based on a critical-collaborative intervention research (Magalhães, 2011). To this end, it brought to bear dialectical historical materialism (Marx & Engels, 1989/2007) as well as some decolonial thinkers as a theoretical base to support this discussion. A synthesis of a workshop developed in 2018 was described so that the praxis of revolutionary activity (Newman & Holzman, 2002) could be exemplified in LACE's theoretical and methodological approach.

Considering that transformative agency implies the dialectics between the subject and the world in shared common practices (Stetsenko, 2017), the space circumscribed by Digitmed becomes a context to strive in an expansive resistance, which provides the participants with interactive and diverse experiences combined with those from their schools. This ongoing movement enables them to reflect on de-encapsulated knowledge in order to expand multiple resources and build possibilities for revolutionary activity not only in schools, but also in different spheres of everyday life.

This activist-interventionist approach in Digitmed seems to be connected to what Santos (2005/2019) points out about building knowledge in the collectivity once it is "incomplete" and ever changing. This epistemological perspective implies that all the participants bring something to share and, therefore, expand the group's understanding and participation. When the participants face dramatic events from their lives during the workshops combined with those they actually go through, they can become activists in the diversity provided in Digitmed Brazil to contribute to their desired future. The various situations they experience with others, in addition to the use of media, performances, and discussions among other activities, give them support to reflect on what they have in their realities and ways they can critically deliberate about what they can do to change their realities.

In this sense, it is possible to say that Digitmed Brazil creates concrete possibilities for this new way of acting in the world – the viable unheard of (Freire, 1970). This framework in LACE is understood as a potential creative action (resist-expand), which is critically thought out so that the participants can reason through what possibilities they have in order to perform an activity. This means that they move beyond their immediate realities because they must consider the broader knowledge available in the world. To the same extent, they rely on everything they have learned so far in their present and past life experiences to come up with possible solutions in facing what the world demands from them now or what they might expect from it. This connection with the past, present, and future helps participants understand that their actions are placed in time and, consequently, are culturally and historically driven towards society.

Note

1 Fernanda Liberali is the coordinator of Digitmed Brazil, which was funded by the Interchange Project Marie Curie International Research Teams, Pipeq and CNPq.

References

Bakhtin, M. M. (Volochínov). (1929). Marxismo e Filosofia da Linguagem. 7th ed. Tradução: Lahud, M., & Frateschi Vieira, Y. (trans.). São Paulo: Hucitec, 1995.

Engestrom, Y. (2002). *Non scholae sed vitae discimus*: Como superar a encapsulação da aprendizagem escolar. In: Daniels, H. (Ed.). Uma introdução a Vygotsky. São Paulo: Loyola.

Freire, P. (1996). Pedagogia da autonomia: Saberes necessários à prática educativa. São Paulo: Paz e Terra.

Freire, P. (2005). Pedagogia do oprimido. 41st ed. São Paulo: Paz e Terra (published in 1970).

González Rey, F. (2016). Advancing the topics of social reality, culture, and subjectivity from a cultural–historical standpoint: Moments, paths, and contradictions. Journal of Theoretical and Philosophical Psychology, 36(3), 175–189. www.fernandogonzalezrey.com/index.php/2015-09-04-16-07-52-artigos/prod-biblio-artigos/prod-biblio-drfernando-artigos-psicologia-cultural-historica.

hooks, b. (1994/2017). Ensinando a transgredir: A educação como prática da liberdade, 2nd ed. Trad. Brandão Cipolla, M. (trans.). São Paulo: WMF Martins Fontes.

Kontopodis, M., Varvantakis, C., & Wulf, C. (2017). Global youth in digital trajectories. London: Routledge.

Liberali, F. C. (2019). Transforming urban education in São Paulo: Insights into a critical-collaborative school project. DELTA [online], 35(3), Apr 18. http://dx.doi.org/10.1590/1678-460x2019350302Magalhães, M. C. C. (2011). Pesquisa crítica de colaboração: Escolhas epistemo-metodológicas na organização e condução de pesquisas de intervenção no contexto escolar. In Magalhães, M. C. C., & Fidalgo, S. S. (Eds.), Questões de método e de linguagem na formação docente. Campinas, SP: Mercado de Letras, pp. 13–40.

Marx, K., & Engels, F. (2007). A ideologia alemã, 3rd ed. Claudio de Castro Costa, L. (trans.). São Paulo: Martins Fontes (published in 1989).

Moita Lopes, L. C. (2006). Linguística aplicada e vida contemporânea: Problematização dos construtos que têm orientado a pesquisa. In Moita Lopes, L. P. (Ed.), Por uma lingüística aplicada indisciplinar. São Paulo: Parábola, pp. 85–107.

Newman, F., & Holzman, L. (2002). Lev Vygotsky: Cientista revolucionário. Bagno, M. (trans.). São Paulo: Edições Loyola.

Rolnik, S. (2018). Esferas da insurreição: Notas para uma vida não cafetinada. São Paulo: N-1 edições.

Romão, J. E., & Gadotti, M. (2012). Paulo Freire e Amílcar Cabral: A descolonização das mentes. São Paulo: Editora e Livraria Instituto Paulo Freire.

Santos, B. S. (2005/2019). Educación para otro mundo posible. Ciudad Autónoma de Buenos Aires: CLACSO; Medellin: CEDALC.

Stetsenko, A. (2016). Vygotsky's theory of method and philosophy of practice: Implications for trans/formative methodology. Educação (Porto Alegre), 39, n. esp. (supl.), s32–s41. http://dx.doi.org/10.15448/1981-2582.2016.s.24385.

Stetsenko, A. (2017). The transformative mind: Expanding Vygotsky's approach to development and education. New York: Cambridge University Press.

Vygotsky, L. S. (1934/2001). A construção do pensamento e da linguagem. Bezerra, P. (trans.). São Paulo: Martins Fontes.

9

STUDENT RESISTANCE AS A PRAXIS AGAINST NEOLIBERALISM

A Critical Analysis of Chilean Public Education from 1980 to 2020

Silvana S. Hernández-Ortiz and María-Constanza Garrido Sierralta

Introduction

The history of Chilean education is an unequivocal expression of the country's political, socioeconomic, and cultural conditions. These multi-faceted inequalities are bound to urban and rural settings, the tripartite schooling system, and the neoliberal policies treating school as another part of the market economy, what we label "market education." Education in Chile cannot be unfastened from the vestiges of neocolonialism, imperialism, dictatorship, and currently, neoliberalism. This study on education, focusing primarily on the public school system, explores interconnected links that confront a present grappling with a troubled past. By way of a new generation of students, hope for a brighter future is on the horizon. In this text, we hope to provide a general account of Chilean public education, and highlight the multiple socio-political milestones achieved by students. Since October 2019, high-school students have become the vanguard embodying a much desired transformation, which translates as fierce resistance and conscious praxis engagement. Their involvement has changed the outlook on public education. The future belongs to them.

Historico-Political Context of the Chilean Education System

In the 19th century, public schooling in Chile had a purely political purpose: the education and formation of citizens that meant consolidating a national identity. At this time, schooling had already a socially unequal origin due to the country's geography and its variant population densities. Rural and geographically distant sectors from the capital were most affected or suffered the most disparities (Serrano et al., 2012). The social inequality of schooling is also showcased in limited access to higher education. Since the 19th century, the country's upper class were the only ones who had access to a university education.

Chilean public education was also the government's response to dealing with poverty. This lower tier of the schooling system was part of the government's undertaking of welfare policies that sought to provide for basic social needs using public spending (Del Valle, 2010; Peña & Toledo, 2017b). Throughout the decades of the country's industrial development, it became necessary to achieve a greater educational coverage throughout the territory. From the 20th century till now, three main demands for public education have constantly arisen. The first focused on the demand for a fair access to education. The latter two are recurrent demands made by Chilean society: to have access to a public education of quality that is also free to all.

In order to understand these last two demands, quality and free education, we must address the three types of school administration: private, subsidized, and public education. These three divisions arose in the second half of the 20th century, during the last years of Augusto Pinochet's dictatorial regime. After his departure and with the return to democracy in the 1990s, education was subordinated to municipal administration and not state intervention (Larrañaga, 1995). This meant that richer municipalities provide better formation and infrastructure than poorer ones, thus accentuating even further the base and superstructural inequalities of Chilean education.

In addition, the decentralization of the state's administration of public education meant delegating the responsibility of choosing a school to the family (Peña, 2011). The school division between private, subsidized, and public; between wealthy and poor municipalities; and now between affluent and impoverished families suggests, yet again, another discriminatory practice with regard to the family's means to choose a school determined solely by their economic ability. Thus, schooling is no longer a right granted by the state, but a commodity to be purchased. However, these issues become even more aggravated given the larger socioeconomic structure. According to Santos and Elacqua (2016), Chile is one of the countries with the highest levels of socioeconomic segregation when compared to countries participating in the Programme for International Student Assessment (PISA). All the same, the state in a more welfare-oriented role grants certain schools a preferential subsidy, with the objective of reducing gaps that exist among school children who enter municipal schools and who do not have sufficient resources for adequate schooling (Peña, 2011).

The state is no longer the guarantor of public education, but renders the education system a part of the *market economy*, wherein the access of students to institutions occurs in an unequal manner determined by their place of origin and their family's socioeconomic level. Sadly, under neoliberalism the most affected students are those who come from low-income and rural communities. This neoliberal education system forces public municipal schools in Chile, unlike private schools, to concentrate on vulnerable and high-risk populations (Martínez Aránguiz et al., 2012; Peña, 2011). Consequently, public municipal schools become educational institutions for those who are not eligible for a paid, or at least subsidized, education. This model generates segregation. First, in terms of the quality of instruction available for these children, but also, because it associates these institutions and children with marginality and poverty (Hernández & Raczynski, 2015; Torrents et al., 2018).

The Chilean neoliberal education system renders competition between different types of school administrations necessary (Peña, 2016). As mentioned, the decision of how much to invest in a child's education is left to the family. Socioeconomic and cultural constraints are assumed as familial responsibilities and not as those of the state. As the school system becomes yet another consumer good in this neoliberal market, education becomes ever more stratified (Bellei, Cabalin, et al., 2018; Zancajo, 2019). The constitutional right to education is not one guaranteed by the state, but determined by wealth and purchasing power. The state makes a minimal investment in children's future since it provides subsidies to select municipal institutions. Private, public, and subsidized educational establishments are then forced to begin competing for public funding (Sisto, 2019; Verger et al., 2016). In this sense, schools start behaving like corporations instead of places for instruction, substituting educational values for monetary ones, treating families and students as clients, and, as a result, the poorest become exceedingly excluded from the benefits of a quality education (Giroux, 2019). Peña and Toledo (2017a) argue that the state is not guaranteeing education as an equal right for all; on the contrary, it has further accentuated segregation. As a result, public education has gradually deteriorated, forcing the middle class to resort to subsidized or private schools. However, this leaves no alternative to Chile's poorest children.

Chile has become a country with a diminishing public education sector. Since 1981, public schools have gone from serving 81 percent of school children to 37 percent in actuality. These are public schools in socioeconomically disadvantaged areas with lower funding. On the other hand, subsidized schools cover 57 percent of school children nowadays (Carrasco & Gunter, 2018). These numbers place Chile as one of the countries with the smallest public education sector in Latin America, and one with the most privatized school systems in the world (Inzunza et al., 2019). Consequently, there exists a social stigma towards public education in correlation to a precarious and low academic standing (Inzunza et al., 2019; Verger et al., 2016).

Neoliberalism as a Vestige of Neocolonialism

Chile has been labeled the most neoliberal country in the world (Cornejo et al., 2011, p. 153), and this is tied to the historical and economic experimentations that occurred before and during the dictatorship era (1973–1990). Chile is a place where most basic resources are privatized. These include, in no exhaustive manner: services (water, electricity, medicine, banks), transportation systems, roads and highways, pensions, the prison system, seawater, healthcare, and education

(Cornejo et al, 2011, p. 153). Moreover, with regards to education, Chile also possesses a 100 percent privatized higher education system, with the average tuition for a Chilean public university reaching the exorbitant amount of $500 per month (Cornejo et al., 2011, p. 153). This amount is exorbitant considering that the current minimum wage in Chile is 320.500 Pesos per month (roughly, $415–420 depending on the fluctuation of the US dollar to Chilean Peso exchange). Also, according to the Chilean National Institute for Statistics (INE, 2020), half of the Chilean workers earn a salary equal, or inferior, to 400.000 Pesos ($518–520) per month. Based on these incomes, no Chilean can afford the current prices to attend a public university without recourse to loans or family wealth. For this reason, October 19th, 2019 was just the *tip of the iceberg* in a continual economic degradation and growing inequality. Income is just one of the many factors Chileans demanded the government to address; other demands included: changing the Constitution which dates back to the military dictatorship; addressing the price hikes in basic necessities like water, electricity, or gas; and restructuring the public sector which includes hospitals, transportation, and educational establishments. This is helpful to understand what led to the Chilean protests of 2019–2020, and which are ongoing. The neoliberal edifice in Chile is rooted in the vestige of neocolonialism and foreign imperialism, which created a deeply segregated structure in this country.

Aníbal Quijano (2007) warns in his text "Coloniality and Modernity/Rationality" that the control of resources and power, as happened during the colonial era, continues in the parasitic capitalist era for it perpetuates a control by "The 'Western' European dominators and their Euro-North American descendants" (p. 168). In effect, we are reminded of Vladimir Lenin's (1975) extensive study of "Imperialism, the Highest Stage of Capitalism," in which he identifies the creation of monopolies as the moment of transition to a higher capitalist system, but also the usurious practice from foreign banks to maintain neocolonial countries in debt and trapped by tricks of finance capital (p. 232). These countries like Chile seemed to see no way out, and Lenin (1975) provides the example of Chile and Germany's cunning banking and loan practices, stating:

> But the facts tells us clearly: the increase in [German] exports is connected with *just these* swindling tricks of finance capital, which is not concerned with bourgeois morality, but with skinning the ox twice—first, it pockets the profits from the loan; then it pockets other profits from the *same* loan.
> *(p. 265, emphasis in original)*

Thus, during imperialism, Chile was converted into a neocolony controlled by foreign banks and companies, a phenomenon we see to this day. In Lenin's (1975) view, imperialism did not care for freedom other than that of the free reign and domination by foreign countries, and reduced enclaves such as Chile to economic dependency (p. 260).

Since the 1960s, North American capitalism became the new *patrón* of world power. As a *patrón*, the US had established a relationship of domination and subordination, particularly with Latin America, its "backyard" (Skidmore et al., 2014, p. 285). As an imperialist power, the US imposed, demanded, and set its firmly gripped claws in subservient countries such as Chile for self-serving purposes. A clearer example of this economic but also political domination was evidenced with Salvador Allende's ousting in 1973 and during Pinochet's military dictatorship (Skidmore et al., 2014, p. 287). Allende brought back an air of national consciousness, or *"Chilenización"* (Skidmore et al., 2014, p. 286), one that was much desired and awaited. Most Chileans between the 1930s and 1970s were growing suspicious of the foreign intervention that had beset the country. Allende wished to regain national control over key sectors in order to give back to the nation what it was rightfully due.

Allende's Marxism was a threat to US economic hegemony and political imperialism. The threat of nationalization and government expropriation troubled the already beneficial exploitation and domination of Chilean resources by the US. In response to Allende's policies, the US pressured Chile economically by shutting down assistance and discouraging investments. Throughout left-wing anti-imperialist campaigns, the US government watched closely the unfolding of elections and intervened, by way of the CIA, in funding right-wing parties, media, and landowners to undermine counter-hegemonic efforts. Declassified documents state (Chile 1964, 2004): "The CIA spent a total of $2.6 million directly underwriting the campaign. An additional $3 million was spent on anti-Allende propaganda activities designed to scare voters away from Allende's FRAP [*Frente de Acción Popular*: Popular Action Front] coalition".

Back in 1964, Allende ran as the candidate for the FRAP, a left-wing coalition. In 1970, new alliances forged when the Socialist, Communist, Radical, and Social Democratic parties, along with the Independent Popular Action (IPA) and the *Movimiento de Acción Popular Unitario* (Popular Unitary Action Movement: MAPU) joined forces and created the *Unidad Popular*. Chile was headed towards a liberation the US did not approve of. The price to safeguard US interests was one of imposed occupation, repression, torture, and the suspension of democratic principles. With the installation of Pinochet, the US made sure their interests were defended and allowed to reign.

A new era of economic experimentation initiated with University of Chicago-trained technocrats, which included Sebastián Piñera's own brother José, implemented extensive changes to the intentionally destroyed Chilean economy. Neoliberalism was first tried in Chile, and opened the country to the world market by "drastically reducing tariff protection, government subsidies, and the size of the public sector" (Skidmore et al., 2014, p. 291). Unlike the previous democratically elected government, during Pinochet's reign of terror the word of the day was *privatization*. All was to be privatized once more, except for copper. To this day, *la Corporación Nacional del Cobre de Chile* (National Copper

Corporation of Chile: CODELCO) remains a state-owned enterprise and the largest producer of copper in the world (Skidmore et al., 2014, p. 291). However, we should not be fooled; CODELCO is national only by name given that transnational companies have gained concession of 70 percent of the industry since Pinochet's regime and this *modus operandi* remains in place to this day (Caputo & Galarce, 2011, p. 55).

As neoliberal policies were implemented during the military dictatorship, other neoliberal policies reformed the country's political and cultural landscape. Soon after Pinochet took power, Congress was dissolved, unions and parties outlawed, and a systematic hunt for opposition members initiated. The discourse had changed, now imposed with an iron fist. The new historical bloc was just the old oligarchic and imperialist one, disguised and rearticulated. The old hegemonic discourse was an utter rejection of all things socialist. It served the country on a silver platter to the US, through the use of violence. Far from emancipation from domination, the heralded freedom was that of individualism and competitiveness. Furthermore, neoliberalism reproduced an ideology that transformed and molded subjectivities. This was apparent in education, which became the government's main public apparatus for transmitting and shaping the youth's values with a selective common core. The dictatorship extended its grip over this instrumental factor. As Cornejo et al. (2011) state, "Chile has been a real laboratory for the application of neoliberal educational formulas" (p. 154). Thus, in education, stark contrasts and inequalities are apparent today, which are in origin violent and segregationist.

Inequality and Segregation in Chilean Education

The schooling process in Chile, which is the pedagogical formation of children from preschool till high-school graduation (OCDE, 2017), is seen in terms of the socioeconomic progress it contributes to the country. Furthermore, this process underlies an implicit promise of an education that will grant learners a fairer and more inclusive engagement in society (OCDE, 2017). However, according to the Organization for Economic Co-operation and Development (Martínez Aránguiz et al., 2012), Chile showcases the highest levels of inequality in terms of economic income, educational attainment, gender gaps, and segregation, especially when considering the most vulnerable populations. Factors such as these actually restrict learners' socioeconomic development. According to the three types of schools, the classifying of students based on their family income and socio-demographic location, marks their social positioning and identity (Domingo, 2016; Rujas Martínez-Novillo, 2017; Wright et al., 2016). One of the psychological effects on learners is the creation and formation of neoliberal subjectivities, which imply that individuals begin to comprehend themselves in terms of "private property" (Foucault, 2016; Peña, 2019). Thus, much like in a market economy, subjectivities are "handled" according to their abilities and interests. The handling of subjectivities resembles that of biopolitics, it is intrinsically motivated by a logic of competition and individualism (Peña & Toledo, 2017b).

Foucault proposes that the subject constructs him/herself (Howell, 2013) through processes of subjectivation (Stewart & Roy, 2014), by way of relations of power and the resistances that emerge. Chilean education should be oriented towards the transformation of the individual, which implies them taking a critical position that reflects on these experiences (González-Rey et al., 2016). Analyzing the constructive processes of subjectivity, within the Chilean education context, demands the acknowledgment of school children as socially active subjects (Pavez, 2012) with abilities to confront and transform realities (Lay-Lisboa & Montañés, 2018). Their abilities to shape new realities have allowed Chilean students to contest numerous forms of oppression. In fact, even Salvador Allende (1970) acknowledged the youth as the vanguard leading the country. In his victory speech delivered at the balcony of the *FeCh* (University of Chile Student Federation), he stated, "Because we all know: the youth of this country were the vanguard in this great battle, which was not the battle of a single man, but rather the battle of an entire people." In the last 20 years, multiple student protests have left decisive imprints, transforming into major political events. Working-class students, who have expressed their discontent towards various democratic governments, have primarily led these.

As mentioned earlier, Chile remains a country where wealth distribution is uneven, and what seem to increase are disparities. The most noteworthy gap in Chilean education remains that of inequality with regard to quality of learning, which continues to be one of the highest inequalities registered amongst children when compared to other countries analyzed by the OCDE. Chile's participation in PISA in 2015 confirmed that the socioeconomic context influences a student's academic performance. Compared to the OCDE's general level of variation (13 percent), a Chilean student's performance in science, for instance, reaches a 17 percent variation based on their socioeconomic context. Some have called this unfavorable division "a type of educational apartheid" (Cornejo et al., 2011, p. 156), which is still tied to the Constitution promulgated under Pinochet's dictatorship. The Constitutional Organic Law of Education (LOCE) was passed without changes, one day before Pinochet's exit. The new General Law of Education (LGE), which has now been approved, came only to consolidate the neoliberal education system.

The Neoliberal Market Education System

The neoliberal educational policies were developed under the military dictatorship from the 1980s (Carrasco & Gunter, 2018; Inzunza et al., 2019; Peña, 2019; Verger et al., 2016; Zancajo, 2019). As mentioned, these neoliberal policies advocated the privatization of all social services and the commodification of education (Bellei, Contreras, et al., 2018; Inzunza et al., 2019; Zancajo, 2019). In this manner, the effects of the market economy, neoliberal policies, and privatization begin to structure the families' responsibilities and learners around an "educational market."

To understand how the most important policies and rebellions have developed in Chilean education, we need to look at the beginning of the 1980s. On May 2, 1980, the Ministry of Education established the *municipalization* of education, which implied the transfer of school administration from the Ministry of Education to the municipality in which schools are located. This significantly widened the gap in terms of the quality of public education versus private (Puga, 2010; Torche, 2005). The richer municipalities distribute more resources to their schools in comparison to the poorer municipalities. Furthermore, this implies incorporating the private sector as one of the providers of subsidized private education, where the state provides a subsidy per student, promoting competition among educational establishments at the level of attraction, retention, and performance (Larrañaga, 1995).

In the 1990s, on the last day of the military dictatorship, the LOCE was established (Falabella et al., 2015). According to this law, complete freedom is granted to establishments to educate without basic regulatory measures. In this sense, education under private administration, financed with public money, may be entitled to generate profit (Montt et al., 2006). There lies the beginning of "market education." The following decade was marked by a series of reforms such as the PSU (university selection test), which restricted even further students' access to better higher education institutions (Koljatic & Silva, 2010). Students at the lower echelon of the education system found themselves at a greater disadvantage since reasoning was replaced by a series of structured tests in different subjects, such as language, mathematics, science, history, and the social sciences. Only a minimum compulsory content is prescribed during secondary education. The schools with better teachers, better funding, and better infrastructure are likely to see their students succeed. This comes to undermine the most vulnerable groups' fair access to university, where academic subjects are partially taught (Koljatic & Silva, 2010).

The 2000s marked the beginning of decades of revolt, beginning with the 2006 Penguin Revolution. This first massive uprising by Chilean secondary school students demanded the right to free and quality education. This was the long overdue response to Chilean privatized education (Falabella et al., 2015; Garretón, 2007; Somma, 2012), and until 2019, was considered the largest protest in the country's history. The *pingüinos* grouped more than a million students who sought the repeal of the LOCE, the end of the *municipalization* and privatization of schools, and the doing away with paying registration fees for taking the PSU (Millaleo, 2011; Vogler, 2006). This battle culminated in 2009 with the establishment of the LGE. This new law maintains educational commoditization, but creates important modifications in the admission processes, curriculum, and accreditation of educational establishments. Establishments were now evaluated and accredited based on their students' levels of performance, which might face closure or suspension if these deliver unsatisfactory results. The state becomes arbiter and evaluator of the "market education" (Falabella et al., 2015). The 2011 protests caught the world's attention, when the CONFECh (Confederation of Chilean students) demanded free education, but also opposed the government's prospects to construct five dams in native land with the HydroAysen project (Zibechi, 2012). The student protests unleashed a social movement that defied privatization and joined forces with social organizations that ranged from environmentalists to unions, but also included common folks. These protests sought substantial educational, economic, social, and political reforms, something that was recently manifested in 2019.

The *30 Pesos Revolution* and the PSU 2020 Boycott

The high-school students' movement continues to be the most recent demonstration of discontent and disapproval of a system that generates deep crevices among the country's population. Precariousness, insecurity, the changing and elimination of curricular subjects, and gaps in funding have driven protesters to demand a real change that would benefit those most in need. These demonstrations are *political events* that rightfully transgress suffocating and oppressive policies. As mentioned earlier, economic inequality continues to persistently grow, with the population still living under the poverty line, that is, with a minimum level of income deemed adequate to survive, the ridiculous sum of 320.500 Pesos a month ($ 415–420).

The *30 Pesos Revolution* began in response to an increase of 30 Pesos (equivalent to $0.04) in the ticket price for the public transportation system in Santiago. This increase took effect on October 6th, 2019. The overall reaction to this measure gave hundreds of high-school students the incentive to organize a mass sit-in at metro stations and evade paying for their tickets (Baeza, 2019). The *evasión massiva* (massive evasion) in Santiago's metro stations caused the shutdown of the capital's entire underground transportation system. In addition, the event brought with it numerous clashes between the protesters and the militarized police (*carabineros*), which have become increasingly violent across the country ever since. To this end, president Piñera established, on Saturday, October 19th, 2019, a state of emergency and curfew in Santiago. Far from appeasing the situation in the capital, protests and demonstrations spread to five other regions of the country and, by October 23rd, a state of emergency had been declared in 15 of the 16 regional capitals. The declaration of a curfew was highly significant, as it was the first time since returning to democracy that it had been declared—this time for reasons of civil disorder. The state of emergency was widely used during the military dictatorship of 1973–1990, rekindling the wounds of a dictatorship that is ever present in the Chilean unconscious.

Again, the large gaps that Chile's education portrays are deep and have been ongoing for more than 40 years. The flipside to this is that such inequality has also driven high-school students to become the main drivers of each protest against Chile's neoliberal system and petrified governments. The students have also stood in solidarity with a variety of groups, like the constantly harassed native Mapuches. The students as the vanguards and drivers of protests have demonstrated that these new social movements are not solely focused on education, but that the objectives of emancipation are common goals. The taking of the emblematic *Plaza Italia* by this new populist mass marks today a new Chile. The Chilean flag, waved second to the Mapuche flag, the *Wenufoye*, symbolizes that the struggle begins by liberating those who have historically suffered most from oppression. This spark of optimism is what remains undefeated. These new protests mark a new moment, emerging from the ruins of a broken system. As Victor Orellana (2019) maintains, "thanks to the ongoing protest movement in Chile, the legitimacy of the country's neoliberal model is currently on trial—reason enough to feel hopeful". As Orellana (2019) states, it is the emergence of a new people, because

> For the first time, society sees its own image reflected in the protests. There is an "us"—all those who make a living from their labor, be it professional or unskilled—and a "them"—the political class, the military, and the rentier business class.

Neoliberalism's hegemonic dominance is currently being contested and, with COVID-19, economic conditions have further deteriorated. Students and the people continue to demonstrate at the now renamed *Plaza Dignidad* (formerly *Plaza Italia*), for the struggle continues until demands are met.

Conclusions: Resistance and Praxis in Public Education

The Chilean student movement portrays the resistance and struggle against the overarching inequality of the country. This movement is validated and supported by the people, and while it has no leader, it certainly has concrete demands. The student resistance movement arose from exclusion, from children feeling marginalized in a system that continuously disregards them. Today, Chilean students are the ones putting the entire neoliberal system on trial. They will no longer accept being subordinated and oppressed. The future is theirs to determine, to shape and mold as they wish. Even the younger students are active subjects aware of their choices, the system, and their possibilities.

The Chilean education system is a control device (Peña, 2010). The conscious resistance praxis of students is an example of how the Chilean neoliberal experiment has bruised generations, who are dissatisfied beyond the classroom. The student resistance movement embraces the demands of an entire nation, who will no longer succumb to segregation, discrimination, and blind obedience to power.

References

Allende, S. (1970). *Victory Speech*. Retrieved 03/07 from www.marxists.org/archive/allende/1970/september/victory-speech.htm

Baeza, A. (2019). Instituto Nacional en el Metro Termina con Denuncia en Fiscalía y Medidas de Contención. *La Tercera*. www.latercera.com/nacional/noticia/evasion-masiva-alumnos-del-instituto-nacional-metro-termina-denuncia-fiscalia-medidas-contencion/857409/

Bellei, C., Cabalin, C., & Orellana, V. (2018). The Student Movements to Transform the Chilean Market-Oriented Education System. In R. Cortina & C. Lafuente (Eds.), *Civil Society Organizations in Latin American Education. Case Studies and Perspectives on Advocacy* (pp. 63–84). New York: Routledge. https://doi.org/10.4324/9781315104874

Bellei, C., Contreras, M., Canales, M., & Orellana, V. (2018). The Production of Socioeconomic Segregation in Chilean Education. School Choice, Social Class and Market Dynamics. In X. Bonal & C. Bellei (Eds.), *Understanding School Segregation. Patterns, Causes, and Consequences of Spatial Inequalities in Education*. London: Bloomsbury.

Caputo, O., & Galarce, G. (2011). Chile's Neoliberal Reversion of Salvador Allende's Copper Nationalization. In X. Barra (Ed.), *Neoliberalism's Fractured Showcase: Another Chile is Possible* (pp. 47–71). The Netherlands: BRILL.

Carrasco, A., & Gunter, H. M. (2018). The "Private" in the Privatisation of Schools: The Case of Chile. *Educational Review, 71*(1), 67–80. https://doi.org/10.1080/00131911.2019.1522035

Chile 1964: CIA Covert Support in Frei Election Detailed. (2004, September 27). Retrieved from https://nsarchive2.gwu.edu//news/20040925/index.htm

Cornejo, R., Gonzalez, J., Sanchez, R., Sobarzo, M., & Opech, C. (2011). The Struggle for Education and the Neoliberal Reaction. In X. Barra (Ed.), *Neoliberalism's Fractured Showcase: Another Chile is Possible* (pp. 153–177). The Netherlands: BRILL.

Del Valle, A. (2010). Comparando Regímenes de Bienestar en América Latina. *European Review of Latin American and Caribbean Studies, 88*, 61–76.

Domingo, J., & y Martos, J. M. (2016). Análisis del Discurso Político en España sobre el Fracaso Escolar en Twitter. *Archivos Analíticos de Políticas Educativas, 24*(70), 1–31. https://doi.org/10.14507/epaa.24. 2357

Falabella, A., Seppänen, P., & Raczynski, D. (2015). Growing Tolerance of Pupil Selection: Parental Discourses and Exclusionary Practices in Chile and Finland. In P. Seppänen, A. Carrasco, M. Kalalahti, R. Rinne, & H. Simola (Eds.), *Contrasting Dynamics in Education Politics of Extremes: School Choice in Finland and Chile* (pp. 121–138). Rotterdam: SENSE publishers.

Foucault, M. (2016). *Vigilar y Castigar*. Buenos Aires: Siglo XXI.

Garretón, M. (2007). *Del Postpinochetismo a la Sociedad Democrática. Globalización y Política en el Bicentenario*. Santiago de Chile: Debate.

Giroux, H. A. (2019). *La Guerra del Neoliberalismo Contra la Educación Superior*. Barcelona: Herder.

González-Rey, F., Mitjáns-Martínez, A., & Bezerra, M. (2016). Psicología en la Educación: Implicaciones de la Subjetividad en una Perspectiva Cultural-Histórica. *Revista Puertorriqueña de Psicología, 27*(2), 260–274.

Hernández, M., & Raczynski, D. (2015). School Choice in Chile: From Distinction and Exclusion to the Social Segregation of the School System. *Estudios Pedagógicos, 41*(2), 127–141. https://doi.org/10.4067/S0718-07052015000200008

Howell, K. (2013). *An Introduction to the Philosophy of Methodology*. India: SAGE.

INE. (2020). *Ingreso y Gastos de las Personas*. www.ine.cl/estadisticas/sociales/ingresos-y-gastos
Inzunza, J., Assael, J., Cornejo, R., & Redondo, J. (2019). Public Education and Student Movements: The Chilean Rebellion Under a Neoliberal Experiment. *British Journal of Sociology of Education, 40*(4), 490–506. https://doi.org/10.1080/01425692.2019.1590179
Koljatic, M., & Silva, M. (2010). Algunas Reflexiones a Siete Años de la Implementación de la PSU. *Estudios Públicos, 120*, 1–22.
Larrañaga, O. (1995). Descentralización de la Educación en Chile: Una Evaluación Económica. *Estudios Públicos, 60*, 243–286. www.cepchile.cl/cep/site/docs/20160303/20160303183955/rev60_OLarranaga.pdf
Lay-Lisboa, S., & Montañés, M. (2018). De la Participación Adultocéntrica a la Disidente: La Otra Participación Infantil. *Psicoperspectivas, 17*(2). https://doi.org/10.5027/psicoperspectivas-vol17-issue2fulltext-1176
Lenin, V. I. (1975). Imperialism, the Highest Stage of Capitalism. In R. C. Tucker (Ed.), *The Lenin Anthology* (pp. 204–274). New York: W.W. Norton.
Martínez Aránguiz, N., Aguayo Ormeño, I., Castro Paredes, L., Fernández Lores, G., Goldstein Braunfeld, E., Mardones Galleguillos, F., Muñoz Ortiz, A., & Salinas Berríos, M. (2012). *Retrato de la Desigualdad en Chile* (2nd ed.). Santiago de Chile: Biblioteca del Congreso Nacional. www.bcn.cl/obtienearchivo?id=documentos/10221.1/43431/4/PDF%20Retrato%20de%20la%20Desigualdad%20en%20Chile%20Baja.pdf
Millaleo, S. (2011). La Ciberpolítica de los Movimientos Sociales en Chile: Algunas Reflexiones y Experiencias. *Revista Anales de la Universidad de Chile, 7*(2), 89–104. https://doi.org/10.5354/0717-8883.2011.17301
Montt, P., Elacqua, G., González, P., & Raczynski, D. (2006). *Hacia un Sistema Escolar Descentralizado, Sólido y Fuerte*. Santiago de Chile: MINEDUC.
OCDE. (2017). *Educación en Chile, Evaluaciones de Políticas Nacionales de Educación*. Paris: OECD.
Orellana, V. (2019). *A New People is Born in Chile*. Retrieved 02/11/19 from www.jacobinmag.com/2019/11/chile-protests-frente-amplio-neoliberalism
Pavez, I. (2012). Sociología de la Infancia: Las Niñas y los Niños Como Actores Sociales. *Revista de Sociología, 27*, 81–102. https://doi.org/10.5354/0719-529x.2012.27479
Peña, M. (2010). Towards a Recovery of Subjectivity in the Process of Learning in the School Context: The Question of the Children's Knowledge in the Chilean Primary School. *Estudios Pedagógicos, 36*(2), 195–211.
Peña, M. (2011). Sujeto Político y Vida Pública: Privatización de la Educación en Chile y sus Consecuencias en los Sujetos que se Educan. *Polis, Revista de la Universidad Bolivariana, 10*(30), 199–215. https://doi.org/10.4067/S0718-65682011000300010
Peña, M. (2016). Ellos Contra Nosotros: Un Análisis Crítico de Discurso Desde los Sostenedores Privados y los Niños Segregados en la Educación Chilena. *Polis, Revista Universidad Bolivariana, 15*(45), 385–403. https://doi.org/10.4067/S0718-65682016000300019
Peña, M. (2019). El Análisis Crítico del Discurso en Textos de Políticas Públicas: Lineamientos para una Praxis Investigativa. *La Trama de la Comunicación, 23*(1), 31–46.
Peña, M., & Toledo, C. (2017a). Discursos sobre Clase Social y Meritocracia de Escolares Vulnerables en Chile. *Cadernos de Pesquisa, 47*(164), 496–518. https://doi.org/10.1590/198053143752
Peña, M., & Toledo, C. (2017b). Ser Pobre en el Chile Neoliberal: Estudio Discursivo en una Escuela Vulnerable. *Revista Latinoamericana de Ciencias Sociales, Niñez y Juventud, 15*(1), 207–218. https://doi.org/10.11600/1692715x.1511225012016

Puga, I. (2010). School and Social Stratification in Chile: What is the Role of "Municipalización" and the Subsidized Private Education in the Reproduction of Social Inequalities? *Estudios Pedagógicos, 37*(2), 213–232.

Quijano, A. (2007). Coloniality and Modernity/Rationality. *Cultural Studies of Science Education, 21*(2–3), 168–178. https://doi.org/10.1080/09502380601164353

Rujas Martínez-Novillo, J. (2017). La Construcción del Fracaso Escolar en España. Génesis y Cristalización de un Problema Social. *Papers. Revista de Sociologia, 102*(3), 477–507. https://doi.org/10.5565/rev/papers.2297

Santos, H., & Elacqua, G. (2016). Segregación Socioeconómica Escolar en Chile: Elección de la Escuela por los Padres y un Análisis Contrafactual Teórico. *Revista CEPAL, 119*, 113–148. https://repositorio.cepal.org/handle/11362/40396

Serrano, S., Ponce de León, M., & Renginfo, F. (2012). *Historia de la Educación en Chile (1810–2010)* (Vol. 1). Santiago de Chile: Taurus.

Sisto, V. (2019). Inclusión "a la Chilena": La Inclusión Escolar en un Contexto de Políticas Neoliberales Avanzadas. *Education Policy Analysis Archives, 27*(23). https://doi.org/10.14507/epaa.27.3044

Skidmore, T. E., Smith, P. H., & Green, J. N. (2014). Chile: Repression and Democracy. In *Modern Latin America* (pp. 268–295). Oxford: Oxford University Press.

Somma, N. (2012). The Chilean Student Movement of 2011–2012: Challenging the Marketization of Education. *Interface, 4*(2), 296–309.

Stewart, E., & Roy, A. D. (2014). Subjectification. In T. Teo (Ed.), *Encyclopedia of Critical Psychology* (pp. 1876–1880). New York: Springer. https://doi.org/10.1007/978-1-4614-5583-7

Torche, F. (2005). Privatization Reform and Inequality of Educational Opportunity: The Case of Chile. *Sociology of Education, 78*(4), 316–343.

Torrents, D., Merino, R., Garcia, M., & Valls, O. (2018). El Peso del Origen Social y del Centro Escolar en la Desigualdad de Resultados al Final de la Escuela Obligatoria. *Papers. Revista de Sociologia, 103*(1), 29–50. https://doi.org/10.5565/rev/papers.2300

Verger, A., Bonal, X., & Zancajo, A. (2016). Recontextualización de Políticas y (Cuasi) mercados Educativos. Un Análisis de las Dinámicas de Demanda y Oferta Escolar en Chile. *Education Policy Analysis Archives, 24*(27). https://doi.org/10.14507/epaa.24.2098

Vogler, J. (2006). *Chile: The Rise of the Penguin Revolution*. Upside Down World. Retrieved 21/06 from http://upsidedownworld.org/archives/chile/chile-the-rise-of-the-penguin-revolution/

Wright, C., Maylor, U., & Becker, S. (2016). Young Black Males: Resilience and the Use of Capital to Transform School 'Failure'. *Critical Studies in Education, 57*(1), 21–34. https://doi.org/10.1080/17508487.2016.1117005

Zancajo, A. (2019). Education Markets and Schools' Mechanisms of Exclusion: The Case of Chile. *Education Policy Analysis Archives, 27*(130), 1–37. https://doi.org/10.14507/epaa.27.4318

Zibechi, R. (2012). *Latin America: A New Cycle of Social Struggles*. NACLA.ORG. https://nacla.org/article/latin-america-new-cycle-social-struggles

10
CRITICAL DECONSTRUCTION OF "EAST MEETS WEST"

The Lesson from Hong Kong

Fu Wai

Technical Notes

There are three types of critical psychologies, all of which interact with each other, but sometimes they intersect or exclude one another:

1. Criticizing *psychology* (in terms of epistemology, or praxis, or social and cultural implications)
2. *Psychology* as criticism (in whatever form, positivistic, historical, or psychoanalytic, etc.) regarding important but often overlooked issues, including justice, human rights, cultural preservation, environmental protection, inequality
3. *Criticism* as psychology (in which criticism is based on various perspectives in philosophy, Marxism and critical theories, psychoanalysis, and Indigenous philosophies) to analyze issues relevant to *Homo sapiens*.

Though ancient Indigenous thoughts could be as alienating as any other criticisms in non-positivistic traditions, this chapter is a trespassing between these three versions of critical psychology. The collage of theories, narratives, history, commentaries, and shifting between main text and endnotes aims to provide a fluid deconstruction of the *East meets West* mythology at a time when Hong Kong is undergoing a quantum leap of *The North vs. X*, which has been an irreversible ongoing trend between 2014 and 2019. This piece of writing is a souvenir of the moment when the relic of colonial Hong Kong was brutally replaced by "post"(?)-colonial directives to eliminate itself, yet at the same time in the void blossoms a new reactionary imagery of a new *We* as the opposition of *The North*. In this way, this humble contribution may be relevant to the objective of this collection: praxis in critical psychology.

In most translations of ancient Chinese philosophical propositions, or protest slogans, direct translation – which may be grammatically incorrect in English but nonetheless closer to the original meaning – will be adopted.

Prelude: A Snapshot of Hong Kong

Whether in colonial, or post-1997, Hong Kong, democracy was/is absent here, either in the form of no open seats, less than half of the council seats being up for election (with the remaining seats comprising government officers or appointed representatives), or half of the seats being dominated by *functional constituencies*, which are not in the form of one-person-one-vote but in the form of one-company-one-vote. In order to maintain their prospects, majority companies vote for pro-government parties.

During colonial years (1841–1997), colonials claimed that any substantial change towards full autonomy (for example, universal suffrage) would lead to the undesirable outcome of immediate Chinese invasion. The only formal proposal, Young's proposal for universal suffrage of the Legislative Council and Governor of 1946, was withdrawn by the succeeding Governor Sir Alexander Grantham on the basis of it not receiving support from the British government, local British merchants, and local Chinese groups (Tsang, 2019).

After the handover of Hong Kong sovereignty to Communist China in 1997, the Chinese government claimed that Hong Kong was under a high level of autonomy. Nonetheless, the communist government refused universal suffrage of the chief executive and rejected the idea of opening all legislative council seats for public voting. On August 15, 2014, The National People's Congress of the People's Republic of China announced the decision that the election of the chief executive (counterpart of the governor in colonial days) had to be exclusively decided by the 1200 members of the election committee, and only pro-communist representatives would be included. No universal suffrage would be allowed (The Standing Committee of the National People's Congress on Issues Relating to the Selection of the Chief Executive of the HKSAR by Universal Suffrage and on the Method for Forming the Legislative Council of the HKSAR in the Year 2016, 2014).[1] This eventually led to the 79-day protest (Umbrella Movement) in 2014.

After the Umbrella Movement, conflicts between traditional pro-democracy parties and self-determination groups weakened the bargaining power of pan-democracy parties in Hong Kong. In 2019, Chief Executive Carrie Lam proposed changing existing extradition law to allow direct extradition to China. From this point on various pro-democracy groups joined forces, which led to the formation of the ongoing protest movement since June 12, 2019.

The movement experienced 2 million strong demonstrations, there were 21 attacks in July from aggressors, fighting took place at various Lennon Walls[2] of pro-democracy artworks, there were mysterious cases involving falling and drowning, local and international reporters were injured by police forces, and there was a siege at a university campus. Protesters advocated for forming a *yellow economy circle*, represented by a frog, nicknamed *Pepe for the people*. In the district board election, a local consultancy constitution, with no power to legislate, saw massive gains for pro-democracy groups, for the first time in the history of Hong Kong (Figures 10.1).

Finally, after the outbreak of Covid-19 (previously called "Wuhan coronavirus" in Hong Kong local news), the Communist Central Government suddenly announced, on June 30, 2020, the implementation of the National Security Law, which allowed direct intervention from mainland China in any alleged cases that initiate conflicts between citizens and the government (BBC, 2020). Many countries, including the US and the UK, condemned this decision, for it violates the Joint Declaration of the Government of the United Kingdom of Great Britain and Northern Ireland and the Government of the People's Republic of China on the Question of Hong Kong (1984, hereinafter "Joint Declaration"), and calls for canceling various agreements with Hong Kong that are based on the assumption that Hong Kong is an autonomous zone.

In reaction to the National Security Law's implementation, the pan-democratic parties called for a July preliminary election for the Legislative Council election in September 2020. The results found that self-determination groups, which called for a referendum on the independence of Hong Kong, gained the majority of votes. The mottos of these groups, *Hong Kong, not China* and *Liberate Hong Kong, revolution now*, were first raised by Edward Leung Tin-Kei, the leader of Hong Kong Indigenous – the most prominent advocacy group for suffrage and independence, established in 2016.

On July 30, 2020, the Hong Kong government disqualified 12 candidates for their anti-National Security Law position. On the next day, the government

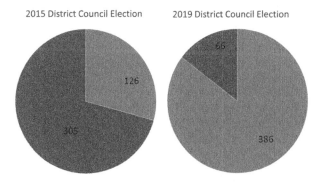

FIGURE 10.1 (a, b) Seats in the district council dominated by pro-government parties (305 & 66) and pan-democratic groups (126 & 386). (a) The result of the 2015 election, which was a year after the Umbrella Movement; (b) the result of the 2019 election amidst the ongoing Anti-Extradition Movement

even announced a one-year deferment of the election for the legislative council, claiming that this was an essential preventive measure in the context of Covid-19 (BBC, 2020).

Separtition

For a long time, the people of Hong Kong could be regarded as undergoing what Jacques Lacan (2017), in *Seminar X, L'angoisse, 1962–1963*, described as separtition: "not separation but partition on the inside" (p. 237). For Lacan (2017), "separtition is what finds itself inscribed right back at the origin" (p. 237).

In the case of Hong Kong, the origin of separtition was not the time of January 26, 1841, when the British army launched Hong Kong Island, but in the 1967 leftist riot when individuals needed to decide if they were communist Chinese or not. The "not" gradually developed into the statement: "we are Chinese, but not communist Chinese because we live in Hong Kong," which finally became part of the *East meets West* discourse (Zhu, 1998).

The second otherness originates, not on July 1, 1997, when the red flag replaced the flag of the Royal Colony with Bauhinia and when Hong Kong was renamed *Hong Kong Special Administrative Region* (SAR), but on the dawn of June 4, 1989, when the Tiananmen Massacre reminded the Hong Kong people that they can either turn a blind eye to it with "the desire not to see" (Lacan, 2017, p. 332), or realize that recolonization by *the North* will not be a better alternative to colonial rule.

The final point of demarcation was June 12, 2019, when society was not only divided by pro-communist and anti-communist groups, but more profoundly divided by those who wanted to keep their dream of old Hong Kong, and those who wanted to deconstruct not only such a dream, but also the concept of a seemingly existing Hong Kong SAR in the world's perception. This is now what activists are calling *Lam chau* or laam5-2 caau2 (攬炒) in Hong Kong Cantonese dialect: if we burn, you burn with us.

The Creation of the *East meets West* mythology

The communist government always condemned the Hong Kong people for their "nostalgic remembrance of British colonial days," and claimed that "it was the 1967 Communist revolt that pressured the British Colonial Government to improve the Hong Kong people's life"; therefore, these articles usually ended with the question: "why, when the British Colonial Government only granted you a second tier citizenship, you still love your enemy, but not your mother country?" (Taikungpao, 2017).

Fermi Wong (2017), founder of Hong Kong Unison, provided a vivid answer: "compare two evils, at least one is a modernized country with democracy, but another one is a place of totalitarianism and brutality. That is why people feel alienated". She explained that it was not a kind of protest against Chinese identity, but sadly that the Communist Party hijacks Chinese identity "just like a rapist said why don't you love me, and feel jealous that I love other one, claiming that 'you are my daughter, you must love me'."

It was true that, during colonist years, before 1967, the situation in Hong Kong was not good. Standards that were not allowed in the UK (e.g., bribery, drug trafficking, and poor hygiene) were all happening in colonial Hong Kong. It is also true that Hong Kong was having high income inequality, which persists to this day, for Hong Kong still has one of the highest Gini coefficients of income inequality in the world. According to the official report of the Gini index, the Hong Kong situation is the worst among Asian countries (Hong Kong Census and Statistics Department, 2017). With a score of 0.539 (cf. the Philippines' 0.444, which is the second worst in Asia), Hong Kong has one of the highest income inequality scores in Organisation for Economic Co-operation and Development (OECD) regions (Oxfam, 2019).

Although there was no official policy of segregation in colonial days, as English was the only official language until 1974, there were huge differences in terms of access to education and opportunity. The majority of refugees, who came from China, regarded Hong Kong as merely a place of asylum during wartime (Faure, 1997).

The *East meets West* mythology was created, and, in large part, completed during Governor Murray MacLehose's term (1971–1982). The strategy to conceal the crisis, which would be disclosed in 1984, was to turn the city inside out by transforming the old drug-fueled and bribery-breeding ground (old Hong Kong) into a modernized metropolis. The strategies MacLehose adopted were a big gamble: to let the already-swollen city become more swollen, so that the desire to buy an apartment comes to be ethically mandatory.

The *Touch-Based Policy*, which allowed illegal refugees to have the right to stay in Hong Kong, increased the population by 600,000 during its six years of implementation (1974–1980) (Faure, 1997). Major changes were going on: building public housing for rent and for sale, allowing local developers to construct the New Towns, building a subway system, completing the cross-harbor tunnel, building the Hong Kong Coliseum and various town halls, and establishing various country parks and mountain trails. Therefore, even to this day, the Hong Kong colonial flag is still adopted as a symbol of resistance to the Hong Kong SAR government, which is seen as a puppet of mainland China (BBC Chinese, 2019, July 5).

The changes in civil works were accompanied with cultural changes that fostered a local Hong Kong identity. For example, the Chinese language was granted official status alongside English and the dungeon in Kowloon Walled City was removed, although citizens are still allowed to live inside the area (Figure 10.2). During colonial days, Kowloon Walled City remained a dissimulated stain on Hong Kong since it is a miniature of Hong Kong that is totally at odds with *East meets West* romanticism. Therefore, it was determined that the Kowloon Walled

FIGURE 10.2 (a) A snapshot of Kwong Ming Street in Kowloon Walled City after the 1974 raid of the heroin dungeons. Kwong Ming, or light, means candlelight used for "chasing the dragon" (taking heroin). (Courtesy of Ian Lambo) (b) Panoramic view of Kowloon Walled City. At least 14,639 households (Hong Kong Legislative Council, 1993, document number H931117) lived in the 0.026-km² area (about the size of two standard football fields). (Courtesy of Ian Lambo) (c) Kowloon Walled City was demolished in 1991 and turned into a park. (Courtesy of the author)

City would be demolished in 1991, not long before the handover of sovereignty to China.

The status of Kowloon Walled City in the British government's eyes is the same as how Hong Kong is viewed by the Chinese Government. The keyword, in both cases, is *the dirt*[3] or, in Sophocles's language, πίνος. The new city identity was consolidated with the establishment of the Independent Committee Against Corruption. Also, the Chinese language, for the first time, was recognized as an official language alongside English. The Governor also organized two large-scale Hong Kong Festivals (in 1971 and 1973), and even Queen Elizabeth II came to visit Hong Kong in 1975 (Faure, 1997). Most importantly, during MacLehose's time, Hong Kong was lucky enough to have Bruce Lee as an internationally

FIGURE 10.3 (a) The Lion Rock, a location in Hong Kong, bears the symbolic meaning of "Lion Rock Spirit," which is presented in government propaganda and TV programs. Therefore, protestors were determined to redefine "Lion Rock Spirit" as a symbol of resistance. (Courtesy of the author) (b) The Lion Rock is a symbol of resistance; protestors lifted an 80-kg statue of a protester taking a flag bearing the slogan: "Liberate Hong Kong, the revolution of our times," which was coined by Edward Leung Tin-Kei, a young leader of the local political group Hong Kong Indigenous. (Courtesy of Lady Liberty (event organizer), posted on LIHKG for public sharing)

famous ambassador of Kung-Fu (Chinese martial arts) – to demonstrate how *the East* could cross over with *the West*. In the local scene, the *Below the Lion Rock* film programs (Radio and Television of Hong Kong, since 1972) promoted the discourse of work hard, leave public housing, and buy a new apartment (Zhu, 1998).[4] The theme song, *Below the Lion Rock*,[5] includes this line: "citizens of Hong Kong, put down our differences, live in harmony below the Lion Rock, become a living legend." The song is utilized by the government when they want to present a vision of *harmony* for the general public (Figure 10.3), and as a theme song for anti-Covid-19 campaigns, as always.

The guiding principle of these policies, as admitted by the Secretary for Home Affairs Mr. Denis Bray (Bray, 1973), was to give up the expectation of a paternalistic government and build a society on the move. The establishment of academic psychology is also part of the policy of creating the *East meets West* mythology.

The Department of Psychology was established in 1968, after the Hong Kong Government commissioned a report from Professor R.C. Tress, Dean of Faculty of Social Sciences, University of Bristol, to set up the Faculty of Social Sciences to investigate ways to cope with social unrest (Mellor, 1981). The first Chair and Head of the Department of Psychology was an Australian cross-cultural psychologist by the name of John Dawson. He established the Hong Kong Psychological Society in 1968, planned for the first Master's degree program in clinical psychology in 1971 (so graduates from the first cohort could get the through train), and facilitated the formation of the International Association of Cross-Cultural Psychology in August of 1972, which was inaugurated at the University of Hong Kong (Blowers, 1987). Chinese psychologists in Hong Kong and Taiwan later criticized his vision of cross-cultural psychology, and they adopted Indigenous psychology as a reaction against it.

The idea of Indigenous psychology could be traced back to Virgilio Gaspar Enriquez (1942–1994), a psychologist in the Philippines, who utilized Indigenous ideas and psychological constructs as a way of counteracting neocolonial forms of academic hegemony (Enriquez, 1992; Ho, 1998). The Hong Kong psychology field was also connected to the Republic of China (in Taiwan), which joined forces with leading figures, like Yang Kuo-Shu (1932–2018) and Hwang Kwang-Kuo, who confronted the Western vision of cross-cultural psychology with Indigenous psychology, though Yang was more concerned about modifying positivistic methodology while Hwang was more concerned about challenging the ideology behind positivism in mainstream psychology (see Hwang, 2005a). In this way, Hong Kong contributes to *East meets West* in academia by fueling logical positivism with Indigenous psychology. The most common way of fusion is to adopt methodologies from logical positivism but with a mixed bag of constructs from ancient Chinese philosophy. Sadly, during this process, the original idea of liberation was largely reduced in the subsequent development of Indigenous psychology (particularly in the Asian context) (Hwang, 2005b). This is somewhat a disappointment for Virgilio Gaspar Enriquez's original idea that Indigenous thinking should be the vital force in decolonizing psychology in its epistemological ground. Here, we will try to explore this possibility with an ancient philosophical framework from Gongsun Longzi (c. 325–250 BCE).

White Horse is Not Horse[6]

While the *Hong Kong not China*[7] proposition was abhorred by the Chinese Communist Party and the Government of the People's Republic of China, this is the *sine qua non* of why Hong Kong could be regarded as an *independent entity* that qualified for a mutual tax arrangement, a mutual extradition agreement, and membership of various international organizations such as OECD and Asia Pacific Economic Cooperation (APEC), and having a separate entity in the Olympic Games and other major sports events. The differences between Hong Kong and other cities could also be found in the name *Hong Kong SAR*, which was regarded as having the same status as *Macau SAR*, but nonetheless, in comparison to Macau, which is treated internationally much less differently, Hong Kong was at least *different* from mainland China in the West's consciousness. Therefore, the recent implementation of the National Security Law in Hong Kong was like the dropping of a bomb that shocked the world.

Interestingly, this could substantiate one of the most important propositions in the ancient Chinese history of ideas: Gongsun Long's 'White horse is not horse' (see *Gongsun Longzi*, Chapter 1: 'White Horse'). Gongsun Long was the leader of the School of Names in the warring-states era (c. 475–221 BCE). *Gongsun Longzi*, his major work, of which only six chapters out of the original 14 chapters remain today, covers five important propositions, including white horse is not horse;

everything is a signifier that signifies beyond signified; there is no one in two; hardiness, color, and stone are three different aspects; and language shapes reality.

Traditional understanding of the *white horse is not horse* proposition is based on set theories demonstrated using Venn diagrams (e.g., Fung Yu-lan; see Fung, 1948). However, Chad Hensen (2007) has challenged this, arguing that such an understanding overlooks that in the whole chapter the idea of natural categories was attacked by Gongsun Long. The statement is not about natural category. The major idea from Gongsun Long was a signifier of demarcation (*you-qu*, "distinction"). The proposition is about the concept of Otherness, and Otherness arises when one abandons the real issue by treating it as if it is a natural, or mandatory, category, or as if it is a logical, ethical, or legal problem. A manifestation of the proposition can be found in current social movements (e.g., Black Lives Matter), and similarly in the *Hong Kong not China* slogan. We should not deal with it from the perspective of *part–whole* and use *the whole* to enmesh within it *the part*; on the contrary, the idea is that Otherness could be found in this demarcation line (–) between the part and the whole.

Another important contribution from Gongsun Long to the situation of Hong Kong is *there is no one in two*. This proposition included Gongsun Long's argument that, while criteria to include different elements in a category could be random, once a schism occurs the pursuit of *commonality* (one) in the *separated polarity* (two) is irrelevant because whatever the illustration of such a commonality may be, it simply overlooks the Otherness that is constructed between each other. Ultimate change would only come after the enmeshment of polarity (not the co-existence of polarity) to allow for a new entity.

In this sense, as *China–Hong Kong* is now becoming *two*, talking about *oneness* is not meaningful any more, unless both parties could emerge into a new entity that gives up construal of *China* and *Hong Kong*. The schism is bilateral. On the one hand, in official Chinese orthodoxy, the history of colonialism is dirt, πινος, something to be washed with a "happily ever after" discourse that "one is doing better now than in the colonial days" (Xinhua Press, 2017, June 28). Sadly, what is untold is that the agreement of "one country, two systems" is based on the signing of a fragile contract with the stated end-date of June 30, 2047, but before that, nothing, so just *viva la vida*.

On the Hong Kong side, it is a matter of maintaining its identity by preserving its originality, and refusing to think and behave in a *Chinese* way.

The origin of this polarity should not be understood as simply China vs. Hong Kong, but as more deeply rooted in history, *the North vs. the South*. Later *the South* is replaced, first, by *X* (unknown), then, by *We*. This is far beyond the realm of mainstream psychology and could only be understood from a critical perspective.

From *East meets West* to *North vs. South*

Throughout Chinese history, the battle between *the North* (the barbarian) and *the South* (the civilized who lacks military strength) went as far as the Jin Dynasty (266–420 CE), Southern–Northern Dynasties (420–589 CE), Song Dynasty

(960–1279 CE), Ming Dynasty (1368–1644 CE), and Republican China (1911–1949 CE) (Huang, 1988). *North vs. South* is also part of the post-1997 discourse, when Horace Chin Wan-kan advocated the emergence of a "new Hong Kong identity." In *On the Hong Kong City State* (Chin, 2011), he suggested that Hong Kong is the gate-holder of ancient pagan culture of Guangdong province, which is under threat from Northern rule. Therefore, he wrote about his idea of Hong Kong qua *city state* that could use its economic position as the entrepôt to negotiate with China and provide *a real contract* that allows the continuation of its city state status.

The book condemned the problem of "people from the North," which was at times full of racism, but it also touched on the fact of re-colonization, or, more precisely, *hypercolonization*.[8] Colonization is admitted by the UK, and the Whig history on the "Joint Declaration" and the "East meets West" success story could be regarded as a nostalgia for things past. Yet in the "post"-colonial era (i.e., post-1997), the form of power structure has not changed: Hong Kong people cannot affect the mainland's decision, and it is not even possible to join the Communist Party as it does not exist in Hong Kong. Now the dilation (εκτασία), or more accurately, ectasia of Hong Kong is not about the influx of asylum seekers, but customers and consumers from the North who bought everything, including property. The Hong Kong people perceived that their living conditions were under "total control" due to the changing economic structure, and the status quo that the "North" is ruling, which is officially mandated by the Hong Kong people's love and subduing. Therefore, the new colonialism, which is executed in the form of its denial, apparent absence, and aims at total domination, is the characteristic of *hypercolonialism*. This sentiment came across in the contemporary social movement (e.g., the anti-national education movement in 2012), and it is in this context that Chin's *On the Hong Kong City State* accumulated resonance with a current fan base, one of whom is Edward Leung Tin-Kei, who became the leader of the self-determination group that later abandoned Chin's idea in pursuit of a self-determination referendum on deciding Hong Kong's fate.

Though criticized by pan-democratic parties as having his head in the clouds, the imagination of Hong Kong as a bearer of Southern culture was despised even among separation activists. The idea of Hong Kong as a city state with equal status within the mainland Chinese government initiated the spark of the self-determination movement, which never took off in Hong Kong except in a little-known attempt by Ma Man-fai (1905–1994), who called for treating Hong Kong as a British protectorate (Tsang, 2019). However, Chin's city state was under the assumption that a contract with the Chinese government is reliable, which was soon liquidized in 2014 as the Chinese government – or, to be precise, it was officially a decision by The Standing Committee of the National People's Congress (NPCSC) – claimed that universal suffrage of the Chief Executive was not liable to the Basic Law, which could only allow for the election of the Chief Executive within the 1200-member "selection committee" whose membership is highly selective. As a form of public repercussion, the North vs. South discourse soon evolved into North vs. X, with X being something unclear (self-determination), an unknown identity yet to develop at that time. This would soon be realized in the 2019 outbreak of the anti-extradition movement, which is a movement against *the Name-of-the-Grandfather*.

The Name-of-the-Grandfather

In Hong Kong, *the North*, the Chinese government, is always called the *Grandfather* (by both pro-government parties and pan-democratic groups). No one has ever had direct access to what is called the Grandfather (President) but everyone interprets and conjectures about the will of the President as a warning to the Hong Kong people to follow orders. The *Name-of-the-Grandfather* is nowhere and everywhere.

The major difference between Lacan's *Name-of-the-Father* (*nom-du-père*) and the Name-of-the-Grandfather (*nom-du-grand-père*) is that the former bears no name – the name is registered in the unconscious, and is even unrecognizable in the form of a voice (*voix*), so that what we inhibit, we distinguish and identify (Lacan & Miller, 1993).

The Name-of-the-Grandfather is different. Grandfather is a euphemism for the Emperor in different dynasties (note: the term still applies in the case of the *de facto* ruler Empress Dowager Cixi in late Qing dynasty, who was called *Lao Foye*, Buddha Grandfather). The castrated eunuch brought the order of the emperor somewhere in the name of "Grandfather," as if it were a powerful and real order, but actually no one knows if the order was real or not, and no one really understood it since the Emperor's instructions were usually ambiguous and open to fabricated interpretation. However, the Name-of-the-Grandfather is real and conscious, for it is not *the father* that makes the name powerful, but the situation that *the name* is already the father. This person does not supervise all things, nor do most people have access to *this person*. The person behind the name must make individuals feel that they are operating an all-inclusive panopticism along with a method of mocking ubiquity and random prosecutions (e.g., Reign of Terror). Therefore, the father of father is Grand, as in *the Grand Other*, who is always linked to grandiosity. This goes beyond what Hannah Arendt described in *The Origins of Totalitarianism* as *totaler Herrschaft* or total dominance (Arendt, 1951). Reign of Terror, for sure it is, but ideology is not necessary. Only the Name-of-the-Grandfather suffices.

The difference between the Name-of-the-Father and the Name-of-the-Grandfather could be found between the Common Law System (in Colonial Hong Kong) and the Basic Law. The former is black and white, with as little room for interpretation as possible, so this rule is a "yes or no," and "yes" must be a total "yes." For the Basic Law, this "yes/no" question is not a question of "yes/no" but a matter of degree. For example, with freedom of publishing, there is "some freedom" until it has been dropped to zero (i.e., you still have the right to publish "something," such as pro-national propaganda, which goes to show that you "have" the right to publish). The same applies to freedom of speech, freedom of organizing political parties, freedom of religion, and freedom of access to information, which are all reducible to a gray zone of interpretation through the lens of the Name-of-the-Grandfather.

Just as in the case of the National Security Law (implemented on June 30, 2020), the only reference to the Basic Law are *Articles 158, 159,* and *160*. *Article 158* stated that the NPCSC has the right to interpret the Basic Law. *Article 159* stated that NPCSC has the right to amend, revise, and introduce new articles as annexes and instruments to the Basic Law. *Article 160* stated that:

> Documents, certificates, contracts, and rights and obligations valid under the laws previously in force in Hong Kong shall continue to be valid and be recognized and protected by the Hong Kong Special Administrative Region, *provided that they do not contravene this Law*. (emphasis added)

In fact, even the Department of Justice of Hong Kong government openly stated on June 14, 2020, "it would be unrealistic to expect common law system could be applied to National Security Law as this is not the practice of legal system of Chinese Government" (Department of Justice HKSAR, 2020). In this way the final mask of *East meets West* mythology – the Common Law system – was taken off.

Before the announcement of the National Security Law, the world was unaware that *Hong Kong* was no longer the entity promised in the *Joint Declaration*. Maybe not due to a lack of awareness, but as a result of an inhibition rooted in the desire not to see, which was accompanied by misrecognition and wishful thinking that the international declaration would be followed by a totalitarian regime, and that this regime would keep on promoting the Common Law system (i.e., the rule of/by law) and its various freedoms (of speech, of information, of belief, of resentment, etc.). The brutal reality is, on June 30, 2017, the communist government openly announced that the *Joint Declaration* is just an obsolete "historical document" that "did not have any rights to restrict the Central Chinese Government over the guidance of Hong Kong affairs" (BBC Chinese 2020). This is exactly what the self-determination groups are now aiming at: to tell the world that their *fantasmatic* Hong Kong no longer exists; therefore, there is no need to provide any benefits to Hong Kong (since it is actually benefiting China), which was formerly established on the assumption of *Hong Kong not China*.

Criticizing Psychological Research in Hong Kong

Since 2014, there have been many so-called psychological studies that framed social movements as "correlating with poor mental health, stress, anxiety, depression, suicide cases, and poor family relationship" (e.g., Hou et al. 2015; Ni et al.

2020).⁹ The message is simple: social movements are not healthy. One should, therefore, restore harmony. They call for *oneness* in the parties involved in the *social cleavage*, and they warn that anger is a threat, if not a sin, to mental health and harmonic relationships. The sources of pain (e.g., inequality, injustice, brutality, hopelessness, and, more importantly, the Name-of-the-Grandfather, of course) have never been mentioned in these so-called value-free academic studies.

On August 28, 2020, The Hong Kong Psychological Society organized an interdisciplinary press conference, which included the Hong Kong Association of Heads of Secondary Schools (HKAHSS), The Hong Kong Council of Social Services (HKCSS), and the Division of Clinical Psychology in the Hong Kong Psychological Society (DCP-HKPS) (Hong Kong Psychological Society, 2019). They called for listening to students' voices and emotional needs, watching out for psychological or mental health, yet at the same time, "by all means to prevent politics to enter the school campus." In this sense, psychology became a service that helped the students by "not letting politics enter the campus." In this tame press release, of course, the sources of emotional upheaval (i.e., injustice, inequality, etc.) are not disclosed. Students were regarded as lacking political subjectivity and are, consequently, susceptible of being manipulated and brainwashed by outside political parties.

At the same time, social psychology in the local institutions of Hong Kong received funding to create a mirage of post-colonial Hong Kong by swiftly transferring *Hong Kong identification* (pre-1997-funded projects) to theme-based projects (e.g., youth identity) that blame the crisis on the blockage of upward mobility, with the "ultimate solution" being house ownership. Since these strategies are clichéd, there are some new strategies to try to help the government to make some excuses. For example, Shek (2020) claims that the perceived lack of upward mobility, lack of identification with Chinese nationality, economic stress, and mental illness are a "context of social unrest." Then he goes on to suggest that lack of "national education" is the root of all problems. In the article, he attempts to make some suggestions, for example:

> The reasoning is that by highlighting the message that the "one country, two systems" arrangement does not work, the President of Taiwan (Tsai Ing Wen) would get more support in the presidential election in 2020. Although these conspiracy conjectures make sense on the surface, we need empirical evidence that cannot be easily substantiated.
>
> *(Shek, 2020, p. 622)*

On the "alleged" police violence, which was undeniable in the live broadcasts during the 2019 social movement, he wrote:

> On the other hand, it should be noted that "innocence before proven guilty" is the cornerstone of the Common Law and the establishment of police

violence and brutality requires evidence beyond reasonable doubt. Besides, objectivity of some videos uploaded to the Internet is not clear.

(Shek, 2020, p. 628)

Shek (2020) suggests "trust of the central government," "national identity," and "political wellbeing" are the solutions to the "crisis on the quality of life and wellbeing" (Shek, 2020, pp. 631–632). The warts-and-all attitude presented in this article indicated the bankruptcy of value-free objectivism and professionalism.

All of these research reports ignored the fact that, as Martín-Baró suggests, it is abnormal to react normally to abnormality. Abnormality, rooted in oppression, should not be addressed as a mental health issue in disguise. Liberation psychologists' primary role is to, at least, facilitate the process of debunking the ideology of normality transmitted in state propaganda (Martín-Baró, 1994).

The limitation of mainstream psychology lies in its ignorance of Gongsun Long's proposition: *There is no one in two*. One could be subdued by the North and live in the fantasy of being linked to an almighty nation that brought forth an unsusceptible bright future, or choose to burst such a fantasy by counteracting the North with X – the micro-politics that gives X a new *We*: the Pepe.

Epilogue: History and Psychology of the Frog

The history of the *Frog* mentioned in the following section may mark the beginning of this irreversible psychological process. The birth of the *Frog*, a key feature of the Hong Kong democracy movement, is one of the most important psychological phenomena in the history of Hong Kong that has never been addressed properly by academic psychologists.

In 2005, Matt Furie created Pepe the Frog, and it was frequently adopted as a widely circulated Internet meme. The far right adopted it as a racist symbol, and this led to the "mercy-killing" of Pepe by Matt Furie in 2017. Yet, in 2019, Pepe was resurrected and given new meaning. The Frog is the shape of the Hong Kong Island, and it is also the main character of the boiling frog fable.

The members of LIHKG[10] even sent copies of Pepe artworks to Matt Furie for approval of usage, and Matt reflected that he was very happy that Pepe was resurrected as a symbol of Hong Kong democracy (LIHKG, 2019). The Frog became frequently adopted in protest art (Figures 10.4).

In July of 2019, the Frog was given a new meaning. In LIHKG discussion groups, there were calls to organize the *yellow economy circle* by encouraging restaurants and shops to openly display protest art: mostly significantly, Pepe the Frog, but also Peggie. Identifying with Peggie exhibits the Hong Kong people's dark sense of humor, wherein previously we were *the Hong Kong Pig* (eating and sleeping, aloof to forthcoming execution), which became enlightened in the Year of the Pig (2019) following the Chinese Zodiac. The hidden masterminds behind Pepe and Peggie, who may or may not include psychologists, are

"East Meets West" 127

FIGURE 10.4 (a) The Frog on Lennon Wall in a tunnel in Shek-Lei public estate, Hong Kong. From the beginning of the civic movement in Hong Kong, Pepe the Frog suddenly appeared as the symbol of the movement, and is often represented on Lennon Wall, named by Hong Kong protesters for pop-up displays of pro-democratic artworks. (Courtesy of a confidential author; photo for public sharing posted at https://lihkg.com/thread/1646838/page/1). (b) Mocking the first of May Golden Week (the practice in Mainland China of having one week of holiday between May 1 and 8), which is a week of shopping sprees in Mainland China. The "Pepe" and "Piggy" stickers, which identify the "yellow economy circle," were given to restaurants and shops that supported the social movement. (Courtesy of confidential author; photo in pop-up Instagram account Ngyatwongkamchow (now defunct) for public sharing)

contributing to the discussion on how to mobilize micro-politics to debunk the Name-of-the-Grandfather.

The opposition not only considers Pepe the Frog a bad joke, they also despise its ugliness. Yet this is exactly the sense of humor reflected in the resistance and the real resilience that brings the *We* identity against *the North*. It is, by now, much more than a question of sovereignty, but a question of subjectivity. The seemingly fragile creatures, as a rule of nature, are also the most imaginative. The yellow economy zone now has more than 4383 shops and restaurants, which can potentially generate an annual revenue of $1.2 billion USD (Business Week Talks, 2020). The movement did not die out but, in fact, it is blossoming.

Unknown to the majority of people in Hong Kong, Nobel Laureate Mo Yan, a mainland Chinese writer, wrote about the *Frog* (Mo, 2009/2014): a story of coercive sterilization, a policy that is still enforced in rural China yet largely abandoned in large cities under the name of the one child policy.[11] People were in a muddied state of repressed anger due to losing fertility, but they found relief in snitching on those who are *illegally* pregnant. In the novel, the Frog represents this dream that human beings could reproduce through external fertilization in order for them to be free from controlled sexuality. At the same time, the Frog is the mascot of a factory that trades illegally in surrogate mothers and artificial insemination to produce new children for sale.

Without any reference to Slavoj Žižek, Mo Yan's *Frog* represents a vivid image of Žižek's verdict: *The Big Other is obscene* (Žižek, Santner & Reinhard, 2005). Frog (pronounced as *wa* in Mandarin), in Mo Yan's novel, is a homonym and metonym of baby (also pronounced as *wa* in Mandarin, but not a common usage in Cantonese, the dialect adopted in Hong Kong). This is a stark depiction of how the invisible (but omnipresent) Big Other is regulating the desire of the population through birth control.

The difference between the joyful Pepe and Mo Yan's grotesque and repressive frogs illustrates the logic of *there is no one in two*, which is evident in the new discourse of *North vs. We*, and should be of major interest to future critical psychologists. All of this begins with Sigmund Freud's motto: "*Wo Es war, soll Ich werden*" (wherever the "Other" is, the "I" will return) (Freud, 1933/1949, p. 86) – or, in Hong Kong's context: *Where It (Pepe) was, I must come into being.*

Acknowledgment

This chapter is dedicated to all the people of Hong Kong who lost their lives, freedom, prospect, and dignity, in a known or unknown manner, to the new visionaries, and to all those in different parts of the world who are in a similar situation.

Notes

1 Lengthy titles and sentences are a major linguistic feature of the Chinese government's official announcement. This structure is very common in the Chinese legal system, which creates room for interpretation that is not allowed in the common-law system since it emphasizes precision.
2 Lennon Wall (which firstly originated in Prague to memorialize the murder of John Lennon, later became a wall on which to stick home-made political drawings).
3 The dirt, in Sophocles' *Oedipus at Colonus*, is πίνος:

> ὃν ξένης ἐπὶ χθονὸς
> σὺν σφῷν ἐφηύρηκ' ἐνθάδ' ἐκβεβλημένον
> ἐσθῆτι σὺν τοιᾷδε, τῆς ὁ δυσφιλὴς
> γέρων γέροντι συγκατῴκηκεν πίνος
> πλευρὰν μαραίνων, κρατὶ δ' ὀμματοστερεῖ
> κόμη δι' αὔρας ἀκτένιστος ᾄσσεται.

> (I have come upon him in this foreign land,
> tossed out here with you two, wearing such clothes,

on which the unkind *dirt* has settled as old as the old man,
infecting his breast, and on his eyeless head
his uncombed hair flutters in the breeze.)
(lines 1256–1261, translated by N. Worman, 2014, p. 8)

The dirt is not only something that must be washed, but it must be incorporated into different elements: Oedipus, Colonus (Colony), shame, guilt, insult, desire of removal, and sin. This is much more complicated than the simple idea of dirt (see Worman, 2014, p. 8).

4 Hong Kong Public Housing is notorious for its lack of personal space. According to the Hong Kong Housing Authority website (www.housingauthority.gov.hk/tc/global-elements/estate-locator/standard-block-typical-floor-plans/index.html), the average living space per capita is capped at 7.5 square meters per person, including public space.
5 *Below the Lion Rock* was sung by Roman Tam, composed by Joseph Koo, and lyrics were written by James Wong (EMI, 1979).
6 This is grammatically incorrect in English, but is an example of a typical ancient language, wherein collective nouns and specific nouns are inseparable, and allow multiple interpretations and deciphering.
7 This is grammatically incorrect in the English language, but it is the exact term adopted in Hong Kong during the recent political movement.
8 Homage to Jean Baudrillard's "Hyperreality" – the state of "more real than real" (see Baudrillard, 1981/1994, pp. 12–14).
9 For example, in Ni et al. (2020), which claimed to be a "systematic review," the authors argue: "We identified 52 studies (n = 57,487 participants) from 20 countries/regions. The prevalence of post-traumatic stress disorder (PTSD) ranged from 4% to 41% in riot affected areas. Following a major protest, the prevalence of probable major depression increased by 7%, regardless of personal involvement in the protests, suggestive of community spillover effects," and the conclusion was "protest, even non-violent ones, can be associated with adverse mental health outcomes." Similar studies include that of Hou et al. (2015). In that article the researchers regard the "link" between social protest and mental health, like PTSD, as strong.
10 LIHKG.com is a popular multi-category forum website in Hong Kong that requires registration of membership.
11 Birth control represented the ultimate dominance of the female body and sexuality. Although the Two Child Policy replaced the One Child Policy in 2016, the nature of control and oppression never changed. Those who live in villages in rural areas suffered more than those who live in large cities, where the law was somewhat lenient (see Scharping, 2017).

References

Arendt, H. (1951). *The Origins of Totalitarianism*. New York: Schocken Books.
Baudrillard, J. (1981/1994). *Simulation and Simulacra* (trans. S. F. Glaser). Ann Arbor, MI: The University of Michigan Press (pp. 12–14).
BBC. (2020, Jun 30). *Hong Kong Security Law: Life Sentences for Breaking China-imposed Law*. www.bbc.com/news/world-asia-china-53238004
BBC. (2020, Aug 9). *Hong Kong Elections: UK and Allies Condemn Moves to 'Undermine Democracy'*. www.bbc.com/news/world-asia-china-53716538

BBC Chinese. (2019, Jul 5). *Colonial Hong Kong Flag in Anti-extradition Protest: Love for Colonial Past or Showing Resentment?* www.bbc.com/zhongwen/trad/chinese-news-48865476

BBC Chinese. (2020, Jul 1). *Observation: How to Make Sense of China's Statement that Joint Declaration is Already Obsolete?* www.bbc.com/zhongwen/trad/chinese-news-40471315

Blowers, G. H. (1987). To Know the Heart: Psychology in Hong Kong. In G. H. Blowers & A. M. Turtle (eds.), *Psychology Moving East: The Status of Western Psychology in Asia and Oceania* (pp. 139–161). Sydney, Australia: Sydney University Press.

Bray, D. (1973, Nov 29). Speech from Secretary of Home Affairs Department in Legislative Council meeting on 29 November 1973. *Legislative Council Archive.* Retrieved from www.legco.gov.hk/yr73-74/h731129.pdf

Business Week Talks. (2020, May 26). *How Yellow Economy Circle Works.* www.businessweekly.com.tw/international/blog/3002579

Chin, W. K. (2011). *On the Hong Kong City State.* Hong Kong: Enrich Culture (in Chinese).

Department of Justice HKSAR (2020, 14 Jun). *It is Unrealistic to Expect the National Security Law Would be Restricted by Common Law System.* Retrieved from www.news.gov.hk/chi/2020/06/20200614/20200614_151729_152.html

Enriquez, V. G. (1992). *From Colonial to Liberation Psychology: The Philippine Experience.* Quezon City, Philippines: University of the Philippines Press.

Faure, D. (1997). *A Documentary History of Hong Kong Society.* Hong Kong: The University of Hong Kong Press.

Freud, S. (1933/1949). *Gesammelte Werke Bd. 15: Neue Folge der Vorlesungen zur Einführung in die Psychoanalyse.* Frankfurt am Main: Fischer Verlag.

Fung, Y. L. (1948). *A Short Introduction to Chinese Philosophy.* New York: Macmillan.

Gongsun Longzi, Ancient Text in Orthodox Taoist Collection, Chinese University Digital Project. https://ctext.org/library.pl?if=gb&file=100261&page=9 (in Chinese).

Hensen, C. (2007). Prolegomena to Future Solutions to "White-Horse not Horse" (Gongsun Long). *Journal of Chinese Philosophy, 34(4),* 473–491.

Ho, D. F. (1998). Indigenous Psychologies: Asian Perspectives. *Journal of Cross-cultural Psychology, 29(1),* 88–103.

Hong Kong Census and Statistics Department. (2017). *2016 Population By-census Household Income Distribution in Hong Kong.* Hong Kong: Hong Kong Census and Statistics Department.

Hong Kong Legislative Council (1993). Minutes of Meeting on 17 November 1993. Hong Kong: Hong Kong Legislative Council (document number H931117).

Hong Kong Psychological Society (2019). *Press Conference on Interdisciplinary HKAHSS (Hong Kong Association of Heads of Secondary Schools), HKCSS (The Hong Kong Council of Social Services) and DCP-HKPS (Division of Clinical Psychology Hong Kong Psychological Society on 28 Aug, 2019.* Retrieved from https://hkps-dcp.org.hk/en/

Hou, W. K., Hall, B. J., Canetti, D., Lau, K. M., Ng, S. M., & Hobfoll, S. E. (2015). Threat to Democracy: Physical and Mental Health Impact of Democracy Movement in Hong Kong. *Journal of Affective Disorder, 186,* 74–82.

Huang, R. (1988). *China: A Macro History.* Armonk, NY: M.E. Sharpe.

Hwang, K. K. (2005a). A Philosophical Reflection on the Epistemology and Methodology of Indigenous Psychologies. *Asian Journal of Social Psychology, 8(1),* 5–17.

Hwang, K. K. (2005b). From Anticolonialism to Postcolonialism: The Emergence of Chinese Indigenous Psychology in Taiwan. *International Journal of Psychology, 40(4),* 228–238.

Lacan, J. (2017). *Anxiety: The Seminar of Jacques Lacan Book X* (trans. A. R. Price). Malden, MA: Polity Press.

Lacan, J., & Miller, J.-A. (Ed.). (1993). *The Seminar of Jacques Lacan, Book 3: The Psychoses 1955–1956* (trans. R. Grigg). New York: W.W. Norton.
LIHKG (2019, Aug 20). *Father of Pepe Replied: Pepe Stands with Hong Kong People.* Retrieved from https://lihkg.com/thread/1490019/page/1.
Martín-Baró, I. (1994). *Writing for a Liberation Psychology* (A. Aron & S. Shawn, eds.) Cambridge, MA: Harvard University Press.
Mellor, B. (1981). *The University of Hong Kong: An Information History.* Hong Kong: Hong Kong University Press.
Mo, Y. (2009/2014). *Frog.* London: Hamish Hamilton.
Ni, M. Y., Kim, Y., McDowell, I., Wong, S., Qiu, H., Wong, I. O., Galea, S., & Leung, G. M. (2020). Mental Health During and After Protests, Riots and Revolutions: A Systematic Review. *Australian and New Zealand Journal of Psychiatry, 54(3),* 232–243. doi.org/10.1177/0004867419899165.
Oxfam Hong Kong (2019). *Hong Kong Inequality Report.* Hong Kong: Oxfam Hong Kong.
Scharping, T. (2017). Abolishing the One-child Policy: Stages, Issues and the Political Process. *Journal of Contemporary China, 28(117),* 327–347. https://doi.org/10.1080/10670564.2018.1542217
Shek, D. T. L. (2020). Protests in Hong Kong (2019–2020): A Perspective Based on Quality of Life and Well-Being. *Applied Research in Quality of Life, 15,* 619–635. https://doi.org/10.1007/s11482-020-09825-2
Takungpo. (2017, Nov 22). Abnormal Psychology for those who Lingered on Colonial Days Bygone. http://news.takungpao.com/paper/q/2017/1122/3517401.html (in Chinese)
The Standing Committee of the National People's Congress on Issues Relating to the Selection of the Chief Executive of the HKSAR by Universal Suffrage and on the Method for Forming the Legislative Council of the HKSAR in the Year 2016 (2014). *Decision of the Standing Committee of the National People's Congress on Issues Relating to the Selection of the Chief Executive of the HKSAR by Universal Suffrage and on the Method for Forming the Legislative Council of the HKSAR in the Year 2016.* Beijing, China: National People's Congress.
Tsang, Y. M. (2019). *Early Political Groups in Hong Kong: Reform Club of Hong Kong and Hong Kong Civic Association.* Hong Kong: Chung Wa Press (in Chinese).
Wong, W. F. F. (2017, Sep 17). Recolonization: A Rapist who Pursues for Victim's Love. *Next Magazine.* https://hk.nextmgz.com/article/2_547322_0
Worman, N. (2014). Oedipus Abuser: Insult and Embodied Aesthetics in Sophocles. Cahiers Mondes Anciens, 2014(5), 1237. Retrieved from http://journals.openedition.org/mondesanciens/1237; doi: 10.4000/mondesanciens.1237
Xinhua Press (2017, Jun 28). *Celebrating 20th Anniversary of Hong Kong's Return to China.* http://finance.sina.com.cn/roll/2017-06-28/doc-ifyhmtrw4310952.shtml
Zhu, Y. W. (1998). *Investigation of Lyrics of Hong Kong Popular Songs, 1949–1997.* Hong Kong: Joint Publishing (in Chinese).
Žižek, S., Santner, E. L., & Reinhard, K. (2005). *The Neighbour: Three Inquiries in Political Enquiry.* Chicago: The University of Chicago Press.

11

DECOLONIZING THE INTERSECTION

Black Male Studies as a Critique of Intersectionality's Indebtedness to Subculture of Violence Theory

Tommy J. Curry

Introduction

In 2017, *The Man-Not: Race, Class, Genre, and the Dilemmas of Black Manhood* introduced the first reading of Kimberlé Crenshaw's theory of intersectionality as an extension of Catherine MacKinnon's dominance theory (Curry, 2017, pp. 208–220). Whereas previous discussions of intersectionality argued that the theory was anti-essentialist and thereby incompatible with essentialist conceptualizations of race, class, or gender, my reading argues that the gender category, specifically the concept of woman deployed by Crenshaw, presumes a rigid historical, cultural, and sociological hierarchy of subordination of women to men. This conceptualization of "women" requires men to exhibit various group-based behaviors and motivations that can be theorized as an effect of patriarchy (Curry, 2017, pp. 197–228). Consequently, intersectionality relies on a conceptualization of gender that allows the reconstitution of Black female identity around sameness and difference (with Black men and white women) while requiring Black males to be theorized primarily through the sameness they share with "men" as patriarchs. Under intersectionality Black males are denied the reformulations afforded to Black females. Because gender operates analytically, as an assertion of Black males' hierarchical location above and privilege over Black women, Black males are depicted as being less powerful than, but nonetheless the same as, white men who strive for the patriarchal domination of women. In this sense, intersectionality functions as an analytic dictum rather than an explanatory theory, since it requires the subordination of women to be a historically salient and structural feature as well as a replicative activity within racial groups in every analysis.[1]

The gender category deployed in intersectional analyses of Black males not only asserts intuitively that Black men and boys are privileged compared to Black women and girls, but elide empiricism and sociological contextualization that explain why various forms of evidence continue to demonstrate greater Black male disadvantage in health, education, economic (downward) mobility, mortality, police homicide, and imprisonment (Curry, 2017, 2018; Harris, 2000; Mutua, 2013). When such empirical arguments showing the peculiar and perilous condition of being Black and male in the United States are presented they are often framed as contributing to the idea that Black males are an endangered species and by effect deemed to be outside of intersectional analysis (Butler, 2013; Carbado, Crenshaw, Mays, & Tomlinson, 2013). Even when intersectional theorists concede that Black men are the primary targets of lethal violence and greater victims of patriarchal oppression in the United States, the claims concerning male privilege and dominance remain unaffected by such evidence (Purdie-Vaughns & Eibach, 2008).

Black males lack structural power over Black women in American society (Johnson, 2018; Lemelle, 2010). Consequently, many of the analyses concerning Black male privilege and Black patriarchy focus on the physical threats Black males are thought to pose to Black female, queer, and trans-bodies interpersonally rather than systemic advantages in employment, economic mobility, or wealth. This article argues that the understanding of Black male patriarchy through violence within intersectional analyses is a product of Black feminism's reliance on subculture of violence theory and what came to be understood as racial-sexual stratification within racial minority groups. This article argues that the criminological formulation of Black maleness *as a threat to women* explains the seemingly fixed perspective of intersectional analyses on the sexual pathology and social deviance of Black men and boys. As such, I argue that Kimberlé Crenshaw's initial formulation of intersectional analysis depends on an understanding of racial patriarchy that is inextricably tied to dominance feminism's emphasis on physical violence and the criminological construct of the intra-racial rapist. The purpose of this chapter is to understand the content of the gender category deployed within intersectional analyses that produce an understanding of Black males' violence as an outgrowth of patriarchal oppression.

Intra-Racial Violence and the Theory of (Black) Male Dominance in Intersectionality

Throughout Crenshaw's corpus, she has commented upon the affinity shared between her theory of intersectionality and MacKinnon's dominance feminism (Cho, Crenshaw, & McCall, 2013; Crenshaw, 2010). Recognizing the interface between intersectionality and dominance theory allows Crenshaw (2010) to conceive of the two theories "not as intractably oppositional but as setting forth similar critiques at different levels of abstraction" (p. 156). Crenshaw has described how her thinking was influenced by MacKinnon's theorization of gender and patriarchy broadly and specifically within the law. She writes, "I found MacKinnon's stance to be a compelling parallel to that of Derrick Bell's in the context of his writings on race and the law" (Crenshaw, 2010, p. 159). Where others might have seen tension—if not a contradiction—between Bell's racial account and MacKinnon's gender account, Crenshaw (2010) found coherence: "having learned to think in institutional and structural terms about the everyday features of American racial stratification, MacKinnon's efforts to do the same with respect to gender seemed perfectly reasonable to me" (p. 160). Crenshaw (2010) found resonance between the group-based analysis that she found most illuminating in theories of racial subordination and MacKinnon's group-based analysis of gender and power (p. 160). Part of the work intersectionality does, in Crenshaw's (2010) view, is to illuminate how group-based theories of racial subordination are rarely met with the criticisms of their essentialism while MacKinnon's analysis of gender subordination usually is (pp. 161–162).

MacKinnon's dominance theory argues that women are a class defined by their subordination in a patriarchal world ruled by men. In this view, womanhood is defined by, and understood because of, its susceptibility to rape and sexual violence. MacKinnon (1989) explains: "if sexuality is central to women's definition and forced sex is central to sexuality, rape is indigenous, not exceptional, to women's social condition" (p. 172). This argument suggests that "woman" is an entity that is forced to relate to the world not only through asymmetrical relationships with men but defined by their susceptibility to violence from men. MacKinnon (1989) explains, "In life, 'woman' and 'man' are widely experienced as features of being, not constructs of perception, cultural interventions, or forced identities. Gender, in other words, is lived as ontology, not as epistemology" (p. 237). When we think, or speak, of the oppression of women being the effect of how we conceptualize women and the "women particularly present" in our analysis of the real world, we are thinking about the violence affecting women that marks out their difference from other kinds of beings. As MacKinnon (1989) argues:

> To speak of being treated "as a woman" is to make an empirical statement about reality, to describe the realities of women's situation. In this country, with parallels in other cultures, women's situation combines unequal pay with allocation to disrespected work, sexual targeting for rape, domestic battering, sexual abuse as children, and systematic sexual harassment; depersonalization, demeaned physical characteristics, use in denigrating entertainment, deprivation of reproductive control, and forced prostitution. To see that these practices are done by men to women is to see these abuses as forming a system, a hierarchy of inequality.
>
> *(p. 15)*

This idea of "woman" qua subordination has been deployed throughout Crenshaw's reflections of intersectional subordination within the Black race, specifically regarding the issues of domestic abuse and rape Black women and women of color generally face. Contrary to the reading of MacKinnon as a gender essentialist whose idea of womanhood centers on white women's experience (Harris, 1990), Crenshaw sees the dominance frame of MacKinnon as a theory articulating the susceptibility womanhood has to violence such that all bodies designated by "woman" are also designated in relation to "men" and other bodies by the violence "women" experience. MacKinnon explains that her abstraction of "woman" operates as a composite unit that applies to all women but is not limited to any woman who claims it. So, for MacKinnon (1989):

> When African-American women are raped two times as often as white women, aren't they raped as women? That does not mean that their race is irrelevant and it does not mean that their injuries can be understood outside a racial context. Rather, it means that "sex" is made up of the reality of the experiences of all women, including theirs.
>
> *(p. 20)*

This generality of the concept of women suggests that dominance feminism is essentialist, but not exclusively so.

Crenshaw has utilized this conceptualization of women from dominance feminism to explain Black women's sex oppression within the Black community. Emphasizing the sameness that Black women have with other women is important to understanding how sexual oppression operates in intersectionality theory. Crenshaw (2010) explains that, "Efforts to create sameness sensibility can sometimes be productive, especially in resistance to cultural and political histories that have foregrounded difference to justify or normalize dominance" (p. 179). Because Black women are sometimes oppressed as women, there is a need to articulate what oppression as woman entails in relation to men and under the system of patriarchy. In "Mapping the margins," Crenshaw (1991) analyzes a specific example of sexual dominance concerning Black women which draws from the previous work done by white feminists concerning the role that domestic violence and rape play in maintaining the subordination of women within racial groups. Crenshaw begins her analysis stating that "battering and rape, once seen as private (family matters) and aberrational (errant sexual aggression), are now largely recognized as part of a broad-scale system of domination that affects women as a class" (p. 1241). Echoing MacKinnon, *woman* is an essential category of being that explains a particular subjugation for Crenshaw. By exploring where two subordinate classes of racial subjugation and gender subjugation intersect, Crenshaw posits that at that point you would find the Black woman and the domination of women complicated by the particular subjugation of racial groups.

Crenshaw's effort to bring attention to the intra-racial dynamics of rape in the Black community relies on white feminist theories. She claims that "[h]istorically, the dominant conceptualization of rape as quintessentially Black offender/white victim has left Black men subject to legal and extralegal violence" (Crenshaw,

1991, p. 1266), so scholars were not able to understand occurrences of rape within the Black community or theorize intra-racial rape. The intersectional explanation that Crenshaw offers however relies on theories that make the subordination of women within the Black community dependent on racist theories of Black male savagery and criminality. Crenshaw (1991) insists that:

> [g]enerations of critics and activists have criticized dominant conceptualizations of rape as racist and sexist. [And that] these efforts have been important in revealing the way in which representations of rape both reflect and reproduce race and gender hierarchies in American society.
>
> *(p. 1266)*

However, the previous literature Crenshaw relies on to substantiate this argument depicts Black males as brutish sexual predators and deviants. Crenshaw (1991) claims that "the use of rape to legitimize efforts to control and discipline the Black community is well established in historical literature on rape and race" (p. 1266), but this argument was far from well-established and was extremely idiosyncratic in the 1970s and 1980s since it was only beginning to be advanced by white feminist sociologists attempting to integrate subculture of violence theory into their gender analyses.

The only source Crenshaw gives to substantiate this "well established" fact is Joyce Williams and Karen Holmes's (1981) *The Second Assault,* which aimed to introduce a new theory of racial sexual stratification and to show that Black men used rape for the patriarchal oppression of Black women. While this may be a now popularly accepted feminist ideology, it was rooted primarily in the subculture of violence theories about Black men's compensatory masculinity, not any concrete scientific evidence. To get the results it desires, intersectionality must not only describe the sexual vulnerability of women and girls in the Black community but assume *as fact* that Black men rape purely for patriarchal power, as white feminists have previously theorized. In constructing sameness with white women "as women," intersectionality consequently constructs sameness between Black men and white men as "men" and "patriarchs."

Previous theorizations of intersectionality have only considered the construction of Black female vulnerability to patriarchy as worthy of concern. No attention has been paid to the kinds of (racist) theories intersectional feminists utilized in the *politicized* construction of Black men as perpetrators of violence against women or as participants in the group of "men" who dominate and subjugate women. Enabled by a mimetic theory of Black manhood, or a theory based on the idea that Black males aspire to imitate white masculinity and produce a culturally peculiar facsimile of white patriarchy in response to their negation under anti-Black racism, intersectionality has deployed various caricatures of Black men and boys and speculative accounts of deviance that simply cannot be reconciled with the existing empirical literature.

The Intersectionality of Black Males: bell hooks's Role in Mimetic Theory

More contemporary theorists of intersectionality such as Frank Rudy Cooper have continued to endorse the racist theory that Black male identity is primarily driven by the imitation of white masculine norms and power. In his article "Against bipolar masculinity: Intersectionality, assimilation, identity performance, and hierarchy," Cooper (2006) claims that

> heterosexual black men will feel compelled to prove their manhood through acts that distance them from marginalized others. Emulation of normative masculinity thus makes it more likely heterosexual black men will seek to offset their feelings of powerlessness by subordinating others.
>
> *(p. 900)*

This need to subordinate others leads Black men to oppress Black women and Black gays to prove their self-worth (p. 859). This claim rests solely on bell hooks's (2004) theorization of Black men in *We Real Cool: Black Men and Masculinity*.

According to bell hooks, the history of racism and Jim Crow segregation gave rise to Black hypersexuality and forced Black men to construct a compensatory phallic identity. hooks (2004) writes:

> Much of the subculture of blackness in the early years of the twentieth century was created in reaction and resistance to the culture whites sought to impose on black folks. Since whiteness had repressed black sexuality, in the subculture space of blackness, sexual desire was expressed with degrees of abandon unheard of in white society.
>
> *(p. 66)*

Sexuality became a compensatory trait of Black men according to hooks. "The black male body, deemed demonic in the eyes of white racist sexist stereotypes, was in the world of segregated black culture deemed erotic, sensual, capable of giving and receiving pleasure," she writes (hooks, 2004, p. 66). Because white men dictated the terms of masculinity and controlled the social, economic, and political resources that made attaining manhood impossible for Black men, hooks (2004) suggests that Black men began "equating manhood with fucking, [and] saw status and economic success as synonymous with endless sexual conquest" (p. 66). The deviance and sexual obsession of Black males were conceptualized by hooks as a product of their incompleteness—*their lack of true manhood*. Throughout hooks's corpus, Black men and Black men's responses to white oppression are depicted in negative terms. She writes: "Precisely because black males have suffered and do suffer so much dehumanization in the context of imperialist white supremacist capitalist patriarchy, they have brought to the realm of the sexual a level of compulsion that is oftentimes pathological" (p. 69).

Because Black men have no positive psychical or cultural resources of resistance in hooks's work that can serve as the foundation of Black manhood, Black males tend to exaggerate the most deleterious aspects of white masculinity. Asserted to be vacuous, Black masculinity assimilates white masculinity to give itself content. As such, Black masculinity became obsessed with patriarchal sex to cope with racist oppression. According to hooks (2004):

> In segregated African-American life, patriarchal sex was not only the medium for the assertion of manhood; it was also reconceptualized in the space of blackness as entitled pleasure for black males who were not getting all the perks of patriarchal maleness in arenas where white men were still controlling the show.
>
> *(p. 67)*

Despite the negative societal conditions Black males find themselves in, hooks emphasizes the pathological nature of Black maleness rather than the oppressive conditions constraining Black males. Whereas subculture of violence theories focus specifically on poor, young, Black males, hooks suggests that *all* Black masculinity is sexually coercive. This point deserves emphasis. While class status accounted for the different behaviors of various groups of Black males in white sociological and criminological theories, hooks suggests the origin of Black male sexual pathology and aggression is masculinity itself. For hooks (2004), "black males from any class, whether individually or in groups, could find affirmation of their power in sexual conquests" (p. 67). In short, hooks understands Black male resistance to white supremacy and social marginalization as the internalization of the racist tropes about Black masculinity offered by white society. Black masculinity, for hooks, is merely the extent to which Black men embrace and absorb the *imago* offered by white society. hooks (2004) writes, "Through the dominant culture's fascination with the black male as a super sexual stud, [Black men] are able to mask their sense of powerlessness, their psychological sexual impotency, as well as their obsessive compulsive dysfunctional sexual habits" (p. 70).

These writings by hooks suggest that Black male violence can be best understood through mimesis (Curry, 2017). Without a culturally positive concept of Black manhood available, Black males seek to imitate the masculinity of white males. From boyhood, Black males are socialized to aspire to the violence performed by white men for hooks. She writes:

> Young black males, like all boys in patriarchal culture, learn early that manhood is synonymous with the domination and control over others, that simply by being male they are in a position of authority that gives them the

right to assert their will over others, to use coercion and/or violence to gain and maintain power.

(hooks, 2004, p. 83)

Consequently, Black manhood is rooted in the emulation of white patriarchal violence. As hooks (2004) says, "Black male violence simply mirrors the styles and habits of white male violence. It is not unique" (p. 61). Poverty and social marginalization only exacerbate the violent tendencies of Black males in this view; they do not cause violence because the violence being amplified by social disadvantage is *already there*, latent but endemic to Black masculinity. Whereas compensatory violence has historically been offered as an explanation of male deviance (Cohen, 1955; Hannerz, 1969), hooks argues that for Black men societal negation is even direr because Black males embrace the racialized caricature of the beast. According to hooks (2004):

> many black males explain their decision to become the "beast" as a surrender to realities they cannot change. And if you are going to be seen as a beast you may as well act like one. Young black males, particularly underclass males, often derive a sense of satisfaction from being able to create fear in others, particularly in white folks ... Showing aggression is the simplest way to assert patriarchal manhood. Men of all classes know this. As a consequence, all men living in a culture of violence must demonstrate at some point in their lives that they are capable of being violent.
>
> *(p. 45)*

The disproportionate rates of violence committed by Black men as well as their "gangsta behavior" are accounted for in hooks's (2004) work by the sexist ideations of patriarchal masculinity. She asserts:

> Overall the facts reveal that black males are more violent than ever before in this nation. And they are more likely to be violent toward another black person whom they deem less powerful. Much black male violence is directed toward females. Sexism and the assumption of the male right to dominate serves as the catalyst for this violence.
>
> *(hooks, 2004, p. 52)*

These descriptions of Black masculinity proposed by bell hooks replicate the pathological descriptions of Black manhood offered by Martin Wolfgang and Franco Ferracuti (1967) as examples of the Black subculture of violence. Subcultures were *distinct and separate* from the dominant culture and were marked primarily by the "potent theme of violence current in the cluster of values that make up the lifestyle, the socialization process, the interpersonal relationships of individuals living in similar conditions" (Wolfgang & Ferracuti, 1967, p. 140).

Wolfgang and Ferracuti (1967) emphasized that the "overt use of force or violence, either in interpersonal relationships or in group interaction" (p. 158) is a product of the normative system's operation within the subcultural grouping and reflects the psychological traits and a particular worldview quite distant from the dominant or parent culture. The primary consideration of Wolfgang and Ferracuti's theory was homicide. They were interested in why Black men and Black women disproportionately utilized lethal violence and aggression regularly within their communities (Wolfgang & Ferracuti, 1967, p. 154). In 1971, Menachem Amir's *Patterns in Forcible Rape* introduced a subculture of violence theory claiming to explain why poor Black men became accustomed to committing rape and how Black women as mothers and partners contributed to the transmission of these values from childhood to adulthood (p. 324).

Amir introduced the most prominent cultural explanation of Black male sexual aggression in the 20th century. Whereas previous ethnological formulations of the Black male rapist relied on ontogenic accounts of racial development, Amir introduced a theory that focused on the deviant values of Negroes and how these racial norms within the Black race produced Black male rapists (cf. Howard, 1903). He writes:

> The Negro subculture is an historically unique subculture which embodies all the characteristics of a lower-class subculture but has some of its features in a more pronounced form ... The Negro subculture is characterized by the revolving of life around some basic focal concerns which include a search for thrills through aggressive actions and sexual exploits ... The emphasis is given by males to masculinity, and their need to display and defend it through brief and transitory relations with women. Such needs and the subsequent concerns with sex stems from growing up in a family in which the mother is dominant and the father has a marginal position ... Young boys are imbued with negative, or at least ambivalent, feelings toward masculine functions. Sexual and aggressive behavior becomes the main vehicle for asserting their worthiness. They, therefore, idealize personal violence and prowess which substitute for social and economic advantages.
>
> *(Amir, 1971, pp. 327–328)*

Amir suggests that one can understand the sexual violence and social deviance of Blacks as having the same origin. However, the absenteeism of the Black father and the lack of patriarchal structure produced a disfigured, and more feminine, Black masculinity (cf. Brody, 1961). This apatriarchal masculinity was thought to not only produce violence, misogyny, and deviance but also find meaning and purpose in rape (Barclay & Cusumano, 1967; Biller, 1968; Hannerz, 1969; Moran & Barclay, 1988). Black masculinity is presented within this theory as a distorted racial facsimile of white patriarchal culture. True masculinity results in civility and order; Black manhood, as apatriarchal, produces sexual confusion and deviance (Pleck, 1981, pp. 126–128).

American feminists found great utility in Amir's racialist accounts of rape. Amir argued, contrary to the previous racist pseudo-science of the early 20th century, that sociology and criminology show that rape is primarily an intra-racial phenomenon and that rape is produced by the culturally peculiar notions of masculinity found within the Negro subculture. Susan Brownmiller enthusiastically supported subculture of violence explanations for rape in the Black community. Brownmiller praised Wolfang and Ferracuti's ability to create a theory of lower-class male culture linking physical and sexual aggression, gangsterism, and masculinity together. However, it was Menachem Amir's study of rape patterns in Philadelphia that most captured her interest. Brownmiller (1975) writes:

> The single most important contribution of Amir's Philadelphia study was to place the rapist squarely within the subculture of violence. The rapist, it was revealed, had no separate identifiable pathology aside from the individual quirks and personality disturbances that might characterize any single offender who commits any sort of crime.
>
> *(p. 181)*

Amir theorized that the same subcultural values Wolfgang and Ferracuti believed produced criminality could also explain the occurrence of rape. Amir's work offered a new territory for feminist accounts of gender to explore. Because his work was based in the study of a major urban center like Philadelphia, he both disproved the longstanding racist trope of the Black male rapist of white women, while nonetheless providing feminists with the construct of the intra-racial rapist, which would motivate the next several decades of feminist theorization in the United States.

Creating the Intra-Racial Rapist through Contra-Culture Theory

To reformulate the deviant model of the Black male rapist inherited from the work of subculture of violence theorists like Menachem Amir (1971) and Susan Brownmiller (1975), Lynn A. Curtis argued that Black males' distortion of white patriarchy best explained their higher rates of rape perpetration. Throughout the 1970s, feminists reconceptualized Black men as (intra-racial) rapists of Black women rather than (inter-racial) rapists of white women. This idea of the Black male as an intra-racial rapist owes its origin to Menachem Amir's *Patterns of Forcible Rape* but became a cornerstone of American feminists' (both Black and white) theory through the work of Lynn A. Curtis.

Unlike earlier subculture of violence theories (e.g., Wolfgang, Ferracuti, and Amir) which understood the Black male rapist to be a product of socialization, where Black subcultural values emphasizing aggression and violence were taught to young Black men by their mothers and the sexual behaviors of Black women, Curtis argued that the Black male rapist was a unique trait of poor Black male culture. Curtis asserted that Black women had no role in the transmission of subcultural values of violence, because poor Black males—their masculinity alone—were the origin and cause of the disproportionate rates of homicide, rape, and sexual assault compared to other racial groups in the United States. Said differently, Curtis surmised that it was race, class, and gender—poor Black masculinity—that created the most virulent form of rape culture in America.

Lynn A. Curtis disagreed with the idea that white racial patterns of rape were the direst in American society. He specifically took issue with Susan Griffin's (1971) *Ramparts* editorial "Rape: An all-American crime." In this article, Griffin (1971) argued that "[t]he same men and power structure who victimize women are engaged in the act of raping Vietnam, raping Black people and the very earth we live upon" (p. 35). Griffin (1971) saw rape as a "classic act of domination" (p. 35). She continued, "As the symbolic expression of the white male hierarchy, rape is the quintessential act of our civilization, one which, Valerie Solanis warns, is in danger of 'humping itself to death'" (Griffin, 1971, p. 35).

Curtis (1976), however, argued that Griffin unfairly places the blame on white men for the practice of forcible rape, because "American feminists tend to gloss over or be unclear about racial patterns in their discussions of sexual assault" (p. 130). These racial patterns exclude what Curtis takes to be the greater frequency and propensity of Black men to rape women more so than white men. In his reply to Griffin, Curtis (1976) wrote:

> In building to this position, Griffin cites national survey findings observing that "90 percent of reported rape is intra- not inter-racial." Yet nowhere does she reveal that 60 of the 90 percent in the national survey involved black men raping black women. Black–white rape is said to be "outrageously exaggerated"—an observation with which we agree, although Griffin is unaware that the reported rate of black–white encounters seems to be rising, at least in some places, and that it is already high in several cities.
>
> *(p. 131)*

Curtis's criticism of Griffin was part of a larger theoretical shift in how rape was being discussed by white criminologists and American feminists. While there was a growing recognition following Amir's *Forcible Patterns of Rape* that the majority of rapes in the United States were intra-racial, there was also an attempt to reconcile the reality that white men were the primary rapists of white women and the historical caricature of Black males as rapists that was rooted in white social and biological sciences since the mid 19th century (Curry, 2017; Lindquist, 2012; Stein, 2015).

For example in *Rape: The Politics of Consciousness*, Susan Griffin (1986) argued that "[t]he white man's open rape of Black women, coupled with his overwhelming concern for the chastity and protection of his wife and daughters, represents an extreme of sexist and racist hypocrisy" (p. 20). Griffin (1986) suggests that white men's power over white women was so restrictive that "any deviance from male-defined standards for white womanhood was treated severely" (p. 20). In Griffin's interpretation of white women's sexual victimhood, the racist myth of the Black rapist was due solely to white men inventing and executing this mythology. Because the violence against white women for defying white men was so great, white women had no choice but to accuse innocent Black men of rape. Griffin (1986) writes:

> In the situation where a Black man was found to be having sexual relations with a white woman, the white woman could exercise skin privilege, and claim that she had been raped in which case the Black man was lynched. But if she did not claim rape, she herself was subject to lynching.
>
> *(p. 20)*

In giving this account of racism and sexism she positions the white woman as a victim to white male violence with no agency or ability to resist against the power of the white male. For Griffin (1986), "The white male has created a convenient symbol of his own power which has resulted in Black hostility toward the white bitch" (p. 20). However, she does not leave this racist trope without further comment since she believes that the fear white women have of the Black rapist is rooted in truth. According to Griffin (1986), "It is not surprising that after being told for two centuries that he wants to rape white women, Black men have begun to actually commit the act" (pp. 20–21).

To not perpetuate the myth of the Black rapist of white women, Griffin (1986) says that "[it] is crucial to note that the frequency of this practice is outrageously exaggerated in the white mythos, [since] ninety percent of reported rape is intra- not inter-racial" (p. 21). The configuration of Griffin's account of how racism and sexism have converged throughout history is not to vindicate the Black male from the horrible criminological trope of the Black rapist, but instead to recognize that the Black man may have been a rapist of white women, and as of the mid 20th century, he was primarily a rapist of the Black woman. The primary weakness of Griffin's piece is that it excludes Black male patterns of rape on Black women and focuses solely on rape between white men and white women. Curtis (1976) explains that

> Much of Griffin's focus is on the relationship dynamics between white men and white women. No thought is given to separate black–black patterns, cultural or otherwise, nor to how rape by black men, especially on black women, is the symbolic expression of the white male hierarchy.
>
> *(p. 131)*

Curtis saw no contradiction between the claim that white male patriarchy and sexual dominance were the origin of sexual violence, historically, and that white patriarchy had been adopted and transformed by the aggressive cultural traits of poor Black men. As such, rape became a culturally pervasive trait among poor Black men and boys, so much so that this behavior ostracized them as a counterculture within poor Black ghettos. Curtis (1976) explained, "White males are the power brokers who have erected the racial and economic barriers forcing black adaptations and who have set the sexual exploitation theme in motion—without being able to similarly prevent blacks from expanding upon it" (p. 131). Curtis believed that Black males mutated and degraded white patriarchy, making it more savage and violent. Curtis (1975) presumed that Black male sexuality was compensatory and more exploitative of women than white masculinity (p. 69). As Curtis (1975) explained:

> The theme of contracultural expression by Black males as extended emulation of white males also comes through clearly in the area of sexual exploitation. Few would deny that today many white males sexually exploit women ... In turn, poor Black men experience fewer restraints against expressing masculinity sexually than economically, so they may exaggerate the dominant cultural pattern even more.
>
> *(pp. 70–71)*

Black males consequently possessed a more brutish sexism towards women than white masculinity. Whereas white patriarchy had paternalistic elements that sought to protect and care for women, Curtis insisted that Black masculinity was more criminogenic in nature, predicated solely on deviance, sexual aggression, and the rape of women.

In *Behind Ghetto Walls*, the sociologist Lee Rainwater (1970) suggested, contrary to the rape literature of his day, that despite their sexual objectification of women, Black boys are "remarkably patient in their relationships with girls and they rarely terminate such relationships automatically when intercourse is refused" (p. 297). Curtis insisted that Rainwater was incorrect, because the sexual excitement of poor Black males posed too great of a threat to their female counterpart. According to Curtis (1975):

> It cannot be expected that those poor Black males who are exploitative will always restrain themselves when sexually excited. This is particularly so if they cannot control sex like the successful pimp and must therefore strategize against the controlling female ... On the spot and convinced that he is or should be horny, a male may not feel like leaving a reluctant female for an alternative, even if there may be an abundant supply of more willing women. His greater physical strength and willingness to use it then present a viable option.
>
> *(p. 73)*

Curtis theorized Black males as sexually insatiable beasts whose very identity was tied to their predatory conquests of women. Curtis (1975) imagined Black males as being so tied to their phallus that a woman's refusal of sex, his rejection, would be incapable of being rationally understood and prompt an act of rape (p. 73). The rape of Black females by Black males in "ghetto settings" was a contracultural norm. In other words, there is nothing spectacular or abnormal in these practices since these Black males are socialized to be criminals and rapists. It is not difficult to see the direct connection between the subculture/contraculture theories of the mid-1970s and the cogitations concerning the Black male super-predator of the 1990s (cf. Bennett, Dilulio, & Walters, 1996; Dilulio Jr., 1995, 1996).

Racial–Sexual Stratification Theory as the Basis of Black Patriarchy

Joyce Williams and Karen Holmes (1981) attempted to create a system of understanding how rape acts as a mechanism to maintain social control and dominance within racial subgroups. Influenced by Lorenne Clark and Debra Lewis's (1977) theory that "[a]ll unequal power relationships must, in the end, rely on the threat or reality of violence to maintain themselves" (p. 176), Williams and Holmes (1981) understood violence as making the racial and sexual stratifications in the United States socially actual and psychologically real. Within every racial group, the violence of sexual stratification "lies in the superior physical strength of the male and is manifested in its ultimate form as rape" (Williams & Holmes, 1981, p. 26). Regarding ethnic or racial stratification, Williams and Holmes (1981) believe such violence is used to suppress revolts and explains why the "military and police are controlled by the dominant system" (p. 26). These two systems operate simultaneously in American society but affect racial minorities as well as white men and women in fundamentally different ways. Attempting to get at the ways that sexual stratification operated within racial and ethnic subgroups, Williams and Holmes theorized that the relationships between all the men and women of white dominant racial groups as well as the relationships in subordinate Black and Brown minority groups were determined by the act of rape.

> Rape, or the threat of rape, is an important tool of social control in a complex system of racial–sexual stratification. Fear of rape keeps not only the female in her place, but fear of the accusation of raping a white woman keeps minority males in their place as well.
> *(Williams & Holmes, 1981, p. 26)*

While Black and Brown men were right to fear punishment, lynching, and death for the *inappropriate rape* of white women in a white supremacist system, all women were nonetheless under constant threat of rape from all men because of patriarchy.

All women, regardless of race-ethnicity, live in a white, male-dominated society where the dynamics of male–female interaction are convoluted by the dynamics of racial power. In a racially and sexually stratified society, a high incidence of rape is predictable. Rape symbolizes not only a key element of social control working to maintain the system, but also the anger and violence engendered by such a system. Anglo-females are potentially appropriate victims for Anglo-males and are vulnerable to inappropriate rape by minority males, the latter, no doubt, symbolizing some of the anger and frustration that have grown so naturally in a system of unequal power. Minority females appear to be the appropriate victims of both inter- and intragroup rape. If they are raped by white males, it is assumed that they asked for it or were simply unpaid prostitutes. If they are raped by minority males, police and other public officials have been known to react as if this is typical in-group behavior.

(Williams & Holmes, 1981, p. 27)

Williams and Holmes (1981) suggested that "in raping minority women, minority males frequently are doing no more than imitating the white male" (p. 27). Williams and Holmes found the contracultural analysis of Curtis more amenable to their feminist anti-rape ideology because Curtis eliminated the role attributed to Black women in sustaining subcultures of violence. Contraculture theory emphasized how the sexual aggression and violence of Black males were due to the internalization of white patriarchal norms, not the subcultural values shared by all members of poor Black communities. Black women are outside of the contracultural frame, which is dominated by Black males, so they are depicted as innocent victims rather than participants in violence, as in the work of Menachem Amir. Williams and Holmes (1981) write:

Although the characteristics of a contraculture are not made entirely clear, it is seemingly comprised largely of young, Black, urban males who are in overt conflict with the dominant culture. For example, Curtis explains that the subculture of violence includes some Black females, while the contraculture is primarily a male bastion. By definition, males rape females (most of whom are also Black) outside the contraculture, and this is why "sizable numbers report to the predominantly white American police institution."

(pp. 8–9)

Racial–sexual stratification theory created a feminist account of intra-racial rape that depended on socialization, where "masculinity" became an idea shared between the dominant and subordinate groups. This idea of a shared masculinity, which is not *distinct or separate*, allowed white and Black masculinity to be theorized as the same—both being the origin of rape and sexual assault. Consequently, "the system of racial–sexual stratification has assigned Black females to be victims and Black males to victimize" (Williams & Holmes, 1981, p. 37). Such a theory allowed the greater frequency of sexual violence, homicide, and deviance in Black communities to be interpreted as the consequence of gender rather than racism and poverty. By offering a feminist analysis in which patriarchy was the engine driving intra-racial gender dynamics, Black masculinity became a hierarchically fixed positionality within the Black race that operated the same way as in the white race due to its mimetic tendencies.

Williams and Holmes (1981) understood that "the Black male is less powerless today than ever before, but he is not powerful. The system in which he has social and economic well-being is still controlled by white males" (p. 30). Because Black males could not escape poverty (ghetto culture) some turned to violence, deviance, and alcoholism, while others adapted by "cultivating an exacerbated male sexuality which represents a kind of self-fulfilling prophecy for whites" (Williams & Holmes, 1981, p. 30). Williams and Holmes (1981) suggest that whites may have initially encouraged the uninhibited sexuality of Black males during slavery for breeding and later to bolster the idea of the Black rapist as a "means of maintaining control over all Blacks as well as over white females" (p. 31). Williams and Holmes (1981) argue that

> the male sex organ became the identity of the Black male as well as his tenuous link with life itself, for while he might be given approval for uninhibited sexual activity with Black women, the least suggestion of sexual behavior with white women was to invite castration and/or death.
>
> *(p. 31)*

In this sense, the sexual mania of the Black male was the creation of white society, a Frankenstein of white male power, that rejected the civility of the white master. While the authors admit that at the time they wrote their book "there is no empirical evidence … nor is there any empirical validation for either the myth of Black male sexuality or that of sex as compensatory behavior" (Williams & Holmes, 1981, p. 35), these claims served as the motivating factors behind Black males' alleged propensity to rape Black women and remain a cornerstone of contemporary intersectional feminist thought.

Despite *The Second Assault: Rape and Public Attitudes* not being well reviewed by sociologists and rape scholars during the 1980s (e.g., Barlow, 1983; Bunting, 1983; Holmstrom, 1983), it has served as the basis of claiming that patriarchy operates in Black and Brown culture in ways that mirror that of whites.[2] However, rarely did these arguments follow the data presented by Williams and Holmes (1981). For instance, white males had the most feminist definition of rape, meaning that they viewed rape as "sex without the woman's consent" and were the only group to reject the idea that women's behavior was responsible for their rape (Williams & Holmes, 1981, pp. 70–71, 118–120). Black men were suggested to be the most traditional of all the sex groups concerning sex roles beliefs and, along with Black women, showed the most support for women's liberation over whites and Mexican-Americans (Williams & Holmes, 1981, p. 132). Williams and Holmes (1981) claimed that whites and Black women appeared to be more feminist than previous research had revealed, while "only Black males demonstrated strong support for the belief that women are curious and excited about rape" (p. 134).

Hugh Barlow's (1983) review of *The Second Assault* best summarizes these contradictory findings. He writes:

> Demographic factors were significant predictors in 19 of 27 regression equations, but half the time in a direction opposite to that expected; sex-role attitudes, beliefs about male–female sexuality, and minority-related rape risks each predicted some attitudes for some of the samples some of the time—but, again, often in the "wrong" direction.
>
> *(p. 949)*

Barlow (1983) claims that the authors knew that their data "seem[ed] inconsistent with the theoretical arguments about racial–sexual stratification" (p. 949), but refused to explain or explore why their work seemed to offer support for subculture of violence theories of race. Throughout Williams and Holmes's work there is an insistence that, while white male patriarchy is structurally and theoretically of national and global concern, the Black male is the most pressing social threat to, and political problem for, women.

Black Male Studies as Rupture: Decolonizing Intersectional Theory

The last 30 years of intersectionality theory have shown remarkable continuity with the preexisting theories developed by racist criminologists and white feminists throughout the 1970s. Rooted primarily in the racist construct of Black manhood as imitative, a deviant mimetic imaginary of white masculinity, contemporary intersectional analyses of Black males posit their existence as primarily compensatory. While these theories of Black masculinity have endured for the last several decades, no additional evidence has emerged to support a compensatory account of Black maleness that was put forth in the 1970s. The gender theories that have produced this specific account of Black masculinity as wanting to imitate white masculinity are primarily ideological. As the sociologists Andrea Hunter and James Davis (1994) explain:

> Studies of Black women emphasize how out of oppression a unique definition of womanhood was forged, one in which adversity gave rise to strength. However, the discourse around men and oppression focuses on the stripping away of manhood. It is a perspective that casts Black men

as victims and ignores their capacity to define themselves under difficult circumstances.

(p. 21)

The current gender theories begin with the assumption that Black male identity is incomplete—the expression of a negated and distorted form. Black men are interpreted as not being "real" men, but *voids of being* constructed by the discourse others have of them. There is no logical reason for theorizing Black women by their positive attributes while conceptualizing Black males through negative stigmas. One could just as easily point to disproportionate rates of crime, abuse, and deviance among Black women as the elements of abstraction. However, this approach is avoided for Black women and embraced for Black men.

The misandry aimed at Black men throughout society is reflected within *theory*. The theories about Black men in the academy, which are deployed throughout feminist and intersectional theory, reflect the popularly accepted racist myths about Black males as inferior and violent. Because these descriptions of Black males are called *theory* and are given disciplinary consensus, anti-Black misandry, or "the cumulative assertions of Black male inferiority due to errant psychologies of lack, dispositions of deviance, or hyper-personality traits (e.g., hyper-sexuality, hyper-masculinity) which rationalize the criminalization, phobics, and sanctioning of Black male life" (Curry, 2018, p. 267), is made axiomatic rather than objective. The hatred, fear, and negation of Black males produce frameworks that are set within disciplines and have become the cornerstone of intersectional literature and various feminist theories. While the *empirical evidence* of Black men's attitudes, psychological orientation, and behavior disproving these myths have sometimes been written by feminist authors (e.g., Harnois, 2010, 2014, 2016; Simien, 2006, 2007), these findings have not been allowed to redirect the anti-Black misandry replicated by *theory*.

The politicized constructions of Black males as perpetrators of violence against women generally, but Black women specifically, pay no attention to the empirical incongruence of such projects. Black males have endured being often erased by well-documented histories of rape and sexual mutilation at the hands of white men and women throughout slavery and Jim Crow. For over a hundred years, sociology, psychology, criminology, and anthropology construed Black males as feminine men and apatriarchal. Within their communities, Black boys have suffered heinous amounts of sexual violence at the hands of women, and continue to experience disproportionately high rates of statutory rape and sexual abuse compared to their female counterparts (Curry & Utley, 2018; Hernandez, Lodico, & DiClemente, 1993).

Black men report a higher 12-month prevalence of domestic violence victimization, rape/made to penetrate violence, and sexual coercion where women are committing a vast majority of these sexual and physical violations in the United States (Curry, 2019; Smith et al., 2017). Despite these realities, which are well documented and evident to those who care to look, intersectionality theory has remained unquestioned concerning the psychologism at work in the constructing of Black men and boys as "patriarchal men committed to dominance," or the assumptions operating to substantiate the compensatory logic of "Black masculinity." This inability for Black men to be understood as *substantively different* from "men" of the dominant group is what has been referred to as intersectionality's Black male problem (Curry, 2017; Oluwayomi, 2020).

Despite the great variety between Black men throughout American society, "many of the studies that theorize about Black manhood fail to elucidate the meaning of manhood for African American men from different socioeconomic backgrounds who undoubtedly grapple with racism but do so via a range of different vantage points" (Hammond & Mattis, 2005, p. 116). Conceptualizing Black males through negation, or their lack of manhood under racism, permits caricature to stand in for character. Starting with pathological presumptions about Black males allows theorists to imagine them as tragic figures who can only attain their humanity by enacting violence against other groups. This pathological theorization of Black male identity is not an attempt to conceptualize the humanity or cognition motivating Black men and boys, but a speculative psychology of Black male criminality. These abstractions attempt to explain the deviant behavior and the disproportionate rates of violence among a small number of Black males as character traits of the whole group.

Numerous studies have shown that Black men emphasize *manhood* over *masculinity* and view Black manhood as an interdependent and spiritual connection to their families and communities. Black manhood is a proactive and adaptive identity that anticipates and reflects upon the obstacles and barriers placed before Black men. Notwithstanding the barriers confronting Black men and boys collectively, Black males have developed a social and political consciousness that emphasizes the uplift of the whole community, sexual egalitarianism, and the importance of fatherhood within the Black community.[3] There is overwhelming evidence showing that the values of Black manhood are positive, functional, and humanist. However, these empirical findings have not been integrated or accounted for within contemporary intersectionality theory given intersectionality's emphasis on the criminological and the mimetic.

Black Male Studies merely exposes this ideological determinism operating within our current gender paradigms and provides the substance for the categories being deployed in intersectional analyses of Black manhood. Black Male Studies argues that Black manhood exceeds the conceptual foundations of gender theory. Because Black males are understood as adaptive and dynamic entities, Black Male Studies requires a reconstituting of the object—a freeing of constructs applied to what is thought of as object and not subject and consequently how one comes to imagine the character and attribute the traits of the group being theorized. The Black male "is not-man, but he demonstrates himself as something more than the representations offered by the West's imagination" (Curry, 2017, p. 227). The liminality of the Black male is not set upon a geography of thought, but rather introduces cosmogonic considerations of Black male realities. As I have explained previously, Black males perceive "the world from an undisclosed place where thinking is needed but that theory/thought/reason has not yet corrupted" (Curry, 2017, p. 227).

Conclusion

Intersectionality has utilized various feminist theories that continue subculture of violence thinking about Black men and boys. While intersectional feminists often claim that intersectionality leads to a clearer social analysis of power and hierarchies throughout society and within groups, the categories and claims of intersectionality fail to distinguish themselves from previously racist theories that sought to explain race, class, and gender based on subcultural values. This chapter is the first to interrogate the theories used to construct the gendered categories and the assumptions behind Black male positionality under intersectional analyses. Contrary to its promises for more liberated Black identities, intersectionality merely replicates the pseudo-science of racist criminology and presents decades-old theories as cutting-edge gender analyses. In short, while intersectionality has allowed Black women to create nuanced experiences and epistemological accounts of Black womanhood, the very same theory has confined Black male experience to the perpetration of violence and defined Black manhood as *lesser*—merely the exemplification of white masculinity's pathological excess.

Notes

1 Two years after *The Man-Not* introduced a reading of intersectionality alongside MacKinnon's (1989) dominance theory, Devon Carbado and Cheryl Harris (2019) incorrectly insisted they were the first to consider this relationship.
2 I could only find three published reviews of this work (Barlow, 1983; Bunting, 1983; Holmstrom, 1983).
3 There is overwhelming evidence that Black men are the most gender-egalitarian and politically progressive group in the United States (Blee & Tickamyer, 1995; Gooley, 1989; Hunter & Davis, 1992; Hunter & Sellers, 1998). There is also substantial evidence that Black men are the best fathers and father children in their community who are not their progeny (Jones & Mosher, 2013; McDougal III & George III, 2016).

References

Amir, M. (1971). *Patterns in forcible rape*. Chicago, IL: University of Chicago Press.
Barclay, A., & Cusumano, D. R. (1967). The study of man: Testing masculinity in boys without fathers. *Trans-action*, 5, 33–35.
Barlow, H. D. (1983). Review of *The Second Assault*. *Social Forces, 61*(3), 948–950. doi:10.2307/2578165

Bennett, W. J., Dilulio Jr., J., & Walters, J. P. (1996). *Body count: Moral poverty and how to win America's war against crime and drugs*. New York, NY: Simon & Schuster.
Biller, H. B. (1968). A note on father absence and masculine development in lower-class Negro and white boys. *Child Development*, *39*(3), 1003–1006. doi:10.2307/1127003
Blee, K. M., & Tickamyer, A. R. (1995). Racial differences in men's attitudes about women's gender roles. *Journal of Marriage and the Family*, *57*(1), 21–30. doi:10.2307/353813
Brody, E. B. (1961). Social conflict and schizophrenic behavior in young adult Negro males. *Psychiatry*, *24*(4), 337–346. doi:10.1080/00332747.1961.11023282
Brownmiller, S. (1975). *Against our will: Men, women, and rape*. New York, NY: Simon & Schuster.
Bunting, A. (1983). Review of *The Second Assault*. *Social Science Quarterly*, *64*(2), 428–429.
Butler, P. (2013). Black male exceptionalism? The problems and potential of Black male focused interventions. *Du Bois Review: Social Science Research on Race*, *10*(2), 485–511. doi:10.1017/s1742058x13000222
Carbado, D. W., Crenshaw, K. W., Mays, V. M., & Tomlinson, B. (2013). Intersectionality: Mapping the movements of a theory. *Du Bois Review: Social Science Research on Race*, *10*(2), 303–312. doi:10.1017/s1742058x13000349
Cho, S., Crenshaw, K. W., & McCall, L. (2013). Toward a field of intersectionality studies: Theory, applications, and praxis. *Signs: Journal of Women in Culture and Society*, *38*(4), 785–810. doi:10.1086/669608
Clark, L. M., & Lewis, D. J. (1977). *Rape: The price of coercive sexuality*. Toronto, Canada: The Women's Press.
Cohen, A. K. (1955). *Delinquent boys: The culture of the gang*. Glencoe, IL: The Free Press.
Cooper, F. R. (2006). Against bipolar masculinity: Intersectionality, assimilation, identity performance, and hierarchy. *University of California Davis Law Review*, *39*, 853–906.
Crenshaw, K. W. (1991). Mapping the margins: Intersectionality, identity politics, and violence against women of color. *Stanford Law Review*, *43*(6), 1241–1299. doi:10.2307/1229039
Crenshaw, K. W. (2010). Close encounters of three kinds: On teaching dominance feminism and intersectionality. *Tulsa Law Review*, *46*(1), 151–189.
Curry, T. J. (2017). *The man-not : Race, class, genre, and the dilemmas of Black manhood*. Philadelphia, PA : Temple University Press.
Curry, T. J. (2018). Killing boogeymen: Phallicism and the misandric mischaracterizations of Black males in theory. *Res Philosophica*, *95*(2), 235–272. doi:10.11612/resphil.1612
Curry, T. J. (2019). Expendables for whom: Terry Crews and the erasure of Black male victims of sexual assault and rape. *Women's Studies in Communication*, *42*(3), 287–307. doi:10.1080/07491409.2019.1641874
Curry, T. J., & Utley, E. A. (2018). She touched me: Five snapshots of adult sexual violations of Black boys. *Kennedy Institute of Ethics Journal*, *28*(2), 205–241. doi:10.1353/ken.2018.0014
Curtis, L. A. (1975). *Violence, race, and culture*. Lexington, MA: Lexington Books.
Curtis, L. A. (1976). Rape, race, and culture: Some speculations in search of a theory. In M. J. Walker & S. L. Brodsky (Eds.), *Sexual assault: The victim and the rapist* (pp. 117–134). Lexington, MA: Lexington Books.
Dilulio Jr., J. (1995, November 27). The coming of the super-predators. *The Weekly Standard*, *1*(11).
Dilulio Jr., J. (1996). My black crime problem, and ours. *City Journal*, *6*(2), 14–28.
Gooley, R. L. (1989). The role of Black women in social change. *The Western Journal of Black Studies*, *13*(4), 165–172.

Griffin, S. (1971). Rape: An all-American crime. *Ramparts, 10*(3), 26–56.
Griffin, S. (1986). *Rape: The politics of consciousness.* San Francisco, CA: Harper & Row.
Hammond, W. P., & Mattis, J. S. (2005). Being a man about it: Manhood meaning among African American men. *Psychology of Men & Masculinity, 6*(2), 114–126. doi:10.1037/1524-9220.6.2.114
Hannerz, U. (1969). *Soulside: Inquiries into ghetto culture and community.* New York, NY: Columbia University Press.
Harnois, C. E. (2010). Race, gender, and the Black women's standpoint. *Sociological Forum, 25*(1), 68–85. doi:10.1111/j.1573-7861.2009.01157.x
Harnois, C. E. (2014). Complexity within and similarity across: Interpreting Black men's support of gender justice, amidst cultural representations that suggest otherwise. In B. C. Slatton & K. Spates (Eds.), *Hyper sexual, hyper masculine?: Gender, race and sexuality in the identities of contemporary Black men* (pp. 85–102). Burlington, VA: Ashgate Publishing.
Harnois, C. E. (2016). Intersectional masculinities and gendered political consciousness: How do race, ethnicity and sexuality shape men's awareness of gender inequality and support for gender activism? *Sex Roles, 77*(3–4), 141–154. doi:10.1007/s11199-016-0702-2
Harris, A. P. (1990). Race and essentialism in feminist legal theory. *Stanford Law Review, 42*(3), 581–616.
Harris, A. P. (2000). Gender, violence, race, and criminal justice. *Stanford Law Review, 52*, 777–807.
Hernandez, J. T., Lodico, M., & DiCelemente, R. J. (1993). The effects of child abuse and race on risk-taking in male adolescents. *Journal of the National Medical Association, 85*(8), 593–597.
Holmstrom, L. L. (1983). Review of *The Second Assault*. *Contemporary Sociology, 12*(5), 527–528. doi:10.2307/2068690
hooks, b. (2004). *We real cool: Black men and masculinity.* Abingdon, UK: Routledge.
Howard, W. L. (1903). The Negro as a distinct ethnic factor in civilization. *Medicine, 9*, 423–426.
Hunter, A. G., & Davis, J. E. (1992). Constructing gender: An exploration of Afro-American men's conceptualization of manhood. *Gender & Society, 6*(3), 464–479. doi:10.1177/089124392006003007
Hunter, A. G., & Davis, J. E. (1994). Hidden voices of Black men: The meaning, structure, and complexity of manhood. *Journal of Black Studies, 25*(1), 20–40. doi:10.1177/002193479402500102
Hunter, A. G., & Sellers, S. L. (1998). Feminist attitudes among African American women and men. *Gender & Society, 12*(1), 81–99. doi:10.1177/089124398012001005
Johnson, T. H. (2018). Challenging the myth of Black male privilege. *Spectrum: A Journal on Black Men, 6*(2), 21–42. doi:10.2979/spectrum.6.2.02
Jones, J., & Mosher, W. D. (2013). Fathers' involvement with their children: United States, 2006–2010. *National Health Statistics Reports*, (71), 1–21.
Lemelle, A. J. (2010). *Black masculinity and sexual politics.* Abingdon, UK: Routledge.
Lindquist, M. A. (2012). *Race, social science and the crisis of manhood, 1890–1970: We are the supermen.* Abingdon, UK: Routledge.
MacKinnon, C. A. (1989). *Toward a feminist theory of the state.* Cambridge, MA: Harvard University Press.
McDougal III, S., & George III, C. (2016). "I wanted to return the favor". *Journal of Black Studies, 47*(6), 524–549. doi:10.1177/0021934716653346
Moran, P., & Barclay, A. (1988). Effect of fathers' absence on delinquent boys: Dependency and hypermasculinity. *Psychological Reports, 62*(1), 115–121. doi:10.2466/pr0.1988.62.1.115

Mutua, A. (2013). Multidimensionality is to masculinities what intersectionality is to feminism. *Nevada Law Review, 13*, 341–367.
Oluwayomi, A. (2020). The man-not and the inapplicability of intersectionality to the dilemmas of Black manhood. *The Journal of Men's Studies, 28*(2), 183–205. doi:10.1177/1060826519896566
Pleck, J. H. (1981). *The myth of masculinity*. Cambridge, MA: MIT Press.
Purdie-Vaughns, V., & Eibach, R. P. (2008). Intersectional invisibility: The distinctive advantages and disadvantages of multiple subordinate-group identities. *Sex Roles, 59*(5–6), 377–391. doi:10.1007/s11199-008-9424-4
Rainwater, L. (1970). *Behind ghetto walls: Black families in a federal slum*. Chicago, IL: Aldine Publishing Company.
Simien, E. M. (2006). *Black feminist voices in politics*. Albany, NY: SUNY Press.
Simien, E. M. (2007). A Black gender gap? Continuity and change in attitudes to Black feminism. In W. C. Rich (Ed.), *African American perspectives on political science* (pp. 130–150). Philadelphia, PA: Temple University Press.
Smith, S. G., Basile, K. C., Gilbert, L. K., Merrick, M. T., Patel, N., Walling, M., & Jain, A. (2017). *National intimate partner and sexual violence survey (NISVS): 2010–2012 state report*. Retrieved from National Center for Injury Prevention and Control, Centers for Disease Control and Prevention website: www.cdc.gov/violenceprevention/pdf/NISVS-StateReportBook.pdf
Stein, M. N. (2015). *Measuring manhood: Race and the science of masculinity, 1830–1934*. Minneapolis, MN: University of Minnesota Press.
Williams, J. E., & Holmes, K. A. (1981). *The second assault: Rape and public attitudes*. Santa Barbara, CA: Praeger.
Wolfgang, M. E., & Ferracuti, F. (1967). *The subculture of violence: Towards an integrated theory in criminology*. London, UK: Tavistock Publications.

12
BETWEEN CRITICAL (WORLD) PSYCHOLOGY AND TRANSDISCIPLINARY PRAXIS

Robert K. Beshara

Critical psychology is a critical attitude *vis-à-vis* psychology, but the book's vision is to go further than that: beyond both mainstream and critical (Euro-American) psychology, and even beyond the discipline of psychology altogether. How is your chapter contributing to the actualization of a critical (world) psychology premised on transdisciplinary praxis?

Hans Skott-Myhre and Kathleen Skott-Myhre

The chapter "Subversions of Subjectification" (Chapter 3) goes well beyond a critique of mainstream psychology to call into question the very foundations of psychological concepts such as agency, self, and the individual unconscious. Traversing 21st-century capitalism, the chapter founds its critique of psychology, not in a general critical attitude, but in a definition of critical as inherently Marxist. While its field of inquiry and proposals for praxis are transdisciplinary, its underlying analytics are derived from a Marxist analysis of capitalism. From this perspective, psychology is seen as an instrument of capitalist appropriation, rather than separable from a critique of how capitalism functions. The chapter suggests that a Marxist analysis of 21st-century capitalism must engage the ways in which the mode of production has shifted and morphed, inclusive of modes of subjectivity. To do this, it engages a transdisciplinary set of analytics that include Marxism, post-Marxism, Taoism, post-humanism, post-colonial critique, post-modernism, and theories of immanence. From this analysis a political project is proposed that is intended to be responsive to current capitalist modes of appropriation and control.

Lois Holzman

I doubt that this chapter (Chapter 4) (or any chapter) will have that kind of impact. In terms of actualization, I prefer to speak of the on-the-ground work the chapter describes. With its synthesis of critical psychology, philosophy, and theatre/performance, social therapeutic methodology might very well appear to be an instance of a critical (world) psychology premised on transdisciplinary praxis. However, it isn't. It isn't premised. It is practiced. Transdisciplinary praxis is an after-the-fact descriptor, not something that guided my colleagues and me to our approach. So too is the term I prefer and we aspire to, which is postdisciplinary.

Michael J. Miller

The view of many Lacanians is that psychoanalysis is already quite separate from psychology, and indeed much of Lacan's work revolved around an attempt to resist psychoanalysis's assimilation by that discipline. My chapter (Chapter 5) argues that, out of identification with Lacan, Lacanianism falls short of resistance and critique, instead cutting itself off from the meaningful engagement with psychology that resistance and critique would require. Lacanianism, while it wants to locate itself as "beyond" psychology, cannot claim to occupy that position since it has not encountered psychology since the early 1950s, and even then, did so in a dubious manner. There can be no "beyond" without an encounter. My chapter attempts to critique a structure marked by an interest in mastery and identification, which I posit underlies this lack of engagement. I note ways in which that structure informs the Lacanian approach not just to psychology, but to any number of "others" (for example, transgender people, women, and people with autism), and at the same time precludes reflexivity, and therefore is doomed to be unable to make meaningful critique, let alone intervention, consonant with the project of critical psychology. On the other hand, my hope is that Lacan's work can be taken up quite differently from this, and can be used as a vehicle for self-critique and humility in the face of the other, in the spirit of Lacan's concept of the "analyst's desire": the desire to always hear more, from a radical position of un-knowing. This attitude is clinically and socially potentially quite powerful, and may have a deeply ethical and even liberatory dimension, but it must be divorced from an attachment to mastery and identification to be deployed that way. My chapter is an attempt to invite readers of Lacan to consider that direction for their approach to his work.

Serdar M. Değirmencioğlu

Psychology grew alongside colonial and imperial forces. It served oppressive regimes again and again. Mainstream psychology today operates fully in line with neoliberal capitalism, with entrepreneurs, dealers, and an import–export business. This business is what needs to be disrupted first. Genuine efforts toward psychologies of liberation and decolonization can only emerge from the Global South. This chapter (Chapter 6) offers practical ideas to decolonize psychology. Critical psychology today has to prioritize critical praxis over theoretical sophistication. Critical praxis is urgently needed and it cannot be sustained without genuine solidarity across borders.

Fernanda Liberali, Valdite Pereira Fuga, and José Carlos Barbosa Lopes

The praxis described in our chapter (Chapter 8) illustrates our general attempt to decolonize the lives of students and educators through a critical perspective that aims at the viable unheard of. Participants in this activist-interventionist approach carried out in the Digitmed Program create possibilities to move beyond their immediate realities while they negotiate knowledge to act in the world and to perform different activities in the world. This inevitable cultural and historical connection enables participants to be aware of human experience as part of constant social change and, therefore, the dialectics between the subject and the collectivity.

Silvana S. Hernández Ortiz and María Constanza Garrido Sierralta

Chilean student movements are revitalizing outbursts of resistance to an unending struggle against the overall socioeconomic inequality and the particular educational segregation in public schools. High-school students voice demands that transcend educational frameworks, and include in their needs that of an entire nation that rebels against neoliberalism and petrified policies dating back to Pinochet's dictatorship. Researchers in critical psychology have shown time and time again how dominant developmental psychology perspectives consider students as underage, uncritical, as a subject-in-formation not ready to be agents of change. However, their fierce participation in protests, in actually helping modify political dictates, renders them key actors in long-awaited socioeconomic and political transformations. The social explosion of October 2019 rekindled the wounds left behind by decades of repression, but it also left multiple student-activists blinded by rubber bullets and deceased from police brutality. Piñera's government perpetuated the well-known shock doctrine to student protests, criminalizing their voices and arresting them on false charges. Children/the youth are agents of change, and their rise in these movements recognizes them as legal, autonomous agents, subjects who critically reflect and participate in changing a nation, an example for the rest of the world.

Fu Wai

The chapter (Chapter 10) is a cut-up between the ancient Chinese (critical) philosophy of Gongsun Long, history, psychoanalysis, the ancient Greek idea of πίνος, criticism of mainstream psychology via Ignacio Martín-Baró, Virgilio Gaspar Enriquez, Jacques Lacan, and Slavoj Žižek and not in the way of William S. Burroughs, but in the way of the Frog that witnesses the rise of a new Hong Kong identity. Transdisciplinary praxis goes beyond the boundary of knowledge, beyond truthing and de-truthing; it is a return to its origin: a testimonial.

Tommy J. Curry

"Decolonizing the Intersection" (Chapter 11) dares to insist that the assumptions of Black manhood offered by intersectionality depend on errant feminist theorists dedicated to the scientizing of the myth of the Black male rapist. Because intersectionality depends on a psychologism of male domination, the theories used to construct the idea of a Black masculinity, which imitates white masculinity, must be interrogated. We can only begin to rethink the racialized male once we have reformulated his fundamental drives, his motivations and desires, for humanity. If Black theories like intersectionality merely hide the origin of their Eurocentric assumptions behind the identity of Blackness or Black woman-ness we will never be truly critical of our thinking and myths serving as the basis of our theories. The sacred creeds must be thoroughly investigated for their remnants of colonial thought just as our othered categories of being are. My chapter introduces Black Male Studies as the foundation of this decolonial mandate by bringing history, sociology, criminology, and philosophy to bear on the question of "how should we think of Black manhood?".

INDEX

activity 24, 40, 44–9, 67, 69, 85–8, 90–2, 96–8, 104, 132, 147, 157
Allende 104, 106
Anzaldúa 22–3, 25, 41
authority 26, 44–7, 52, 56, 63, 74, 78, 138

Baudrillard 35, 129
becoming 34, 38, 40, 46–9
Black 2–3, 7–8, 53, 121, 132–51
Black Male Studies xiv, xv, 132, 148, 150, 158
body 6, 30, 34–5, 37, 39–41, 59, 129, 133, 135, 137
Brazil xiv, xv, 49, 85–6, 91

capitalism 1, 3, 5, 8–9, 24, 33
Chican@ studies xiv, xv, 21–3, 31, 35–40, 48–9, 74, 77, 80, 85–6, 89, 103–4, 138, 155–6
Chile xiv, xv, 100–9
Chuang Tzu 36, 38, 41
colonial 2, 4–5, 9, 20, 23, 25–6, 35, 58–9, 66–9, 75–7, 85–6, 103, 113–14, 116–17, 121–3, 125, 155–6, 158
commodification 19–20, 47, 49, 101, 106–7
communication 23, 36, 38–41
creativity 35–6, 39–41, 45–7, 54, 85, 92, 98
Crenshaw 7–8, 132–6
critical psychology xiii, xv–vi, 1–2, 6–9, 13, 44–6, 49, 51, 53, 70, 74–5, 78–9, 86–7, 113, 128, 155–7

decolonial xiv, 1, 4–5, 8–9, 14, 23, 25–6, 68, 70, 73, 75, 77, 79–80, 88–90, 97, 120, 132, 148, 157–8
deconstruction 45, 48–9, 55, 113, 116
Deleuze and Guattari 33–5, 37–9
desire 1, 8, 33–7, 40, 47, 59–60, 63, 74, 78, 90–3, 97, 100, 104, 114, 116–17, 124, 128–9, 136–7, 156, 158
development 2, 4, 14, 45–9, 60, 66–7, 75, 85, 88, 90–2, 101, 105, 117, 140, 157
dialectic 35, 45, 47, 56, 64, 86–8, 90, 97, 157
dictatorship 77, 100–8, 157
displacement 14, 17, 19–21

education 8, 13, 23, 25, 27, 31, 46–8, 70, 72, 78, 85, 87–92, 100–3, 105–9, 117, 122, 125, 133, 157
epistemology xv, 20, 23, 31, 34–5, 44, 46–7, 54–5, 89, 97, 113, 120, 134, 151
Euro 1–2, 4–6, 22, 49, 59–60, 66–8, 74, 88, 91, 103, 155, 158

Fanon 1, 3, 59
feminism xiv, xv, 3, 7, 31, 34, 38, 62–3, 133, 135–6, 141–2, 146–9, 151, 158
Freire 3, 6, 86, 88–92, 97–8

gentrification 13–14, 17, 19–25, 40
Global South 1, 3, 35, 75, 77, 79, 89, 157
Gongsun Long 120–1, 126

Index

Hegemony 5–6, 21, 24–5, 89–90, 104–5, 109, 120
home xv, 13–14, 16, 24–8, 79, 82, 95, 119, 128
Hong Kong xv, 113–29
hooks 87–9, 97, 137–9

imagination 1, 8, 17–23, 25, 28–9, 39, 41, 45–6, 48, 55–6, 58, 60, 122, 127, 145, 148, 150
Indigenous xiii, xv, 2, 14, 17, 21–2, 26–8, 39, 67–8, 83, 113, 115, 119–20
intersectionality 7–8, 41, 132–7, 147–51, 158

Lacan xv, 6, 51–64, 116, 123, 156, 158
language 6, 16, 19–21, 28, 48, 56, 60, 69, 72, 76–7, 86–7, 107, 117–18, 121, 129
liberation 2–5, 8–9, 79, 88, 92, 104, 109, 115, 119–20, 126, 148, 151, 156–7

mainstream psychology 7, 45, 47–8, 68, 120–1, 126, 155–6, 158
manhood 132, 136–9, 141, 148, 150–1
man-not 8, 132, 151
map 8–9, 15, 23, 135
Marx xv, 6, 20, 33, 35–6, 45–6, 49, 86–91, 97, 104, 113, 155
masculinity 136–42, 144, 146–51, 158
master 52, 55–9, 62–3
materiality 4–5, 19–21, 24, 34–5, 37, 86–7, 90–1, 97
Mignolo 2, 4–6, 23

Name-of-the-Father 52, 123–5, 127
Neoliberal 69, 74–5, 77–9, 85, 100–7, 109
New Mexico xiii–v, 1, 13–14, 16–19, 21–8, 30–1, 82
non-alignment 1, 6

ontology 19–20, 24, 34, 40, 44–5, 48–9, 54, 134
oppression 2–3, 5, 9, 36, 61, 67–8, 70, 74, 83, 86–91, 106, 108–9, 126, 129, 133–8, 148, 156

patriarchy 8, 78, 132–6, 138–41, 144–50
pedagogy xiv–v, 3, 25, 86–9, 105
Pepe the Frog 115, 126–8, 158

performance activism 46, 49
place xiii, 1, 14, 16–17, 20–3, 25–8, 66, 95, 98, 102, 105, 116–17, 151
plant 27–31
politics xiv, 1–5, 7–8, 25, 31, 33–41, 46–8, 59, 67–8, 72, 77–8, 85, 87, 89–92, 96–7, 100, 104–6, 108–9, 119, 124–9, 135–7, 143, 148–51
power xiv, 2–3, 20, 22–7, 29, 39, 41, 46–7, 49, 52–3, 57, 61, 63, 69, 72, 75, 77, 85, 89–90, 92, 102–6, 109, 114–15, 122–3, 132–4, 136–9, 142–7, 151
practical-critical 44–7, 49
praxis xiii–vi, 1–6, 8–9, 13–14, 31, 40, 44, 48, 69, 77, 79–80, 88–90, 97, 100, 109, 113, 155–8
psychoanalysis xiv–v, 6, 35, 51–7, 59–63, 113, 156–7
psychosocial 1, 6–7
Pueblo(s) xiv–v, 1, 13, 17, 25–6, 31, 82–4

Quijano 2, 5, 103

racism 3, 5, 53, 67, 73, 78, 89, 122, 126, 136–8, 141, 143, 147–51
reflexivity 55, 57, 62, 156
resistance 38–9, 45, 56, 63, 69, 74–5, 77, 86, 89, 91–2, 97–8, 100, 106, 109, 117, 119, 127, 137–8, 143, 156–7
revolution 8, 33, 41, 45–9, 62, 85–8, 90–1, 97, 107–8, 115, 119
rhetoric 2, 5, 14, 17, 19–25, 56

Santos 89–90, 97
separtition 116
social therapeutics 44, 46, 48–9, 156
space 9, 17, 19–25, 27, 31, 39, 47, 58, 86, 89, 91–2, 97, 129, 137–8
student(s) xiii–v, 1, 3, 13–14, 26–8, 55, 59, 62, 71, 73–7, 86, 89, 91, 93, 96, 100–2, 105–9, 125, 157
subjectivity 4, 6–7, 14, 33, 35–8, 40–1, 54, 57–61, 63, 71, 85–6, 88, 90, 97, 105–9, 125, 127, 135, 143, 150, 155, 157
subversion 33–4, 36–9, 85, 155

transdisciplinary xvi, 1, 7, 155, 156, 158
Turkey 77–9

unconscious 2–3, 5, 7, 33–6, 40, 46, 60,
    108, 123, 155
Unidad Popular 104
United States xiii, xv, 1, 9–10,
    22–3, 56, 68–9, 133, 141–2,
    145, 151
uselessness 28, 36–41

vacuole(s) 39–41
violence 2, 5, 38, 40, 52, 67, 75, 91, 105,
    108, 125–6, 129, 132–6, 138–51
Vygotsky 87–8, 90

white xv, 21, 24, 53, 76, 132, 135–49, 151,
    158

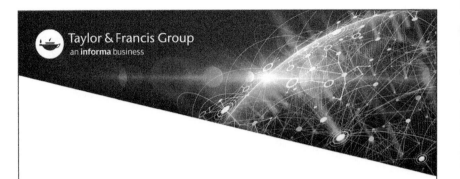

Taylor & Francis eBooks

www.taylorfrancis.com

A single destination for eBooks from Taylor & Francis with increased functionality and an improved user experience to meet the needs of our customers.

90,000+ eBooks of award-winning academic content in Humanities, Social Science, Science, Technology, Engineering, and Medical written by a global network of editors and authors.

TAYLOR & FRANCIS EBOOKS OFFERS:

A streamlined experience for our library customers

A single point of discovery for all of our eBook content

Improved search and discovery of content at both book and chapter level

REQUEST A FREE TRIAL
support@taylorfrancis.com